Thug Life

Thug Life

Race, Gender, and the Meaning of Hip-Hop

MICHAEL P. JEFFRIES

The University of Chicago Press
Chicago and London

Michael P. Jeffries is assistant professor of American studies at Wellesley College.

The University of Chicago Press, Chicago 60637
The University of Chicago Press, Ltd., London
© 2011 by The University of Chicago
All rights reserved. Published 2011
Printed in the United States of America

21 20 19 18 17 16 15 14 13 12 11   1 2 3 4 5

ISBN-13: 978-0-226-39584-5   (cloth)
ISBN-13: 978-0-226-39585-2   (paper)
ISBN-10: 0-226-39584-7   (cloth)
ISBN-10: 0-226-39585-5   (paper)

Library of Congress Cataloging-in-Publication Data

Jeffries, Michael P.
    Thug life : race, gender, and the meaning of hip-hop / Michael P. Jeffries.
        p.   cm.
    Includes bibliographical references and index.
    ISBN-13: 978-0-226-39584-5 (cloth : alk. paper)
    ISBN-13: 978-0-226-39585-2 (pbk. : alk. paper)
    ISBN-10: 0-226-39584-7 (cloth : alk. paper)
    ISBN-10: 0-226-39585-5 (pbk. : alk. paper)   1. Rap (Music)—Social
aspects—United States.   2. Hip-hop—Social aspects—United States.
I. Title.
    ML3918.R37J44   2010
    306.4'842490973—dc22

                                                2010005575

♾ The paper used in this publication meets the minimum requirements of the American National Standard for Information Sciences—Permanence of Paper for Printed Library Materials, ANSI Z39.48-1992.

In memory of my grandparents, and with unending love for my family.

CONTENTS

Acknowledgments / ix

INTRODUCTION / State of the Hip-Hop Union / 1

ONE / The Meaning of Hip-Hop / 23

TWO / From a Cool Complex to Complex Cool / 55

THREE / Thug Life and Social Death / 77

The Bridge: Summary of Chapters Two and Three / 113

FOUR / Hip-Hop Authenticity in Black and White / 117

FIVE / Parental Advisory: Explicit Lyrics / 151

CONCLUSION / The Last Verse / 189

EPILOGUE / Obama as Hip-Hop Icon / 199

Appendix / 207
Notes / 225
References / 235
Discography / 247
Index / 249

ACKNOWLEDGMENTS

I want to start by acknowledging the original practitioners and philosophers of hip-hop. Their names are too many to mention here, so it must suffice to say that this book started decades ago with their courage and creativity. Second, I thank the respondents who shared their time and love of hip-hop with me. Let me also acknowledge all those outside the academy whom I talked to about my work, and all the students I have taught and learned from, who keep the questions in this book alive.

Thanks to Doug Mitchell, Tim McGovern, George Roupe, and the University of Chicago Press for handling this project with such care.

I am grateful for the efforts of Elena Creef, Jonathan Imber, Susan Reverby, and the rest of my colleagues at Wellesley College, who made a place for me and supported me as I finished this book. It is a tremendous privilege to be part of the community at Wellesley.

I warmly thank the African American studies faculty and staff at Harvard University. I continue to benefit from the teaching, research, support, and advocacy of Lawrence Bobo, Glenda Carpio, Michael Dawson, Henry Louis Gates Jr., Evelynn Hammonds, Evelyn Higginbotham, Jennifer Hochschild, and Michele Lamont. Thanks to Tommie Shelby for reviewing a critical slice of the manuscript late in the revision process and to Marcyliena Morgan and the Hiphop Archive for treating hip-hop with the respect it deserves. In addition, I want to thank those with whom I rose through the ranks, Derrick Ashong, Mia Bagneris, Laura Murphy, and Josef Sorett, for the time we shared.

Thanks to A. Kwame Harrison, for his thoughtful notes on my work.

In April 2005, at a conference on hip-hop and feminism, I met Murray Forman for the first time and asked him to review a paper of mine on hip-hop and criminality. Murray worked at a different institution and had his own students to mentor, but he gladly agreed. At the time, it may have seemed like a small act, but it was the spark that eventually led to this book. Murray gave me notes, encouraged me to develop my ideas, and became a trusted adviser as this project developed. I am lucky to count him as a friend and colleague.

Kimberly McClain DaCosta also provided advice, and her support has been indispensable. In addition to expressing my admiration for her work, I want to thank her for helping me keep things in perspective. It is a rare talent to perceive both the forest and the trees, and if I have improved in my capacity to do this, it is no small part due to her example and her wisdom.

William Julius Wilson has been the most formative influence on my professional development. The quality of what he continues to teach me about generosity, mentorship, and the richness of this vocation is equal to that of his research, which has long since assumed its place in the canon of sociology. His efforts have contributed greatly to whatever success I have achieved.

I would be remiss if I failed to mention my friends and mentors at Swarthmore College. Allison Dorsey, Robin Wagner-Pacifici, and Sarah Willie-LeBreton taught me, among many things, that this work is truly human practice.

The names of many of the artists and authors to whom I owe thanks appear in the pages of this book. I have never met most of the people I cite, but this does not diminish my gratitude for their work, and I thank them for holding the conversation I strive to join.

I stand on the shoulders of my parents, Emily and John, and look to my siblings, David and Julia, to find my way. My wife, Sarah, keeps me safe. My deepest thanks and love are not enough for all you have done.

State of the Hip-Hop Union

The white music industry has always denigrated the black community. White corporate America has always feared the black male. It wants to suggest black males are inhuman thugs.

—C. Delores Tucker[1]

More or less, I'll forever be a thug
Shed my blood, for everything I love.

—Jadakiss, "Everything I Love (Remix)" (2006)

The Beginning

As 1970s deindustrialization and new trends in urban planning destroyed impoverished black and Latino/a neighborhoods, residents in New York and other American cities took to the streets, b-boying (also known as break dancing), DJ-ing, and rapping in the face of economic neglect and injustice.[2] In the late 1970s and early 1980s, participants, observers, and documentarians incorporated and recognized graffiti art, which had been around for some time, as the fourth element of what we now call hip-hop.[3] Politics aside, these practices were fundamentally about creativity and play, and the enjoyment that early practitioners derived couldn't be kept on the corner for long. Hip-hop's emergence drew the attention of people outside the urban neighborhoods where it arose, and during the 1980s and 1990s, the recording industry turned hip-hop into big business.

In hip-hop's block party beginnings, the DJ-ing, MC-ing, and dancing were often live and in concert. Until the Sugar Hill Gang's "Rapper's Delight" hit stores in 1979, Public Enemy's Chuck D "did not think it was conceivable that there would be such a thing as a hip-hop record."[4] Today, commercially recorded rap music has largely supplanted the live model of hip-hop interaction, and hip-hop is most frequently witnessed and engaged as a packaged musical commodity. Original b-boys, DJs, and MCs were local celebrities who specialized in public performance, but I never went to such a performance growing up in Brooklyn in the 1980s. I first heard hip-hop at age five on a 45-rpm record of "Walk This Way" (1986) by Run DMC and Aerosmith, and my earliest memory of collective hip-hop practice is singing the *Billboard* chart-topper "Just a Friend" (1989) by Biz Markie on the bus to school with my fourth-grade classmates. I did not listen to rap music regularly until age twelve, when my family moved to the suburbs in New Jersey and I became infatuated with Dr. Dre's *The Chronic* (1992) and A Tribe Called Quest's *Midnight Marauders* (1993) CD. Hip-hop is now a global phenomenon, and from the street corner to the countryside, much of today's younger generation will get its first hip-hop fix from YouTube and digitally recorded MP3s rather than live shows in the park.

Content changes have shadowed the shifts in sites of production and audience demographics. Instead of representing hip-hop as a party-fueling set of face-to-face performative practices or an activity capable of mediating the economic and political neglect and social disorder in depressed communities, an increasing number of popular music artists turned to telling hood stories and glorifying wealth and consumption as hip-hop grew in popularity. Though the original hip-hopper was a local partier, the dominant image of hip-hop commoditized by record companies and amplified by mass media from the mid-1990s on is that of the nationally recognizable urban gangster-celebrity.[5] Tough talk and big spending were the calling cards of self-proclaimed "thugs" in commercially successful hip-hop from 1993 to 2008. But before thug life, there was crossover.

Culture for Sale

Mark Anthony Neal thoroughly and succinctly explains black music's crossover to the mainstream in his 2005 article for *Pop Matters* entitled "Rhythm and Bullshit." In 1972, a group of Harvard Business School students conducted a study at the request of the Columbia Records Group. Their research, which has since come to be known as the Harvard Report, argued that the growth of the black middle class in the post–civil rights era provided record companies with a new consumer base ready to purchase black music recordings. A number of soul and rhythm-and-blues acts that produced such musical commodities had achieved commercial success and fame under contract with smaller, boutique record labels such as Stax and Motown. The report recommended that Columbia partner with these boutique labels rather than purchasing them or attempting to convince their artists to leave and sign with Columbia. As partners, the smaller companies would maintain a high degree of creative autonomy with regard to production, promotion, and artist development, because the boutiques knew the music and its consumer base best. In exchange, Columbia would receive a product from the boutiques ready for commoditization and distribution on a mass scale that boutiques could not possibly achieve on their own. As Neal observes, "The boutique model was not necessarily about crossing R&B over to the mainstream, but rather positioning the larger corporate labels to better control the R&B market."[6] Still, as a result of these developments, consumers across race and class lines gained greater access to traditionally black musical commodities, and white demand for black music skyrocketed.

The Harvard Report set the course for massive changes in the record industry. The global music market is now dominated by four major record labels: Sony Music Entertainment, Electric & Musical Industries Limited (EMI), Universal Music Group, and Warner Music Group, responsible for the licensing and copyright protection of their products. Each of these labels owns myriad smaller companies (Sony now owns Columbia) and boutique labels, including independent hip-hop labels, which handle promotion and artist development. For example, Sony owns GOOD Music, a label founded by Kanye West. Universal owns Interscope Records, which controls the Island Def Jam Music Group and its subsidiaries, including Jay-Z's Roc-A-Fella Records and the labels founded by Eminem and 50 Cent. According to Nielsen SoundScan, the four major record labels controlled over 86 percent of the United States music market as of 2007 (Cashmere 2008).

Record industry consolidation overlays consolidation of the radio airwaves, a trend aided in no small part by the Telecommunications Reform Act of 1996. Traditional thinking on radio programming held that airwaves were not private property, and therefore companies who wish to use them must do so under the pretense that their programming serves the public good. The "public good" refers less to public affairs or community service programming than it does to reflecting the public's taste for programming within a given locale. Before the Telecommunications Reform Act, companies could not own more than two radio stations in one local market or more than twenty-eight nationally, because doing so would prevent them from best serving the local base of each station. Since the act, the most powerful corporations have seized control of radio programming, as the ten largest companies now control over two-thirds of the market.[7]

Neal argues that these developments have two crucial effects on the music industry. First, decisions regarding musical selection rest with a smaller group of program directors than ever before, and the same playlist is distributed to hundreds of outlets throughout the country, so hip-hop radio sounds extremely similar no matter which city is it based in. Second, it is exceedingly difficult to hold program directors responsible for their decisions, because they are not beholden to local constituencies. Not only do program directors operate with the massive financial support of the national media conglomerates that employ them, they perform their jobs in relative anonymity. As 50 Cent notes, "It's easier to attack a individual than it is to attack a corporation, so they point to specific hip-hop artists to go after, [as] opposed to going after Paramount or Columbia Pictures."[8] Should someone object to the lyrical content of the latest hip-hop hit to receive heavy commercial rotation, it is much easier to blame the rapper than to blame a nameless, faceless program director, or the courier of undocumented payola from one of the record companies, or the multinational corporations that employ them both.

As for the measurable impact of corporate control on hip-hop, Jennifer Lena (2006) finds that the explosion of "puerile rap," with content focused on sex and violence, is clearly related to increased investment in and production of hip-hop by major record labels rather than independent labels. As a result of these new trends in content, rap music and those who perform it have become easy and frequent targets for politicians and cultural critics. Even those with affinity for the art wonder if hip-hop has any political potential left now that its production and distribution are controlled by executives with no connection to hip-hop's origins and its consumption is connected to such a broad consumer base. As Queeley explains:

> The corporate appropriation of what began as a powerful expression of the Black and Latino experience of urban poverty has significantly compromised its transformative potential . . . The recurrence of deeply embedded racist stereotypes coupled with the fixation on consumption characterizes corporate control of hip-hop and diminishes its position as a revolutionary art form and burgeoning mass social movement . . . Hip-hop now lives in the ghetto of the white imagination. (2003, 2)

These concerns recall long-standing uneasiness about mass production and the culture industry in the intellectual tradition of Theodor W. Adorno and Max Horkheimer, who argue that mass-produced cultural works are stripped of their creative and intellectual value and distributed to soothe and sedate the public with politically nonthreatening *entertainment* rather than *art*, which has the potential to encourage critical thinking and shake up social relations (Adorno 1938; Adorno and Horkheimer 1947). Queeley's comments foreground the racial politics of this story; it is not simply that hip-hop has been commoditized but that the "white imagination" Queeley speaks of has repeatedly imagined hip-hop culture as synonymous with and exemplified by the domination-driven, exploitative ghetto gangsterism invoked by many of the music's most popular acts.

Whether these trends will continue remains to be seen. Statistics compiled at the end of 2007 point to a significant decline in hip-hop record sales, and the viability of independent labels combined with the emergence of the Internet as a means to promote and distribute music means that the influence of corporate decision makers is significantly diminished (Sanneh 2007b). The notion that an MC might rise to the top of his profession without claiming thug life is more realistic today than at any point in the past fifteen years, and the celebrity of MCs such as Lupe Fiasco, Kanye West, and others who do not fit the mold of the "white racist imagination" proves that more than one model of black masculinity is commercially viable in the mainstream hip-hop marketplace. Still, rumors of the hip-hop thug's demise are greatly exaggerated. *Billboard*'s year-end charts for 2008 list six MCs among the fifty top artists of the year: Lil' Wayne (no. 2), T.I. (no. 10), Flo-Rida (no. 12), Kanye West (no. 18), Plies (no. 37), and Young Jeezy (no. 43) (Pietroluengo 2008). Of these six, only Kanye West does not cast himself as a thug/gangster/ghetto hustler.

The overarching question driving this book is "Should black men's hip-hop thug narratives and performances be considered resistant to or compliant with black subjugation in an era when the range of representations of blackness available for consumption is heavily influenced by white demand?" However, because interpretations of hip-hop cannot be neatly categorized as "resistant" or "compliant," my research questions are more specific: How should we understand narratives about ghetto life, "thuggin'," courtship, and material excess performed by black men in commercially successful hip-hop? And are there significant differences between the ways black and white men interpret rap music and the meaning of hip-hop?

Cultural Appropriation and Masculinity

These research questions are important not just because they satisfy innocent curiosities about hip-hop culture but because they engage racism and culture theft in America. We must recognize the influence of black artistic and cultural traditions on hip-hop, as the dominance of Afro-diasporic speech, music, and dance patterns is distinct and empirically established. Whether studying hip-hop in the United States, Japan (Cornyetz 1994; Condry 2006), Cuba (Fernandes 2006), Brazil (Pardue 2008), or Francophone countries on both sides of the Atlantic (Durand 2002), it is impossible to do so without grappling with African musical aesthetics and questions of the racialization of people of African descent, particularly African Americans. However, one of the primary effects of corporate influence on American hip-hop is the wrongful suppression of nonblack contributions to hip-hop history. The efforts of white, Asian, Hispanic, and indigenous American practitioners are frequently ignored, and the omission of Latino/a hip-hop experiences is especially egregious considering the indispensable role played by so many Latino/a practitioners from the beginning of hip-hop history.

The narrative of black purity in hip-hop is a myth propagated from many points on the ideological spectrum of racial politics. This narrative thrives in the commercial sphere in large part because representations of spectacular, oppositional ghetto blackness are captivating and salable to consumers in a range of social milieus. It is not my intent to deny the experiences of all the other racial and ethnic groups that make up hip-hop communities, nor do I wish to partake in the cementation of an archaic discourse of racial identity that pits whiteness against blackness.[9] Because hip-hop authenticity is contextually and spatially grounded, one's claim to it in specific locales may be determined according to an entirely different racial rubric—blackness does not always reign supreme. Further, different elements of hip-hop are often associated with, and visibly dominated by, particular racial and ethnic groups. For example, Asians and Asian Americans (especially those of Filipino descent) have established a strong foothold in DJ and b-boy culture on the West Coast, while Latinos and Latinas have been holding down the East Coast b-boy scene since before the dance had a name.

Nevertheless, black American men have dominated the landscape of commercially successful rap for the past two decades. The association between popular rap and blackness is due in part to the racial composition of the earliest groups to have major commercial success, especially Run DMC, the first rap group to receive significant exposure on MTV and release a certified multiplatinum album, *Raising Hell* (1986). This connection was further strengthened by black nationalist, Afrocentric, and black-loving content of collectives like Public Enemy and the Native Tongues during the 1980s and by the advent of gangsta and black ghetto "reality" rap in the 1990s, which record companies were quick to push. The association between blackness and MC-ing is also built on the strength of arguments about the indispensability of black vernacular familiarity and rhetorical dexterity to the practice of rapping. My research project is specifically concerned with commercially successful rap music, and because of the considerations mentioned above, as well as my focus on black coolness and white cooptation, there is much to be gained by selecting whiteness and blackness as analytic starting points.

White appropriation of nonwhite cultural products speaks to the invisibility of white racial identity and the power of white supremacy. Like other racial and ethnic identities, whiteness is a localized and fluid concept, experienced and understood only through combination with other identity markers, such as region, class, gender, and sexuality (Frankenberg 1993; Hartigan 1999; McDermott 2006). Of course, many white people who recognize the salience of race and ethnicity as social constructs that impart unjust advantages work to eliminate race-based social injustice. Other whites believe they are less distinct or trendy than nonwhites because there is nothing interesting or important about whiteness. Extensions of this self-concept are the false and socially damaging belief that race and ethnicity have no impact on their lives and a commitment to act as though race does not exist; this is the invisibility of whiteness, or the color-blind ethic. Alternatively, a white person may feel guilty about racism and white supremacy and want to actively disassociate herself from white privilege as much as possible. Whites who say, "I have no culture," "We should all be color-blind," or "I don't like being white" may search for an alternative culture community that allows them to fashion a fulfilling identity.

We all search for cultural niches, or communities of people who affirm our ideas about self and society. In the case of white Americans, however, the cultural identity or community they choose often becomes their primary identity marker, without a racial or ethnic qualifier, because the white body is "normal" and indistinct in the American racial context. In contrast, the identities of nonwhites are frequently dependent on racial markers in majority-white professions or spheres because the bodily stain of blackness (and brownness, redness, and yellowness) cannot be ignored; George W. Bush was just another president, but Barack Obama is the first *black* (or multiracial) president.

The dominant narrative of cultural appropriation and absorption of hip-hop into the mainstream avows that white people, and specifically white men, enjoy a voyeuristic relationship with irreverent and spectacularly cool hip-hop blackness. It is assumed that white male hip-hop fans

consume and derive pleasure from racist representations of black masculinity in order to access a desirable, distinctive, and trendy masculine self-
concept without regard for the poisonous racial and ethnic politics that
enable such consumption. Through hip-hop, white youths escape from
the discipline of suburban and corporate life and wear a mask that allows
them to live "dangerously in the limbic sensuality of the outlaw culture"
without any of the material consequences that young black men identified
with hip-hop must deal with, such as discrimination, incrimination, and
the self-inflicted wounds of social disorder and labor-market detachment
on family life (Patterson 1999, 276). Further, white people who wear hip-
hop clothes and listen to rap music are often regarded as "posers" who do
not possess a great deal of hip-hop knowledge, are not especially invested
in the culture, and do not even understand what they are participating in.

Bakari Kitwana's *Why White Kids Love Hip-Hop: Wankstas, Wiggers, Wannabes, and the New Reality of Race in America* (2005) is the first hip-hop
studies book dedicated primarily to these issues. Kitwana moves beyond
the notion that all white kids like hip-hop solely because they want to be
cool or dangerous, drawing connections between themes of alienation in
hip-hop, the economic alienation that young people of all races and eth-
nicities face, and a new era of racial politics that allows for far more cultural
contact points than previous epochs. Kitwana's book is quite valuable, but
it does not prominently feature the voices of the "white kids" who are the
subject of his study, with the exception of a few narrative vignettes. This
is the greatest contribution of my book: the interview sections provide a
crucial check for my understanding of coolness and racial politics in commercially successful hip-hop, as I document meaning as understood by everyday hip-hop fans for whom hip-hop is a passion but not necessarily a
vocation. This sample composition, which emphasizes consumers rather
than producers, distinguishes this book from outstanding recent American
hip-hop ethnographies (Keyes 2002; Morgan 2009; Schloss 2004, 2009)
focused on professional and semiprofessional hip-hop performers who
frequently practice MC-ing, DJ-ing, or b-boying.

Not only do I contribute to the discussion about "why white kids love
hip-hop," but I investigate why everyday black listeners love hip-hop too.
The voices of black respondents who do not understand themselves as hip-
hop artists are equally important and almost equally ignored by canonical
hip-hop studies. This omission may grow from, or result in, the wrongful presumption that blackness imparts a natural predilection for hip-hop,
and black engagement could not possibly contain the same socially toxic

motivations as white fanaticism. In a worst-case scenario, both black and white respondents might enjoy commercially successful hip-hop primarily because it celebrates the pleasure derived from imposing black masculinity, homophobia, female degradation, and conspicuous consumption. But it is careless to assume that one's racial and ethnic identity dictates the sort of enjoyment one extracts or that these are the only or primary reasons young men become hip-hop enthusiasts.

Racial and gender identities are intersectional, and the contest over cultural appropriation is explicitly concerned with the appropriation of cool *black masculinity* rather than simply blackness. Despite hip-hop's historical ethnoracial hybridity, the innumerable contributions of female practitioners and fans, and the discursive contestation between the sexes embedded in hip-hop texts, most commercially successful American hip-hop has had a black male face, body, and voice. Today, those in charge of the commercial distribution of hip-hop are overwhelmingly male, but the pool of corporate decision makers is significantly less black than the pool of hip-hop celebrities. This is precisely the relationship at the root of the debate over hip-hop as resistance: white men distribute and consume commercially successful rap music, and black men perform it. As Queeley asserts, "Hip-hop now lives in the ghetto of the white imagination" (2003, 2), but it is not simply whites but white *men* who control the corporations that critics believe are destroying the culture. Further, the rap-as-resistance debate implies a struggle against white power, but whiteness alone does not adequately describe the power structure that organizes American society. Hip-hop's struggle is often framed as a guerrilla war against white patriarchy rather than simply whiteness.

This primary rationale, as well as the practical concerns associated with constructing a viable comparative study, results in a sample composed entirely of young men. The cost of this methodological choice is immense in a field and cultural community where women's voices are actively marginalized and disregarded in order to protect male power (see chapter 5) and where hip-hop is often wrongly reduced to an unmediated and uncomplicated manifestation of black masculinity (Rose 1994). I regret that this book might be viewed by some as yet another example of the fortification of heteronormative masculinity, both within and beyond hip-hop communities. However, the value of focusing on representations of men and presenting men's voices is that this method affirms the importance of gender as a construct that shapes everyone's experience rather than just women's experiences.

Taking Sides

Hip-hop detractors and defenders write in a range of styles, but the loudest critics are often those with social and generational distance from hip-hop who are granted a more public forum to voice their remorse about its social effects. The anti-hip-hop crusades of certified stars such as Bill Cosby[10] and Bill O'Reilly[11] are well documented, and journalists repeatedly blame hip-hop for many young black celebrities' fall from grace.[12] I want to briefly touch on the objections of a few prominent researchers and academics who disapprove of hip-hop, as they often explain their positions in more detail than media celebrities. One such commentator, John McWhorter, whose distaste for hip-hop stems from its impact on black behaviors and culture, frankly avers, "Hip-hop creates nothing" in his strongly worded and weakly researched "How Hip-Hop Holds Blacks Back" (2003). He writes:

> The attitude and style expressed in the hip-hop "identity" keeps blacks down . . . [T]he arm-slinging, hand-hurling gestures of rap performers have made their way into many young blacks' casual gesticulations, becoming integral to their self-expression. The problem with such speech and mannerisms is that they make potential employers wary of young black men and can impede a young black's ability to interact comfortably with co-workers and customers. The black community has gone through too much to sacrifice upward mobility to the passing kick of an adversarial hip-hop "identity."

In later work, McWhorter (2008) acknowledges that hip-hop can be attractive as art, and he understands its appeal as a form of popular music. But he insists that hip-hop's primary message is one of empty rage and narcissism rather than anything that constitutes adequate assessment of, or means to ameliorate, the political situation of African Americans. McWhorter also compares rap music to the black music of eras past, as he connects the violent rhythms of hip-hop with the physical presence of stereotypical menacing black manhood. In contrast to "sweet" black soul music of the 1970s, the advent of rap turned "black music [into an] assault on the ears and soul. Anyone who grew up in urban America during the eighties won't soon forget the young men strolling down streets, blaring this sonic weapon from their boom boxes, with defiant glares daring anyone to ask them to turn it down" (McWhorter 2003). For this reason, it may be logical and justifiable that white people are scared of the stereotypical black hip-hop thug. Black male oppositional identity goes by many names, be it "cool pose" (Majors and Bilson 1992) or "street culture" (Elijah Anderson 1990), but the common theme is that hip-hop fills black men's heads with illusions of antiestablishment glory, resulting in behaviors that impede their life chances. If hip-hop "rowdies" (McWhorter's term) fail to shape up their dress, speech, and mannerisms, they will continue to be shut out of jobs and shipped out to prison.

Political scientist Martin Kilson, the first African American professor to be granted tenure at Harvard University, echoes McWhorter's concern across the generational divide in his 2003 piece "The Politics of Hip-Hop and Black Leadership." Kilson argues:

> The "hip-hop worldview" is far from being a viable post–civil rights era message to African-American children and youth. It is seldom a message of self-respect and self-dignity . . . It is ironic, in fact, that Black youth in poverty-level and weak working-class families who struggle to design a regime of self-respect and discipline in matters of education and interpersonal friendship, get no assistance whatever in these respects from hedonistic, materialistic, nihilistic, sadistic, and misogynistic ideas and values propagated by most hip-hop entertainers.

While McWhorter focuses on black men specifically, Kilson comments on hip-hop culture's effects on both men and women who face class disadvantage. Hip-hop oppositional identity emerges as a choice that individuals can accept or reject, as Kilson's rhetoric of individual responsibility, "self-respect," and "discipline" emphasizes. The impetus for Kilson's piece is Todd Boyd's *The New H.N.I.C. (Head Niggas in Charge)* (2002), a text that pits the hip-hop cultural revolution against the civil rights movement. Kilson chides Boyd, Michael Eric Dyson, and other academics who dare assert that hip-hop is usefully oppositional or that the "hip-hop worldview" constitutes a legitimate political philosophy or ethic for any and all who claim it. Such a worldview is "nothing other than an updated face on the old-hat, crude, anti-humanistic values of hedonism and materialism" (Kilson 2003).

Kilson garners support from a number of academics, including Paul Gilroy, who argues that the "attractively packaged pseudo-rebellion" (2000, 179) that is hip-hop holds no political value for blacks hoping to improve their lives and makes for a juvenile exercise in academic inquiry. Adolph Reed holds hip-hop studies in similar contempt, arguing that a chimerical discourse of "cultural politics" disguises the problem of contemporary black political pathology, as identification with a hip-hop "taste community" takes the place of "purposive contests over state action" (1999, 206).

bell hooks draws her analytic circles slightly larger, as she criticizes hip-hop's destructive gangsterism, calling attention not only to the damaging effects of heartless hip-hop rebellion but also to the ways in which the hallmarks of hip-hop hedonism—violence and sexism—reflect the values of the "white supremacist capitalist patriarchy" that is America (1994, 116). Such an argument adds a new dimension to the hip-hop problem for the black male hip-hop fan, who must not only find the personal strength to make the individual behavioral choice to stop acting irresponsibly (McWhorter 2003) and get serious about politics (Reed) but must also holistically combat the diseased cultural context in which hateful hip-hop is created.

Contrary to Reed's argument, there are multiple examples of hip-hop communities actively engaging the state, even if such political action is not the primary purpose of hip-hop practice. Russell Simmons's Hip-Hop Summit Action Network's campaign against New York State's Rockefeller drug laws, P. Diddy's "Vote or Die" campaign, the Black August Hip-Hop Project's ongoing efforts to raise awareness about political prisoners, and institutionalized partnerships between hip-hop acts and government institutions in Brazil (Pardue 2008) and Cuba (Fernandes 2006) constitute but a few examples of such engagement. However, most hip-hop scholars concede that direct action aimed at governments and political institutions is not elemental to hip-hop's definition or practice. When discussing the politics of hip-hop, most academics do not refer to the empirically demonstrable impact of hip-hop on material efforts to regulate or influence government. Instead, to Reed's dismay, the discussion is primarily about cultural politics or "contestations over meanings, over borders and boundaries, over the ways we make sense of our worlds, and the ways we live our lives" (Mitchell 2000, 159).[13] Thus the title of this book, which directs attention to the *meaning*(s) of hip-hop.

Hip-hop journalist Jeff Chang employs the idea of the "hip-hop generation" to describe the unbounded, multiracial collection of people who grew up witnessing hip-hop's expansion and to capture "the turn from politics to culture" (2005, 2). Chang demonstrates this "turn" not by separating politics (government and state action) from culture (meaning-making) and hip-hop but by showing how large-scale political and economic processes are manifest in hip-hop practice from the 1960s through today. That is, he enables us to understand politics through cultural events and phenomena and illustrates the ways politics and culture interact.

While Chang's text is among the best book-length accounts of hip-hop history, it is by no means the first. British musician and journalist David Toop published one of the first books on hip-hop's development in 1984, though it took roughly a decade for hip-hop to make serious inroads as a legitimate topic for academic exploration. A number of texts were written in the early and mid-1990s, and the range of topics expanded beyond merely describing hip-hop's birth and growth. Houston Baker's *Black Studies, Rap, and the Academy* (1993) is significant because it explicitly ties the development of hip-hop to the development of the academy and the quest for knowledge. Baker lays what has since become a well-trodden path for hip-hop analysis, arguing that hip-hop is fundamentally oppositional to white mainstream culture, which aligns it with black studies, a discipline designed to oppose and deconstruct the epistemic dominance of white-centered disciplines and scholarly methods.

Black Studies, Rap, and the Academy was much needed and relatively well received by scholars in the field, but at the time of its publication, and perhaps still, Tricia Rose's *Black Noise* (1994) was without question the finest piece of hip-hop scholarship to date. More than fifteen years later, Rose casts a huge shadow in the field, and the comprehensiveness of her text is rarely approached by contemporary hip-hop studies. While *Black Noise* weighs in on a number of issues vital to my study, including black vernacular and the oral storytelling tradition, tropes of black masculinity, and hip-hop's history as an art form created by marginalized populations, her fundamental argument is that hip-hop should be understood as a hidden transcript that "critiques and resists various aspects of social domination" (100).

Hidden transcripts are created in opposition to dominant or public transcripts, which prescribe a discourse that frames power relations in a way that legitimizes society's distribution of resources, both political and material. Rose's public/hidden transcripts framework is adopted from James Scott's *Domination and the Art of Resistance* (1992), as she demonstrates the ways in which rap performance, without being unflinchingly serious, straightforward, or unambiguous, constitutes a dynamic and occasionally playful effort to direct audiences' attention to the inconsistencies of justice, authority, and legitimacy as articulated by those in power. One of Rose's most valuable contributions is her recognition of the ways in which "hidden and popular transcripts are readily absorbed into the public domain and subject to incorporation and invalidation." This absorption results in the resistance paradox, as "contradictions between commodity interests . . . and the desire for social control" emerge as the unending internal struggle played out in the hip-hop music industry (1994, 101).

Rose serves as the standard-bearer in rap music scholarship because she foregrounds hip-hop's diversity and its Jekyll-and-Hyde political potential rather than emphasizing its revolutionary essence. Much of the best work that follows along these lines has been conducted by scholars primarily concerned with sex and gender issues in hip-hop practice and communities. Sex and gender dynamics within mainstream hip-hop seem to be most defenseless against anti-hip-hop attacks, thanks to the rampant objectification and degradation of women in commercial rap music and video. But even this criticism, which is more than fair, may be turned to a potential political strength by scholars who point out discursive battles within hip-hop. Rose notes that the verbal assault on women throughout hip-hop's history is not a one-sided phenomenon but involves give and take between men proclaiming their dominance and women rappers who not only rebuke men's claims but intervene on multiple discourses that address gender relations, challenging the order and the rules of the game. Hip-hop feminists such as Joan Morgan (1999) and Gwendolyn Pough (2002, 2004) point to the ways in which hip-hop forces women (and men) who love the music to come to feminist consciousness in a social and political context devoid of a clearly identifiable or authoritative feminist movement. If hip-hop has emerged as a black public sphere (Dawson 2001; Pough 2004; Harris-Lacewell 2004) with room for dissent, ideological contestation, and the possibility of consensus or resolution, this may be its most important function, particularly for communities of color.

Positioning myself on the political spectrum of hip-hop scholarship is a difficult task. There is certainly a connection between one's aesthetic and affective feelings about the music itself and one's tolerance for hip-hop's shortcomings and evaluation of its political potential. I cannot separate my love of hip-hop music from my defense of its politics because I know that hip-hop played an instrumental role in forming my identity, and I consider myself deeply concerned with social inequality and injustice. But unlike some critics' one-sided disavowal of all things hip-hop, my appreciation for hip-hop culture is reflexive. I concede that some hip-hop, along with other pop cultural phenomena, may have nurtured the most regrettable aspects of my cultural-political personality, especially during adolescence as a heterosexual middle-class black male. Commercially successful rap was not the only reason that I accepted homophobia as a social norm or occasionally rhetorically objectified women during my early teen years, but many of the representations and commodities I consumed failed to deter me from doing so. These contradictions are possible because there is such a wide range of hip-hop and because the mechanics of hip-hop allow for conflict and contestation, even within bounded commodities. Songs and performances, in addition to being polyphonic, are often polytextual, and poly-ideological. There is nothing endemic about hip-hop that leads to morally or politically commendable, or reprehensible, behavior. As Rose (1994), Morgan (1999), Pough (2002, 2004), and others note, one of the gifts of hip-hop for those of us who love it is that it forces personal reckoning with one's beliefs and social habits.

My Contribution

Hip-hop performances have the potential to both intensify and combat black American subjugation.[14] The question of rap music's effect on power relations cannot be answered using textual[15] analysis alone, because texts contain both hegemonic and counterhegemonic elements.[16] While I dedicate two chapters to textual analysis in order to explain my definition of hip-hop coolness, the book moves beyond texts to study commercially successful hip-hop by interviewing everyday rap music listeners and uncovering respondents' conceptions of hip-hop's meaning. This mixed methodology differentiates my work from other projects and commentators in three ways.

First, in the textual analysis in chapters 2 and 3, I do not make sweeping statements that hip-hop functions *mostly* or *primarily* as a means of political resistance without sufficient evidence. My theoretical frame affirms fluid power relations grounded in discourse and multiplicitous subjectivity rather than a zero-sum, haves versus have-nots understanding of power and agency. Such an understanding means that cultural production has the *potential* to trouble social norms and dominant discourses, but there is nothing *essentially* revolutionary or progressive about hip-hop, despite its beginnings as the product of marginalized peoples.

Second, as explained in the appendix, my methodology creates a sample for textual analysis more clearly defined than other studies, which rarely justify the texts they draw from and selectively sample the infinite universe of hip-hop to make their cases. I discuss performances by the artists deemed relevant by my respondents because I want to describe a recognizable fraction of the hip-hop world and unveil commercial rap music's tensions and paradoxes. Anyone with broad exposure to hip-hop music would acknowledge that there are many acts without mass exposure that produce musical products with explicitly revolutionary ideological content. By selecting texts based on respondents' preferences and artists' presence in the commercial hip-hop market from 1993 to 2008, I analyze meaning in a strain of hip-hop that is most often criticized for being politically worthless, if not disgraceful and callous. Ultimately, I argue that even commercially successful hip-hop artists offer performances that challenge previous theories of coolness and force us to reconsider representations of black masculinity.

Third, when scholars and critics perform textual analysis, they are essentially working from a real world sample where $n = 1$ (the scholar himself or herself). My project pits my interpretation against the interpretations of forty other consumers in an attempt to more fully sketch the meanings that listeners draw from popular hip-hop. Though there is a strong theoretical foundation within cultural sociology for both textual and interview-driven data analysis, this is the first book-length study that employs both methods with reference to each other, as my arguments about hip-hop meaning are directly compared with respondents' statements.

Plan of the Book

Interview data drive chapter 1, which asks, "How do young black and white men define, engage, and utilize hip-hop?" Though there are clear differences between the ways white and black respondents define hip-hop, respondents agree that hip-hop is about more than pseudo-oppositional posturing and report multiple uses of hip-hop music as socioemotional technology. This chapter enables us to understand the dynamics of hip-hop identity as an amorphous construct that interacts with racial identity rather than canceling it out.

Chapters 2 and 3 constitute my own analysis of rap music performance. I focus on the relationship between coolness and black masculinity as I argue that hip-hop coolness cannot be adequately characterized either as a tragic coping strategy or as the aspiration to a holistic and spiritually cool state of being. Like all commercially successful performers, rappers are concerned with projecting a cool image, and in many cases this image is politically problematic. But textual analysis in chapter 2 illustrates that rappers produce a collective racial discourse that is not necessarily oppositional. This points us toward a new and more complicated definition of coolness that draws on multiple understandings of black coolness both as the performance of composure and detachment as coping strategy, and as the aspiration to a luminous and perhaps spiritual bodily state.

Chapter 3 examines the historical context and content of representations of thug life in commercially successful rap. These performances seem to fit the oppositional/coping model of black masculinity most seamlessly, casting black men as cool-obsessed outlaws. However, even in the case of hip-hop thugs, the black masculinity prescribed by cool pose is insufficient. Hip-hop thugs build narratives about fear, vulnerability, and love alongside the negative themes reflective of the most objectionable stereotypes of blackness. The simultaneous existence of these different elements within thug performances stands as evidence of a multiplicitous subjectivity, presenting black masculinities full of conflict and possibility rather than an essentialized version of black manhood with prescribed outcomes born from the pressure to cope. I suggest that coolness of the sort we see in hip-hop is better understood as *complex cool* rather than cool pose.

After I have explained my understanding of black male performance in commercially successful rap and provided readers with my take on the major themes in mainstream hip-hop, chapters 4 and 5 present respondents' answers to questions of taste, authenticity, and content. In chapter 4, the canonical work on the sociology of taste serves as a backdrop for respondents' comments about why they like rap and the significance of "keeping it real." Again, similarities and differences emerge between white and black respondents, as signifying and authenticity are solidified as aesthetic principles. However, the meaning of authenticity varies significantly between respondents, and their statements both support and complicate the readings of authenticity I propose in chapters 2 and 3.

The final chapter containing interview data, chapter 5, explicitly addresses three issues that consistently provoke episodes of moral panic about the explicit content in rap music: the place and treatment of women in hip-hop, use of the words *nigger* and *nigga*, and representations of gangsterism and criminality. In this chapter, I provide a final overview of all the qualitative interview data related to authenticity in hip-hop and identify three operative authenticity questions about commercialism, gender, and race. This effort to synchronize and summarize the most salient interview data collected about hip-hop authenticity poses an alternative to the more academic treatment given in chapters 2 and 3.

The conclusion summarizes the key findings of my study and reaffirms the centrality of everyday listeners to the debate over hip-hop's meaning and significance. The importance of balancing textual analysis with in-depth interviews is highlighted, and I make the case that the research design should be copied and expanded to engage other segments of the hip-hop universe. The book closes with an epilogue that tries to make sense of President Barack Obama's rise as a hip-hop icon, given my arguments about complex cool black masculinity in hip-hop. For readers who wish to learn more about the sociological methods employed in the study, the appendix more thoroughly discusses my qualitative methodology in the recruiting and interview processes.

In the remainder of this introduction, I address theoretical matters, beginning with a brief explanation of signifying, and closing with a word on textuality.

Signifying

The exact definition of *signifying* is contested because it is used to refer to so many communicative phenomena, from tongue-in-cheek reference to prior speakers and writers to playfully insulting a conversational adversary. For the purposes of this book, *signifying* refers to an indirect method of communication whereby the speaker builds meaning intended for a restricted audience using signals that only the intended audience will be able to recognize and decode. Signifying may be accomplished through rhyming, mimicry, call and response, repetition, teasing, shouting out (one's name or another phrase), or a variety of other tactics. The effect of signifying is that unfamiliar listeners mistake or fail to grasp the full significance of the communication. The intended audience appreciates the artistry of the signifier, is aware of the vernacular game in play, and can decode hidden meanings. By contrast, the unintended audience, which may be victimized through verbal attack embedded in signifying, is unaware of the game and any artistry or skill employed by the speaker.[17]

This study discusses signifying in two sections. Chapters 2 and 3 affirm the utility of a signifying framework for understanding hip-hop lyrics. I decode signifying by hip-hop performers, asserting myself as one of the intended audience members spoken to by commercially successful MCs. Numerous hip-hop scholars perform similar analyses, and I make only modest contributions to the body of knowledge about signifying and how it is used in hip-hop.

In chapters 1, 4, and 5, in-depth interviews provide the foundation for a comparative study of race and hip-hop meaning and culture. In presenting the interpretations of hip-hop consumers, I steer clear of sweeping, didactic rhetoric about where hip-hop needs to go or what hip-hop truly is. Rather, I use interview data to shed new light on the driving theoretical frames of the project and contribute to ongoing scholarly discussions about masculinity, resistance, authenticity, and reception. I ask listeners what hip-hop is and what performances mean rather than arguing for a universal conclusion that one group is inherently or intellectually capable of recognizing signifying or understanding hip-hop while another is not; neither capacity for nor appreciation of signifying is determined by race. However, findings do reveal differences in the ways in which black and white male listeners activate discourses of race, gender, pleasure, and identity in their discussions of hip-hop, as performances may signify different things to different groups.

The Problem of Textuality

Hip-hop performance is more than text, but we cannot ignore the importance of the words and symbols that are the lifeblood of a vernacular cultural phenomenon. Gilroy urges scholars to

> move beyond an understanding of cultural processes which . . . is currently torn between seeing them either as the expression of an essential, unchanging, sovereign racial self or as the effluent from a constituted subjectivity that emerges contingently from the endless play of racial signification. This is usually conceived solely in terms of the inappropriate model which *textuality* [Gilroy's emphasis] provides. The vitality and complexity of this musical culture offers a means to get beyond the related oppositions between essentialists and pseudo-pluralists on the one hand and between totalizing conceptions of tradition, modernity, and post-modernity on the other. It also provides a model of performance which can supplement and partially displace concern with textuality. (1993, 36)

What are we to make of this warning? Gilroy's primary aim is to arrive at a more productive and accurate notion of black diasporic identity. In fact, Gilroy's main objection to textuality, as articulated above, has less to do with the method of analysis (textual or semiotic) than with the common products of such analysis, which are simplistic notions of black identity as either fundamentally modern/essential/normative or postmodern/transient/pluralistic. So on one hand, we might fairly ask whether this objection to textuality has anything to do with textuality itself or has more to do with Gilroy's objections to the politics and arguments of scholars who frequently employ textuality as they attempt to understand black diasporic experience.

On the other hand, we could focus on Gilroy's distinction between performance and textuality as the key to the foregoing quotation and to his distaste for textual analysis where black music is concerned. Greg Dimitriadis echoes this concern, explaining that "texts—whether symbol systems or lived experiences—are always in performance. They contain no essential or inherent meaning, but are given meaning by people, in particular times, in particular places" (2001, 11). Gilroy, Dimitriadis, and others[18] advance worthy disapproval of isolated or abstracted textuality. But hip-hop scholars must pay attention to texts, first because of the vernacular tradition of hip-hop, and second because they recognize that the text itself *is* a contingent[19] performance rather than a pure expression of selfhood. As Eithne Quinn notes, "In nearly all gangsta rap tracks there are two performances going on simultaneously: the action of the (usually first-person) character within the narrative, and the rhetorical action of rapping itself. That is, the performance *in* the text and the performance *of* the text" (2005, 124). To these two performances, Dimitriadis would add another: the performance inherent in listening to the music at a particular time and place. Recognizing the simultaneity of these performances does not eradicate textuality or render it arbitrary. What I am suggesting is that textuality and performance are not diametrically opposed, and the best studies of hip-hop culture give credence to both.

Our experience with music experience is *formative*; it shapes reality, as one of the forces that colors our perception and experience of ourselves as well as other subjects and objects (DeNora 2003, 61). A component of the formative powers of musical texts and performances is *exploration* as we learn each boast, confession, joke, and jab of a favorite rap song. This exploration is in fact something active, something that we *do*, and the lessons we learn from each musical session and moment may be recontextualized and *transported*. We may find music applicable to places, people, and experiences beyond the possible intentions of its composer and beyond our initial formative experiences with the text or performance in question. We bring our relationship with music to concerts, clubs, and parties where we perform it with others, collectively engaging in its life cycle and reaffirming its resonance. As a researcher concerned with racial identity and politics in the early twenty-first century, I acknowledge my own performative context and recognize that my musical formation, exploration, and transportation is enabled by the commoditized form of thug-era hip-hop and impossible to assess without attention to race, class, and gender.

Summary

Hip-hop's commercial success prompts concerns that the culture is now driven by white consumers who demand objectionable representations of blackness. Further, white men hold significant decision-making power within corporations that control commoditization and distribution of hip-hop, giving nonblacks a major stake in both the production and consumption of what is traditionally conceived as black American cultural product.[20] The questions driving my project are (1) How should we understand black men's hip-hop performances, many of which contain degrading content and themes pertinent to theories and stereotypes of black pathology? (2) Do black male listeners interpret and rearticulate hip-hop's definition, content, and significance differently than white male listeners? And more broadly, (3) What can hip-hop tell us about race, class, and gender?

While I am sensitive to the theoretical and methodological implications of combining textual and ethnographic analyses, these disparate disciplinary and theoretical approaches are reconcilable. One of the goals of the book is to provide a model for methodologically rigorous interdisciplinary work enabled by affirming hip-hop studies as a research field. None of the meanings offered stand as the definitive understanding of what hip-hop truly is, but taken together, data and arguments in the chapters that follow illustrate how hip-hop matters.

ONE

The Meaning of Hip-Hop

Music hath its land of origin; and yet it is also its own country, its own sovereign power, and all may take refuge there, and all, once settled, may claim it as their own, and all may meet there in amity; and these instruments, as surely as instruments of torture, belong to all of us.

—M. T. Anderson, *The Astonishing Life of Octavian Nothing*

I listen to hip-hop every single day of my life.

—Marc (w1)

"I Am Hip-Hop"

Picture the scene at a Jay-Z concert: tens of thousands of people from all walks of life, shoulder to shoulder in a massive sports arena, singing every word of their favorite rap anthems for two hours straight. It makes sense to think of such events as proof that we can be one nation under a groove, connected to each other through the power of music. In these situations, the life experiences and belief systems that divide and differentiate us seem to melt away as we collectively affirm the power of hip-hop. But even in these moments of synchronized mass participation when we are all identified with hip-hop, might we be hearing different things and living through the music in vastly different ways? Or is hip-hop identity strong enough to erode the boundaries between us?

Legendary MC and hip-hop philosopher KRS-One believes that anyone can relate to hip-hop and that hip-hop provides limitless opportunities for those who wish to connect to it or through it:

When it comes to Hip-Hop, there is no race, there's no ethnicity, there's no "this is mine." It's like, I can relate to that, I can relate to that. I can relate to this, I can relate to this. If I can relate to all of this, what does that say about me? And then you go back to your own people and they don't relate to you. Which is where the whole "I am Hip-Hop" philosophy comes from. (quoted in Long 2009)

Controversially, KRS suggests that this process of relating to hip-hop has the potential to throw one's previous sense of self into disarray, revealing that previous affiliations with one's "own people" may fail to provide the same material for relating or connecting as hip-hop. For KRS-One, hip-hop identity becomes the best available identity for sustaining human complexity, as antiquated markers of race and ethnicity pale in comparison.

This chapter tests KRS's thesis, as everyday listeners define hip-hop and talk about how it corresponds to their sense of self. Music constitutes a rich form of symbolic material through which individuals forge identities and locate themselves in society. If hip-hop enables people to find themselves and relate to each other, we should expect to find some elaboration of both personal and collective identity within respondents' descriptions of what hip-hop is and how it is used. The import of such a finding is that these distinctions have undeniable, if unquantifiable, effects not only on respondents' sense of self but on cultural politics and power relations, as they redraw the boundaries around "us" and "them."

As noted in the introduction, those looking for a direct connection between one's status as a hip-hop fan and revolutionary political practice are likely to be disappointed. But as Lawrence Grossberg explains, "Fandom is, at least potentially, the site of the optimism, invigoration and passion which are necessary conditions for any struggle to change the conditions of one's life . . . While there is no guarantee that even the most highly charged moments will become either passive sites of evasion or active sites of resistance, without the affective investments of popular culture the very possibility of such struggles is likely to be drowned in the sea of historical pessimism" (1992a, 65).

I begin with a brief discussion of the application of social movement theory to hip-hop and sketch a basic outline of the relationship between social movements and collective identity. After providing these theoretical frames, I introduce each respondent and explain how the sample is divided into race and class categories. Data reveal listeners' understanding of what "hip-hop" means and how one's affinity for hip-hop and social identity are connected. The chapter closes with a discussion of hip-hop's influence on respondents who engage and use it in multiple ways.

Hip-Hop as a Social Movement

S. Craig Watkins grapples most earnestly with questions of commercialized hip-hop's political import, arguing persuasively for a continued understanding of hip-hop as a unique social movement:[1]

> In many ways, hip hop represents a particular species of social movement . . . First, this particular movement takes place on the field of popular culture, a site not immediately discerned as political, or capable of producing social change. Second, hip hop is invigorated by the creative labor of a constituency not ordinarily regarded as interested in effecting social change: youth. Third, like social movements in general, hip hop enables its participants to imagine themselves as part of a larger community; thus, it produces a sense of collective identity and agency. (1998, 65)

The final sentence of this quotation, about hip-hop's potential to produce collective identity, is the axis on which this chapter spins and is at the core of the academic debate about what a social movement is. Watkins offers a broad definition of social movements, characterizing them as "collective efforts to produce social change" (1998, 65). Charles Tilly (2004) is a bit more specific, emphasizing that those who act and make claims in such movements are ordinary people rather than members of the politically powerful and elite. The trouble comes when questions about the specific challenges posed, groups targeted, and changes achieved take center stage in the debate. Disagreements about challenges, targets, and changes have resulted in a two-pronged typology in social movement literature. "Old" social movements are understood to have occurred primarily in Europe during the nineteenth century and are solely concerned with protest motivated by class interests and carried out by members who share a class status (R. Williams 2004, 92). The goals of these movements are institutional changes that result in political and economic redistribution. "New" social movements offer a corrective to this limited model, expanding the definition of social movements to include those that occur outside of Europe during the twentieth century and focus on "cultural understandings, norms, and identities rather than material interests" (R. Williams 2004, 92). The defining characteristics of new social movements are (1) identity, autonomy, and self-realization; (2) defense rather than offense; (3) politicization of everyday life; (4) nonclass or middle-class mobilization; (5) self-exemplification (organizational forms and styles that mimic the ideology of the movement); (6) unconventional means (as opposed to conventional means such as voting); and (7) partial and overlapping commitments (a web of overlapping memberships rather than party loyalty) (Calhoun 1995).

The differences between old and new social movements are not as great as many believe—many of the old movements were undoubtedly concerned with identity, culture, and language, elements essential to solidifying the collective and forming the message of the movement. Defining social movements as phenomena that deal explicitly and exclusively with class interests constitutes not only an analytic failure but a wrongful effort to exclude the efforts of peoples marginalized by other forms of categorization, such as marginalized racial and ethnic groups in America, from definitions of what constitutes legitimate political action (Calhoun 1995, 176).[2]

From all this, we see that hip-hop's status as a social movement is intimately bound with who hip-hop participants understand themselves to be. For this reason, collective identity is a crucial element in movement production and sustenance. Collective identity is "an individual's cognitive, moral, and emotional connection with a broader community, category, practice, or institution. It is a perception of shared status or relation, which may be imagined rather than experienced directly . . . Collective identities are expressed in cultural materials—names, narratives, symbols, verbal styles, rituals, clothing, and so on—but not all cultural materials express collective identities" (Polletta and Jasper 2001, 84). It is possible to have a personal identity that is not tied to a larger collective, and in part for this reason, one may argue that simply defining oneself does not in and of itself constitute a politically significant act or serve as adequate evidence of a social movement. But as Scott Hunt and Robert Benford observe, "By virtue of constructing and elaborating a sense of who they are, movement participants and adherents also construct a sense of who they are not" (1994, 443). This process of differentiation is an important one and clearly qualifies as politically significant if we keep Calhoun's insights about the defensive character of new social movements in mind.

Ron Eyerman and Andrew Jamison reaffirm that "social movements are the result of an interactional process which centers around the articulation of a collective identity" (1991, 4) and make the case that music is a cognitive phenomenon with tremendous potential to influence social movements by virtue of its "knowledge-building and identity-giving qualities" (1998, 23). When they talk of social movements as knowledge-building collective praxis, Eyerman and Jamison speak of knowledge both as a general worldview and as any specific issue or topic that movement participants are focused on (1991, 3). I sifted through the interview data looking for evidence of both types of knowledge, and while respondents' contributions failed to provide evidence that the hip-hop movement is explicitly concerned with a specific set of social issues or political topics, there is plenty of evidence that suggests respondents use hip-hop to understand their social worlds.

"Collective identities are *talked* into existence" (Hunt and Benford 2004, 445). I set out to hear everyday listeners talk, conducting interviews to uncover respondents' "symbolic work," which Paul Willis explains has four crucial elements: language, the active body, drama, and symbolic creativity (1990, 11). Each of these elements serves as a symbolic resource for human practitioners, but of the four, symbolic creativity emerges as the key concept. Symbolic creativity is an active force that produces identities and orients us in the world.[3] Willis's great contribution here is that that the inspiration for, and ability to perform, identity cultivation inheres in each of us rather than exclusively outside of us. We are not simply products of omnipotent structures that mold us into predetermined social beings.[4] Studying individuals in addition to structural forces and institutions is therefore essential to understanding identity and social life. This is not to say that structural context is irrelevant and human creative capacity reigns supreme in the realm of identity. To the contrary, the point is that each of us exercises symbolic creativity in the context of structural forces using cultural materials to build our sense of self. Symbolic creativity produces individual and collective identities that "affirm our active sense of our own vital capacities, the powers of the self and how they might be applied to the cultural world" (Willis 1990, 12).

With this understanding of symbolic creativity and its connection to social movements in mind, we turn to the list of respondents, their definitions of hip-hop, and their understandings of themselves.

The Respondents

A complete description of recruitment methods and other methodological considerations appears in the appendix. Here it suffices to say that each respondent was recruited in the Boston metropolitan area and is included in the sample because he is someone who regularly enjoys commercially successful hip-hop. Respondents were either approached at a place where such hip-hop is featured or consumed, such as a record store or a club or concert affiliated with the major hip-hop radio station, or recommended by someone at such a site. Placing the young men I spoke with into class categories was a challenging task. Traditional measurements of class are dependent on occupation, income, and education. However, when applied across racial lines, these criteria must be considered with attention to residential space. Poverty, disorder, and ghetto culture are central to analyses of hip-hop meaning, thanks to the symbolic importance of the ghetto as an element of hip-hop authenticity and the historical importance of neglected urban space as the birthplace of hip-hop culture. If I am investigating whether blacks with ghetto experience will understand and describe commercially successful hip-hop in different ways than whites who are alienated from the ghetto, I must be sure that my sample contains a fair number of respondents who fit those descriptions. The list below separates respondents by race and neighborhood experience, based on where each respondent has lived most of his life. No white respondent describes his neighborhood as predominantly black.

White Respondents with Impoverished Neighborhood Experience (7 Total)

ABE is a twenty-year-old construction worker from a largely white and working-class neighborhood in a small city. He is a high school graduate with no college education. He describes growing up as "a little rough" and discusses the presence of drugs and violence in his neighborhood.

ADAM is a twenty-one-year-old construction worker from a working class neighborhood in a small city. He did not complete high school and describes his neighborhood as a mix of working people and poor people. Neighborhood disorder was fairly commonplace, and Adam has served less than a year in jail for selling drugs, an activity he no longer partakes in.

ANTHONY is a twenty-one-year-old full-time college student. He is a Serbian national from an impoverished but safe neighborhood in Serbia who attends college in the United States by virtue of a full athletic scholarship. He describes his family circumstances as "great," despite the considerable hardships they have endured as a result of war and economic instability in his homeland. Because he is Serbian, Anthony does not self-identify as white, but he acknowledges that others see him as white.

CHRIS is a twenty-three-year-old fast-food restaurant worker from a predominantly white working-class neighborhood in a small city. He completed high school but has no college education and still resides in the neighborhood in which he grew up, though he believes far more wealthy people live there now than during his childhood.

FRED is a twenty-four-year-old who works in sales and lives in a working-class and middle-class suburban neighborhood. He holds a high school diploma but has no college education. The neighborhood in which he grew up was almost entirely white and deeply impoverished, with a high volume of drugs and street crime.

JAMES is a twenty-three-year-old high school graduate who attends college part time. He lives in public housing in the neighborhood he grew up in, which is racially mixed but severely impoverished.

KEVIN is a twenty-year-old grocery store clerk who grew up in different neighborhoods, some of which were more comfortable than others. He terminated his high school education after ninth grade because, he says, "It's not that I like going against people, I just don't like to be told what to do." He served more than a year in prison for a drug conviction.

White Respondents without Impoverished Neighborhood Experience (13 Total)

BRANDON is a twenty-three-year old manager at a restaurant and bar. He completed high school but terminated his college education after two years. His home neighborhood was a mostly white middle- to working-class section of a small city, and he lives in a similar neighborhood today.

DAMIEN is twenty years old and currently unemployed. He grew up in a mixed middle- and working-class suburban neighborhood. Damien has a high school degree from what he describes as a "trade school" and no college education.

ERIC is a twenty-three-year-old full-time college student who works part time at a radio station. He grew up in a mostly white middle-class suburb and counts his family among those who live comfortably.

ISAAC is a twenty-three-year-old part-time college student who does not work to support himself. He describes the neighborhood in which he grew up as a mostly white "upper-middle-class" small town.

KENNY is a twenty-two-year-old full-time college student at a prestigious university. He is from what he describes as an upper-middle-class white urban neighborhood.

MARC is twenty-three years old and works in sales. He is a college graduate from a mostly white middle-class suburban community.

PAUL is a twenty-four-year-old computer hardware tester with a college degree. He grew up in a mostly white middle-class suburb.

PETE is twenty-three years old and currently unemployed but financially stable. He completed high school and one year of community college before discontinuing his education. He is from an overwhelmingly white and wealthy suburban community.

RICHARD is a twenty-one-year-old full-time college student at an elite university. He lived and attended high school in a white upper-middle-class suburb.

ROY is twenty-four years old and currently unemployed. He holds a high school degree but terminated his college studies without graduating and now plans to reenroll. He was raised in a predominantly white upper-middle-class suburb, where he still lives.

RUSSELL is a twenty-year-old part-time college student who also holds a full-time job as a chemist in a food-testing facility. As a child, he lived in a number of middle-class neighborhoods, and he resides in a white middle-class neighborhood today.

WALLY is a twenty-year-old full-time college student. He describes the suburban neighborhood in which he grew up as mostly white and middle class and considers his a typical middle-class family from his hometown.

ZACK is twenty-four years old and works in retail. He holds a college degree and described his hometown as middle class, almost entirely white, and suburban.

Black Respondents with Impoverished Neighborhood Experience (12 Total)

ANDRE is a twenty-nine-year-old security guard and part-time DJ. He completed high school and began college but terminated his studies without a degree. He now lives in a predominantly white suburban town but was raised in an impoverished urban black community, where he and much of his family lived in public housing projects.

BEN is twenty-four years old and currently unemployed. He graduated from high school but did not enroll in college. Ben did not go into detail about his home neighborhood, describing it as "the hood, around Boston." In his interview he uses the term "hood" to describe black neighborhoods with high levels of poverty. He now lives with family outside of the city in a racially mixed middle-class suburb.

BILL is a twenty-one-year-old who works at a travel agency. He completed high school but did not enroll in college. He lives in the neighborhood in which he was raised, which is working class and poor, urban, and almost entirely black and Hispanic.

BRIAN is twenty-three years old and currently unemployed. He graduated from high school and a two-year college. He lives with his family, who recently moved from a working-class black urban neighborhood to a middle-class racially mixed neighborhood.

DAVID is a twenty-two-year-old electrician. He completed high school but did not enroll in college. He still lives in his home neighborhood, which is urban, black, and working class to poor, though he commuted to high school in a predominantly white suburban town.

DWAYNE is twenty-five years old and holds a fellowship position with a prisoners' advocacy organization. He left high school before earning his diploma but later attained a GED. The neighborhood in which he grew up is urban, deeply impoverished, almost entirely black, and characterized by high levels of street crime and disorder. He served time in jail as the result of a drug-related conviction.

GEORGE is twenty-two years old and works in a juvenile halfway house. He is a college graduate who still resides in the neighborhood in which he grew up, which is almost entirely black and significantly impoverished, with high levels of disorder and street crime.

GREG is twenty-four years old and currently unemployed. He did not finish high school, and he served time in prison for a drug conviction. The neighborhoods he lived in as a child and adolescent were poor, urban, predominantly black, and home to frequent street crime. He now lives with family in a racially mixed middle-class suburban town.

NEIL is a twenty-five-year-old port authority worker. He finished high school and enrolled in a technical school but did not earn a degree. His family moved frequently during his childhood, and he lived in a variety of working-class and middle-class neighborhoods in different cities and suburbs.

NOLAN is a twenty-two-year-old who works in a community center. He holds a college degree and was raised in an impoverished black urban neighborhood with high levels of disorder and street crime. He attended high school outside of his section of the city in a middle-class, mostly white suburb.

RYAN is a twenty-five-year-old food service worker. He holds a high school degree but did not enroll in college. He is from a racially mixed working-class area of a small city, where he still lives today.

STEVEN is twenty-three years old and currently unemployed. He holds a high school diploma and enrolled in college but terminated his studies without a degree. His family lived in what he described as a poor, black, urban neighborhood but moved to a racially mixed suburb when he was twelve years old.

Black Respondents without Impoverished Neighborhood Experience (8 Total)

ALLEN is a twenty-one-year-old full-time college student from a middle-class, predominantly black urban neighborhood.

DARRYL is a twenty-three-year-old full-time college student from a wealthy, predominantly white suburb.

EVAN is a twenty-five-year-old who works as an audio engineer and producer from a one-room studio in his family's house. He graduated from an audio engineering program at a four-year college and grew up in a racially mixed middle-class suburb.

JACK is a twenty-three-year-old health care lab worker and part-time DJ. He was raised in a predominantly black neighborhood, which he describes as more suburban than urban, though it is within a city. He explains that there are certain sections of his neighborhood with better reputations than others but that he has never had a problem staying out of trouble. He graduated from a private high school outside his neighborhood and enrolled in college but did not graduate.

JASON is a twenty-year-old full-time college student from a racially mixed middle-class suburban neighborhood.

NATE is a twenty-three-year-old who works at a health club. He holds a college degree and was raised in a majority black but racially mixed middle-class suburban neighborhood.

SEAN is twenty-six years old and currently unemployed. He holds a high school degree and enrolled in college for two years before terminating his studies. The neighborhood in which he grew up is predominantly white and middle class.

TIM is a twenty-four-year-old mechanic. He graduated from high school and enrolled in two different four-year colleges but terminated his studies before earning a degree. He is from a middle-class black urban neighborhood, though he attended a mostly white suburban high school.

Neighborhoods matter because respondents are more likely to have witnessed antisocial behavior and to bear the psychosocial effects of poverty in troubled neighborhoods, and one would think that a respondent's understanding of hip-hop is related to his life experience. Neighborhoods also matter because they are crucial to class structure. Social capital transmission in middle-class communities is grounded in teaching children to employ critical thinking, interact on fairly equal footing with authority figures, develop a sense of personal entitlement, and acclimate themselves to a structured daily schedule of work and play. These are not the aims of child socialization in communities of working-class standing and below, where children are taught to defer to authoritative adults, follow instructions, and fill their schedules without regimented, institutional time commitments (Lareau 2003).

Placing each respondent in a specific class category is complicated by educational status, which is crucial to one's class standing and to understanding the ways in which respondents are likely to interpret artistic cultures.[5] Establishing firm class categories with attention to education is especially difficult in the case of my sample, which includes men from privileged backgrounds without a college degree and men from disadvantaged backgrounds who graduated from four-year colleges. For example, George and Nolan each grew up amid poverty, neighborhood disorder, and ghetto culture, and they still lived in those neighborhoods when interviews were conducted. However, each managed to earn a college degree at a school far from his hometown, which places them on an upwardly mobile track despite their neighborhood status. While level of education sometimes complicates the class status picture, in other cases, it firmly solidifies the class standing of upper-middle-class respondents. Based on both neighborhood experience and level of education, each respondent is counted as a member of one of four class categories:

1 CULTURAL ELITE. These are respondents who have had the dual benefit of a middle-class upbringing and college education. Each respondent in this category was raised in a middle-class neighborhood and has either completed college or is currently enrolled in school.

2 STAGNANT MIDDLE CLASS. This is a relatively small group of respondents who were raised in middle-class communities where they still reside but terminated their studies without receiving a college degree.

3 UPWARDLY MOBILE WORKING CLASS. These respondents have come from working-class or impoverished upbringings but are in position to join the middle class by virtue of their education.

4 STAGNANT WORKING CLASS. These respondents have spent the vast majority of their lives in either working-class or impoverished communities and do not have the sort of education likely to result in upward economic mobility.

Social class	Whites	Blacks
1. Cultural elite	(10) Eric, Isaac, Kenny, Marc, Paul, Pete, Richard, Wally, Zack, Russell	(5) Allen, Darryl, Evan, Jason, Nate
2. Stagnant middle	(1) Roy	(3) Jack, Sean, Tim
3. Upward working	(4) Brandon, James, Fred, Anthony	(4) Brian, Dwayne, George, Nolan
4. Stagnant working	(5) Kevin, Chris, Adam, Abe, Damien	(8) Andre, Ben, Bill, David, Greg, Neil, Ryan, Steven

In the chapters that follow, respondents are identified by name, race, and class category as indicated above. For example, Allen, who is black, was raised in a relatively stable neighborhood, is on track to receive a college degree, will be identified as "(Allen, b1)," where "b" stands for black and "1" indicates his position in the most privileged status group.

Hip-Hop Is . . .

Rather than defining hip-hop as a set of artistic practices that fall within the categories of DJ-ing (playing, mixing, and scratching records), MC-ing (rapping), b-boying, and graffiti art, a significant portion of respondents across race and class categories first describe hip-hop as a culture or lifestyle.

> Hip-hop is a cultural way of life. Like KRS said, "Rap is something you do, hip-hop is something you live." You can listen to a hip-hop or rap record and be fine with that but not incorporate it into your life. But what hip-hop means to me is that you wake up and you're a part of hip-hop. You wake up and you know it's part of your life. (Marc, w1)

> I'd say hip-hop is a culture, it's a way of life. It's more than just music, it's a lifestyle, it's how you dress, how you think. (Nolan, b3)

> It's a culture, it's a way of life. It's the way you walk, the way you talk, the way you express yourself. It really is a way of life. Sometimes you can't describe it, but you know it when you see it. (Steven, b4)

> It's a culture, it's a lifestyle, the clothes, the shoes, everything. It's part of who you are. The essentials of it are good music basically. Production combined with good lyrics, that's what hip-hop is to me. (Bill, b4)

> It's a culture, man, I don't know. It started off as something cool, like with dancing, beat boxing, break dancing, all that. It transformed over the years to something different, like controversial with all this using the n-word and derogatory terms for females. I mean it has changed quite a bit but I guess . . . I grew up with it so I adapted to the culture. (Fred, w3)

When asked the open-ended question "How would you define hip-hop, or what does hip-hop mean to you?" none of the respondents define it strictly according to its widely recognized artistic elements (DJ, MC, b-boy, graffiti), and only one respondent mentioned all four elements as part of his definition. So hip-hop is more than just art. "Culture," however, emerges as a common buzzword, and the subjects insist that hip-hop is something they live, not just listen to. However, respondents struggle to describe exactly what the "culture" entails in terms of meanings, behavioral norms, values, and aspirations (Herbert Gans's definition [1991]), and interview data do not reveal a clear pattern of inherited ideas expressed symbolically (Clifford Geertz's definition [1973]).

Another common response evoked by the open-ended question about hip-hop's definition or meaning is respondents' contention that hip-hop is a means of communication and expression. More specifically, multiple respondents discuss hip-hop as a means of physical expression, complete with visual bodily markers of hip-hop style (such as sneakers and baseball caps). Again, this characterization of hip-hop as expression or communication is consistent across a range of race and class categories.

> I would say hip-hop is more of just a rhythm, but when you hear those lyrics, just somebody speaking to you. It's not like singing—rock and roll—it's more like somebody is speaking to you, and you try to listen to that person. (Paul, w1)

> A statement by many people, and they express it many ways. Those that can feel and hear the music can accept it for what it is. That's what hip-hop is to me. Definitely a standpoint from where everybody can speak their mind about what they see and what they going through in life. (Sean, b2)

> MICHAEL: What does hip-hop mean to you?
> DAMIEN (w4): Lifestyle. Music. Trying to get a point across. Clothes, your walk, the way you wear your hat.

> Hip-hop is like an expression of yourself, a representation of the things you think are ill or sick, however you want to say it. You put your words, your thoughts, what you're all about, into rhyme form, to a beat that you think represents the sounds you want to hear. I feel like they're the superheroes of music. You get to say anything, you get to say the most information out of any music. You can make yourself sound like anything. It's the only real music where you talk about yourself while you're singing. You get to describe a whole persona. It's just sick. (Brandon, w3)

Right off the bat, these excerpts confirm hip-hop as a tool for elaborating identity. Brandon, Sean, and Paul all explain that hip-hop is something that allows people to tell the world who they are. Hip-hop as communication is a prevalent theme in the data, and in total, eighteen of the forty respondents invoke communication or expression in comments about what they understand hip-hop to be. This understanding echoes Simon Frith's insistence that music is performative (rather than purely textual) and that "the term 'performance' defines a social—or *communicative*—process. It requires an audience and is dependent, in this sense, on interpretation" (1996, 205; emphasis added). Further, "song words are not about ideas ('content') but about their *expression*" (1996, 164; emphasis added). For example, Frith argues that "songs don't *cause* people to fall in love, but provide people with the means to articulate the feelings associated with being in love" and that songs "don't function to convey ideas or arguments but slogans" (1996, 164–65). The quotations from respondents seem to partially refute Frith, as they emphasize the idea that hip-hop narrators are "trying to get a point across" and that they "try to listen to that person." Such comments could be read as listeners' concern for the message or *content* of a given song, which for Frith is secondary, if not irrelevant. But closer reading of these quotations shows that what listeners concentrate on is the *expression* itself rather than a specific, consistent message that defines hip-hop music or culture. Respondents "try to listen to that person" not because performers deliver specific messages that prescribe beliefs or action but because artists "speak their mind" and "describe a whole persona." So while respondents may have trouble enumerating the cultural axioms of hip-hop when prompted, they clearly see it as a tool for identity building and interpersonal connection.

The idea of hip-hop as communication or expression presents itself in data from both black and white respondents with considerable frequency, but this theme also points to cleavages between racial groups. When respondents describe the "communication" and "culture" in more depth, race and class influence their answers. One question that arises from these data is "Who is doing the communicating when respondents describe hip-hop as communication or expression?" Respondents frequently refer to rap music in their answers to this question, and we can read one reply across both racial groups as "Whoever happens to be rapping on the track or executing the hip-hop performance at hand is doing the communicating." However, respondents also make specific reference to the types of people for whom hip-hop is a voice. Both black and white hip-hop listeners affirm the culture as a voice for economically disadvantaged, urban, or black people as they describe the meaning of hip-hop, but black respondents speak more frequently about the racial identity of hip-hop communicators. The following are all of the excerpts from interviews with white respondents who explicitly refer to the race and class identity of the hip-hop practitioners.

Where it started, like in the seventies, in Brooklyn, DJ Kool Herc and stuff like that, that's when it was really real and wasn't affected by capitalism and commercialism and people just trying to sell it, sell it, sell it. So it started there and was by mostly black urban people. (Pete, w1)

For me it's music of people who struggle. People who struggle throughout their history, struggle throughout time. I mean hip-hop is not how some rappers try to represent right now. Hip-hop is not about girls or cars, it's something else. For me hip-hop started as poor people tried to present to the rest of the world, maybe to other people, how they live. (Anthony, w3)

Me being a white person, I think there's an initial getting past any qualms about listening to a music that was primarily black when it started. (Eric, w1)

It's a relatively young form of popular music. It's always interesting to me to think about how young popular music is anyway. American popular music is basically nascent still. I'd say it's a newer genre of music that primarily arose in New York and featured primarily African Americans. It's heavily rhythmic and features people rhyming over beats. (Richard, w1)

I read a Nas interview, and he was like, "Rap and hip-hop is like music coming out of the crack generation, and that's people rapping about being broke, or hustling, and that's what made them unique. Music that's played now, where you have the rapper rapping and somebody singing the hook, that's great black music, but that's not rap or that's not hip-hop" . . . For me personally I think it's like a cultural thing. As much as I like it, I feel like I'm an outsider to it. (Wally, w1)

Two of the salient themes from this group of excerpts are conceptions of hip-hop as music and as a development affected by capitalism and commerce rather than simply a culture or communication and expression. There is also much to be said about the quotations above as they pertain to race, class, space, and identity. The temporal character of blackness as presented in the excerpts is worth highlighting. In each instance where hip-hop is identified as a black cultural product, white respondents affirm hip-hop blackness in the past tense ("it *started* there and *was* by mostly black urban people"; it "*was* primarily black when it *started*"; and it "*arose* in New York and *featured* primarily African Americans").[6] Both Wally and Eric explicitly mention that they feel a sense of distance from true hip-hop culture because of some combination of their racial and generational identity.

Compare white respondents' invocations of blackness as part of hip-hop history with a collection of quotations from black respondents who mention race and class as they describe hip-hop.

When it first came out, it was a way for urban poor black youths to express themselves in a way that was unique to us. (Andre, b4)

I feel like it's antiestablishment. The art itself is mostly performed by underprivileged persons in America, to a very large extent, who happen to be persons of color. The reason I say it's antiestablishment is [that] in the mainstream, a lot of the stuff that hip-hop communicates is totally unacceptable. (Dwayne, b3)

MICHAEL: What does hip-hop mean to you?

JASON (B1): Mostly like, sending a message, something positive. I'm not sure.

MICHAEL: Can you explain that a bit more?

JASON: Well, now it's, like, different, but back then it was, like, black unity and stuff. Now they might still do that, but it's different, the way they put it out there.

ALLEN (B1): I'd say hip-hop is a voice for disenfranchised people, so they can speak out.

MICHAEL: What does hip-hop make you think about?

ALLEN: Hip-hop could open someone's eyes to minority issues that they were completely blind to. It could also make you think about where you stand in society and the things that you're doing that reflect poorly on the black community around you.

Hip-hop is like a culture, it's a voice for black people to be heard. Our own style, our own music. (Nate, b1)

Hip-hop is a way of life which explains that we have struggled and the way that we have survived and prospered in the urban areas. (George, b3)

MICHAEL: When you say it's "the way you talk, the way you walk," what is that way? What does that mean?

NOLAN (B3): Hip-hop is real innovative. The pioneers of hip-hop and the people they associate with, there's something about them. I guess it's their uniqueness. They have a rich history, they have a story. A lot of people have to find a story, but their story is the plight of African Americans, I'd say. It's not just limited to them, I'll just say minorities, people who know that there's a lot of hardships, more so than with other cultures and races.

It's a way of life. It's our culture, it's black culture. (Ryan, b4)

MICHAEL: What does it mean to you, even if you don't have the perfect definition?
TIM (B2): Think hip-hop, think urban, think rap, think black-oriented style of music.
MICHAEL: What makes it urban or black oriented?
TIM: That would have to do with the artists that does hip-hop, artists that perform hip-hop, the people that listen to hip-hop.

Similarities and differences emerge as black and white men mention race and class when describing hip-hop in these responses. Hip-hop is once again described as a voice for disadvantaged people who struggle, bolstering the argument that hip-hop is understood as a social movement and a means to tell the world who you are. Eleven black respondents discuss race as part of the definition of hip-hop, compared with only three white respondents. With more race-related responses, the range of descriptions given by black respondents is broader than the range given by white respondents. Respondents from each racial group define hip-hop as a type of music and as something that started as an urban, poor, and black phenomenon and grew into something different. In addition to echoing white respondents' belief that hip-hop *began* as black practice, some black respondents affirm hip-hop as black music and black culture in the present day. White respondents do not define hip-hop as something that remains black or "a voice for black people" today in their answers to questions of definition or any other topic during the interviews.

The difference between hip-hop as something that *was* black and hip-hop as something that *is* black is related to the role that hip-hop plays in constructing identity for the men in the study. Both black and white respondents claim that hip-hop is a part of what makes them who they are. Following are examples of such claims by white respondents from a range of class backgrounds.

What hip-hop means to me is that you wake up and you're a part of hip-hop. You wake up and you know it's a part of your life. Like I'll always remember listening to Biggie in second grade. That had an impact on me for the rest of

my life. The way I dress, my mannerisms, the friends I talk to all have a part
of hip-hop. (Marc, w1)

MICHAEL: What does hip-hop mean to you, or how would you define it?
CHRIS (w4): My life, pretty much. Growing up on it I feel like it influenced
    me a lot of ways. Even my other influences in some way, I relate it [other
    influences] to it [hip-hop]. Basically my whole life is hip-hop.

It's like a lifestyle. The way you dress. Like I always have my cap on. Clothes,
like Phat Farm, stuff like that. I mean I'm always listening to it, all my friends
listen to it. I see it as a lifestyle and music, not just music. (James, w3)

It's a culture, it's a lifestyle, the clothes, the shoes, everything. It's part of who
you are. (Paul, w1)

Note that there are both personal and collective identity claims within
these excerpts. White respondents state that they are personally affected by
hip-hop, as they listen to it every day and believe it affects the way they live
their lives. Further, this relationship with hip-hop connects them to other
people who share in the lifestyle, as respondents mention the ways hip-
hop connects them to their friends. However, if these white respondents
affirm personal and collective hip-hop identity, then blackness cannot be
elemental to hip-hop's definition in their minds. If hip-hop identity were
racialized as black by definition, it would be something that could not co-
exist with respondents' conceptions of themselves as white (or at the very
least nonblack).

Interestingly, refusal to identify contemporary hip-hop culture as black
by definition does not indicate a complete denial of any societal association between race and hip-hop for white respondents. As Roy explains, his
hip-hop self-presentation is frequently read by other whites as a ridiculous
or disgraceful desire to embody blackness, and as a white person, he feels
pressure to defend his hip-hop identity from attack.

My parents always had a problem with me listening to rap music. They'd always tell me, "You're not black. Grow up. It's only a phase." My dad still tells
me to this day, he goes, "You're twenty-four years old. Turn your hat straight."
He goes, "Why do you dress like that?" I go, "It's what I'm comfortable in, it's
what I feel like wearing." If I have to go somewhere that I have to be dressed
differently, it's not like I go to a wedding in jeans and a T-shirt. I dress appro-

priately for the situation. But yeah, I'm just going out with my friends, just to hang out some place, I'm going to be comfortable . . . This is what I'm comfortable in. I'm not comfortable with my hat like that [*turns his baseball cap so that the brim is in the front*], it doesn't *feel* right . . . They don't understand. I try to bring it back to my dad all the time. I go, "Dad, when you were growing up and people were wearing tight jeans and bell bottoms, everybody was saying 'you're ridiculous.' What kind of style were you doing? You guys all rebelled against that." And the only thing my dad ever tells me is "We did things, but we did them better and smarter." I'm like, "Well, you know, everybody's got to make their own mistakes, everybody's got to do what they want to do." I'm not ashamed to walk out in public with a shirt that says, "Get every dollar, free the ghetto" [T-shirt he is wearing]. I really don't have a problem with that. Some of my friends see me who are a little more preppy than I am, and my neighbor who I've been friends with my whole entire life, the first day I wore this shirt, he goes, "I would not go out in public with you wearing that shirt." I go, "Why?" He goes, "Because it's just ghetto." I go, "Yeah, you're right, it's ghetto, but you know what? Tommy Hilfiger ain't making major money off this shirt. I paid six dollars for it. I don't have a problem with that." (Roy, w2)

While respondents from both racial groups discuss their style of dress as part of hip-hop identity and state that hip-hop style is frowned upon by people inside and outside of their community, none of the black respondents mention defending their style from attacks that they dress "too black."

White respondents use hip-hop to build their identities, and identification with a hip-hop community is both personal and collective according to their responses. However, white respondents do not feel *racially* connected to other hip-hop fans, hip-hop is not defined as black culture by white respondents who identify with it, and affirmation of hip-hop identity does not result in renouncing one's whiteness.

The importance of hip-hop to elaborations of personal and collective identity is further crystallized by interview data from black respondents who claim hip-hop as their own. The quotations below (five of which are repeated from above) highlight the collective dimension of *black* identity accessed through hip-hop, with emphasis added on collective pronouns. It is important to note that this sense of collective racial identity is affirmed by black respondents from a range of class locations.

When it first came out, it was a way for urban poor *black* youths to express themselves in a way that was unique to *us*. (Andre, b4)

It could also make you think about where you stand in society and the things that you're doing that reflect poorly on the *black* community around you. (Allen, b1)

Hip-hop is like a culture, it's a voice for *black* people to be heard. *Our* own style, *our* own music. (Nate, b1)

Hip-hop is a way of life which explains that *we* have struggled and the way that *we* have survived and prospered in the *urban* areas. (George, b3)

It's a way of life. It's *our* culture, it's *black* culture. (Ryan, b4)

I just feel like it's a medium of communication. People are just talking about what *we* got to deal with. As a young man, growing up in American *cities*, especially New York City, that's how it goes down. (Dwayne, b3)

White respondents claim that they grew up with hip-hop culture, that it stands as a form of expression, and that it influences who they understand themselves to be. We can infer that hip-hop aids in white respondents' construction of collective identity because they repeatedly mention the ways hip-hop connects them to their friends. Black respondents make similar claims, but their affirmation of collectivity is built on the belief that they share these understandings of self with other *black* people who make hip-hop a part of their lives. These findings provide support for affirmations of hip-hop as a crucial ingredient of black cultural capital among young people (Clay 2003; Carter 2005) and speak to the power of hip-hop social capital across class lines. Black respondents' collective racial identity corresponds and operates in concert with their sense of the hip-hop collectivity. Contrary to KRS-One's assertion that hip-hop identity should or will eventually result in a natural disruption or replacement of racial and ethnic identity constructs, these data suggest that hip-hop identity is interwoven with racial identity for many black men who express themselves through the culture.

Two other points are worth noting: First, black respondents' collective claim to hip-hop is, in part, an ownership claim. When white respondents affirm hip-hop as part of their individual identities, they do so without such claims; none of the white respondents say, "Hip-hop is for us," or "I believe hip-hop is made for me." Two black respondents, however, describe hip-hop as "our culture" and "our own music," which not only imparts collectivity through connections to others who share in hip-hop but communicates group ownership. Second, part of what makes hip-hop "black culture" for black respondents who identify it as such is hip-hop narrators' expression of life experiences that black listeners personally relate to. This experiential piece of hip-hop's definition serves as our transition from a discussion about what hip-hop is to how hip-hop affects those who live it.

Feeling It

Tia DeNora writes, "Music needs to be understood in terms of its (non-verbal) capacities for enabling and constraining its user(s). How, then, can this idea be developed and how can music's structuring powers be illuminated at the level of social experience?" (2000, 7). A number of researchers engage these questions of music's "(non-verbal) capacities for enabling and constraining" using the idea of *affect*. Drawing on Gilles Deleuze and Félix Guattari (1980) and Brian Massumi (2002), Eric Shouse explains that affect is "not a personal feeling. Feelings are *personal* and *biographical*, emotions are *social*, and affects are *prepersonal*" (2005; emphasis in original). We cannot explain what affect is, or that affect has influenced us, because once we apprehend affect, we have already processed it and transformed it into feeling or emotion. The first moment music hits us or we are exposed to the shared energy of a crowd at a concert, affect is in play. Affect "always precedes will and consciousness" as "a non-conscious experience of intensity; it is a moment of unformed and unstructured potential" (Shouse 2005).

Shouse asserts that "in a lot of cases, the pleasure that individuals derive from music has less to do with the communication of meaning, and far more to do with the way that a particular piece of music 'moves' them. While it would be wrong to say that meanings do not matter, it would be just as foolish to ignore the role of biology as we try to grasp the cultural effects of music" (2005). This point is well taken, but the fact that we are dealing with fields of pleasure and pain does not undermine the importance of investigating interpretations of music. Hip-hop is certainly driven by perception and affect. It makes listeners feel good, which is connected to its popularity—people want to partake in a pleasurable perceptive or affective experience. Affirming pleasure, however, does not fully explain patterns in hip-hop content and cannot tell us all we need to know about structural, cultural, and discursive forces that influence power relations and identity cultivation. Affect is certainly relevant to hip-hop and its listeners, but there is still good reason to investigate how respondents interpret and articulate the pleasure they feel and what they make of the symbolic patterns and representations present in hip-hop performance. Interview data demonstrate how listeners are affected by hip-hop and how they interpret hip-hop's affective qualities.

So far, we have documented respondents' definitions of hip-hop and highlighted the ways hip-hop serves as a building block for individual and collective identity. Following respondents' understanding of hip-hop as expression or communication, one of the prevalent themes in responses across racial lines is the notion that hip-hop narrators communicate feelings that listeners "relate to" and find appealing.

> I can relate to a lot of the things people say in the songs. Like people in the eighties when they started listening to rock and roll, they were getting rebellious, like they wanted their freedom. Now it's more like things that people say are what people grew up doing, what they see every day; it's more of what I see every day. Not so much of what I grew up going through, because I really didn't have that hard of a life growing up, but I can relate to a lot of the things people say and the feelings that they feel. (Roy, w2)

> KEVIN (w4): Sometimes when I'm sitting there listening to it by myself, you relate to it, your whole body gets a tingle. It just touches you, you know?
> MICHAEL: Do you get that feeling from other things?
> KEVIN: When I can relate to something. They put it in a form where you can relate to every word.
> MICHAEL: Do you get it from other types of music?
> KEVIN: Only hip-hop. There's other stuff that I can relate to it, but it doesn't, like, touch me where my head goes numb and I start to think about it.

> I feel like having hip-hop is a really helpful association because the lyrics speak so much on so many different topics all over the world. You could pick any topic in the world, and I'm sure somebody who knows hip-hop could relate that to a song. (Russell, w1)

> I think hip-hop is struggle, man. Somebody tells you a story about their life, and you're in the struggle, it really gets your ear. It's like, "Oh, he went through all that and he's *still* here?" What doesn't kill you makes you stronger. That's what hip-hop is, really. (Bill, b4)

In the above quotations, respondents talk about relating to hip-hop in general terms. When they listen to hip-hop, these men connect narrators' words to their own emotions, without reference to specific experiences or events from their personal lives or to the scenes described in hip-hop songs. This set of responses, which highlights a nonspecific sense of hip-hop's power to evoke feelings, is a relatively small slice of the data that characterize listeners' experience with hip-hop. However, it is significant in that it hints at the power of music as something that does not simply serve as the expression of preexisting internal emotions but as something that is part of the "reflexive construction of that internal [emotional] state" (DeNora 2000, 57). The nebulous quality of these responses springs in part from the fact that "relating" *to* music is actually relating *with* music—building oneself and one's understanding of life with the aid of musical materials. Both black and white listeners, including those whose words appear above, not only speak of a general sense of hip-hop's potential to make them feel something or to construct emotions, but they indicate that the feelings produced through interaction with hip-hop are tied to specific life experiences or philosophies.

> I don't know if you heard "Every Day I'm Hustling"[7]—that's like the number one single. I fell in love with it, because it's like, that's what life really is, an everyday hustle. You got to make money somehow. Whatever you put your mind to, work with your hands, work with your head, it's all about making that money. (Sean, b2)

> A Jay-Z song that I like is "99 Problems." And the reason that is, is because if you look at, how I feel, a lot of the problems that ensues over anything, a lot of good guys have been locked up or killed, or it could even be gang related, but my whole thing is because a woman is behind it . . . So you could have anything, it could be your job, your car is not working, feeling down because of family, you could have ninety-nine problems, and the chick ain't making it the one hundredth. (Jack, b2)

> My favorite rappers, they have a story to a song or an experience or something that's something I like that I can relate to and listen a lot . . . I'm listening to him and I've been to an exact party like the one he's at, and I'm hearing all the crazy things that's going on. All different drugs and stuff. That's why I like it, he's telling my story. I've been there before. (James, w3)

Respondents identify two connections between "real life" and hip-hop narratives.[8] In one sense, hip-hop narrators express sentiments that reflect the order of the world, as reflected in Jack's comments and in Eyerman and Jamison's theory of social movements as knowledge-building phenomena. It is a fact of life, according to Jack, that women cause problems for men, and Jay-Z's insistence that he will not succumb to women problems constitutes an important life lesson in song. Similarly, it is a fact of life that we all work to live, and Sean hears this truth echoed by Rick Ross in the song "Hustlin'" (2006). This understanding of reality reflected in hip-hop is slightly different than what is communicated by respondents like James who hear stories in hip-hop narratives that are strikingly similar to events from their own lives.

Understanding hip-hop reality as reflective of personal experience or life events brings race back into focus as a force that influences hip-hop interpretations. The following comments are from black respondents.

> JASON (B1): "99 Problems" is a good song.
>
> MICHAEL: Why?
>
> JASON: It's kind of like something that you see every day, kind of.
>
> MICHAEL: What is?
>
> JASON: The racism shit that's going on, those problems.
>
> MICHAEL: Okay, so what is that song about?
>
> JASON: Well I'd have to look at the whole song, but the part I can remember now is the part where you get pulled over and stuff for no reason. That's the stuff you see every single day.
>
> MICHAEL: Has that ever happened to you personally?
>
> JASON: Yes. Way too many times.

> DWAYNE (B3): Some people listen to reggae, which, in a very ironic sense, has the same message, revolutionary message, but not in the same terms. But it's also rebellious.
>
> MICHAEL: What is the revolution that reggae or rap is looking for?
>
> DWAYNE: Barriers, there's a lot of barriers. As a young black man, I could still go to Harvard and graduate with honors and still have a lot of problems in the workplace, like people will never really respect my work. That's talking from a professional sense. To the extent I feel like "What the fuck am I doing here anyway?" You feel like that shit wasn't built for you. That's speaking from a realistic viewpoint.

> MICHAEL: Can you think of a specific lyric from it ["Mr. Nigga" by Mos Def (1999)] that you like, or what about it do you like?
>
> ALLEN (B1): The whole airplane part, where he's talking about how they have laws just for black people. Every time I fly back to Cali, it's a bitch to get through security. It's horrible! Every time! I'm purposely wearing like, basketball shorts and a T-shirt, nice little low-top shoes, and I still get

stopped, make me take my shoes off. It's like I can't really hide anything. That whole song is hilarious. But it's true, I see where he's coming from with that . . . Especially when he goes into first class and gets that look like, "Are you sure you belong here?" I remember the first time, they have these college prep courses, like regular, college prep, called "gate." For some reason, all the colored people in my school have to take a test to get into gate, and the rich white people just get placed in it. So I already had to take a test to get into that class. So I finally get in and I'm the only black person there and my school is 70 percent minority. And the first thing my teacher says is "Are you sure you're supposed to be here?" [*Laughs*.] I can't win! The shit I had to go through to get here! [*Laughs*.] That's why I like that song.

One song I always sing, and I always play it on my birthday too, is from Nas, *Illmatic*, "Life's a Bitch." The title of the song is real gloomy, but I don't feel that way. Yeah, life's a bitch, but it gets better, it's what you make of it. Growing up in the city, a lot of my cousins are locked up for a long time, a couple of my close boys got killed before I went off to college. It's sad too. Any young minority living in an urban area, for you to make it—what am I, twenty-two now?—for you to make it to see twenty-two and be out in the real world, it's a blessing. So many obstacles and so many forces against you, for you to be doing something with yourself and not be strung out on drugs or caught up in the system, it's a blessing right now. So that song always hits me. (Nolan, b3)

None of the white respondents mention their race or racialized experiences when connecting events from their personal life or their outlook on society to their experience with hip-hop. Conversely, Jason, Dwayne, and Nolan refer to their racial identity as they explain the link between the hardships described in hip-hop narratives and those in their personal life. This does not mean that every time black people listen to hip-hop they hear something racially relevant; the four excerpts above represent only a portion of black respondents' interpretations. The point is that the range of black respondents' interpretations looks different from the range of white responses, at least partially because of racial identity and racialized experience. Additionally, the racialized experiences mentioned by black respondents center on what they understand to be race-related hardships or insults rather than celebratory or romantically black elements of their culture. That is, it is conceivable that the real-life experiences referenced by black respondents might equate with presentations, mannerisms, or cultural scripts commonly understood to be unique or dignifying to black people or to performances that allow them to relate to a supercool, "badass" persona. Respondents identify hip-hop as a distinctive culture with a style all its own, but none of the black men report being emotionally touched by black "stylin'" to the degree demonstrated above; these comments deal explicitly with race-based oppression and resistance.

Though race is not mentioned by white respondents who discuss connections between hip-hop and their own life events, white listeners relate hip-hop to their life experiences as well.

MICHAEL: Are there specific songs by Styles that you enjoy?

KEVIN (w4): I always used to listen to a song, "My Brother," on how his brother died. When my uncle died I listened to that a lot.

ABE (w4): I don't know the name of the song where he talks about his girlfriend and his daughter. His girlfriend was getting high when she had his kid around and stuff.

MICHAEL: Why does that speak to you?

ABE: I did that when I had my kid around. I've gotten high and stuff. That's not the right thing to do.

MICHAEL: Eminem is talking about it happening in his life . . .

ABE: And it happened in my life.

MICHAEL: Can you describe what that feeling is?

ABE: You feel like a piece of shit. My daughter don't deserve that, she deserves the best. She doesn't deserve her father getting high and just being a dumb ass.

MICHAEL: That's a really personal example. If it doesn't make you feel happy, why would you choose that song?

ABE: I don't know. Because I went through that situation. It just hits home, you know what I'm saying?

These excerpts clearly show respondents engaging hip-hop for reasons other than its celebration of coolness, ruthless masculinity, and material excess, the themes commonly offered as explanations for young men's fascination with hip-hop.[9] Respondents affirm hip-hop's role in helping them cope with suffering and guilt, affirming their vulnerability as a key element of the connection they feel to hip-hop music and culture. Hip-hop music provides listeners with words and imagery that are connected to feelings and experiences from their personal lives, and the black and white men in the study describe the impact that listening to a song can have on their thoughts and mood. As Abe, Kevin, and Nolan indicate, listeners actively select songs they know they will relate to in specific ways. This is a crucial point, as it speaks to respondents' propensity to listen with a purpose in mind, using hip-hop as an emotional technology that takes them from one emotional state to another and as the material that constitutes the emotional states themselves. Both black and white listeners from a range of class categories speak to this use of hip-hop and affirm the importance of affect and emotion.

> I listen to music primarily to get excited. Not necessarily to get pumped up, but just like emotionally excited. (Richard, w1)

> MICHAEL: Can you define hip-hop? What does hip-hop mean to you?
> ADAM (w4): It means freedom, freedom of speech. It means relief. No, not relief. You know, calming. Because when I listen to music, you know, if I'm having a tough time or it just, like, puts me in another state of mind, you know? Just makes me forget about what's going on in the world, what's going on in my life, or whatever. Puts me in another state of mind and gives me a feeling of relief.

> Three 6 [Mafia] stuff, they're real violent, they get you hyped up. I remember I used to listen to them before football games and stuff, get you real hyped up. (Nolan, b3)

> When you listen in the car, you don't really want to hear a club song, you want to hear a song that will help you go through your day. Different environment, when you're in the club, you want to hear something that will intensify your drunk [laughs]. Make you feel more. Feel the music, feel the bass in your body. You want to enjoy that. (Ben, b4)

> MICHAEL: Can you describe the feeling you get when you hear a hip-hop song you like?
> ERIC (w1): I think I'll probably have a smile on my face, definitely. It's kind of similar with how I react to a lot of music. It's a very body-related experience. A lot of times I've noticed that if I'm not listening to music, and maybe even hip-hop in particular, I'm not in the same frame of mind. I'm not afraid to put something on repeat and listen to it over and over.

One of the songs that always got me going in the past was on Method Man's first CD, *Release Yo Delf* . . . Once I hear that, I'll freak out in my room, like that song is sick. I just want to go snap out. I try to find a good song for any mood that I'm in. I hear the beat, just a low, rolling beat, then you hear that trumpet and it sounds like the king is coming. It's on, I can do anything that day. I get so excited, on the phone, like, "Let's go do something boys! I got to get out of my house and do something now, I don't care what it is!" (Brandon, w3)

Listeners frequently engage hip-hop with purpose. They are aware that it changes their state of mind or the way their body is feeling, and they draw on hip-hop commodities as cultural resources to effect these changes. Hip-hop is used in different ways: some of the interviews identify the music as fuel for emotional excitement, while others suggest the healing and coping potential of hip-hop for young men dealing with pain. Differences in use are evident not only among the full range of all forty respondents but also in the comments of individual respondents who listen to many different types of hip-hop knowing that each type will have a specific affect on them. Once we acknowledge these differences in use, boundaries within hip-hop begin to reveal themselves as respondents distinguish between different types of hip-hop, affect, and audience. The following quotations highlight these internal distinctions and bring questions of taste to the fore.

As far as rap music is concerned, there's different types. Like you know that new Ludacris song, "Runaway Girl," a song that talks about women's struggle, things like that; then you have a song like my boy Project Pat, he has a song that's like, "I Ain't Goin' Back to Jail." You go Three 6 Mafia, they got a song like "Half on a Sack." You're talking about drugs, then you're talking about going to jail, then you're talking about a woman's struggle, then you got Tupac's classic song "Keep Ya Head Up," talking about when you're going through stuff. You def have different kinds of songs. There's a song out there for every type of mood that you could feel. Like if you're a woman that may have got dumped by her boyfriend or cheated on, there's a song for that. If somebody got shot, there's a song for that. Even for the people that are in the hip-hop generation that are getting older, like Jay Z got that song "30 Is the New 20" ["30 Something" (2006)]. There's something out there for everybody. (George, b3)

Like those two songs for instance. One is more for the club, partying and everything is all happy, then the other one is like, "Niggas screw they face up at me!" Like he's talking about what he's feeling, you know what I mean? He's walking, seeing people that's looking at him, and he's like, "On the real son they don't want beef/'cuz when I aim that and cock it out the window." You know what I mean? It's more gutter, it's more like, more gangster I'll say. It's more like what dudes in the hood are thinking, or what they go through every day. The watered-down stuff is more like the club, the party songs, radio, commercials, for people that's into having a good time and can't really relate to that lifestyle. But somebody in the hood could relate to that too, it could make them feel better and bring them out the situation they're going through. When you hear a song like that it makes you smile, or thinking about a girl, a female, forgetting about the drama and the fighting and things like that. (Greg, b4)

Both George and Greg acknowledge that use of music varies according to the mood and self-regulation goals of the listener. But another vital aspect of these excerpts is the sense that one's social status prescribes one's taste or the type of music that is most useful to the listener. Jay-Z's song "30 Something" is for hip-hop fans who are getting older. Gangster songs are targeted at "dudes in the hood," whereas party songs are "for people that's into having a good time and can't really relate to that lifestyle." Deeper investigation of hip-hop content and the sociology of taste follows in forthcoming chapters.

Summary

This chapter asks the questions "How do young black and white men define hip-hop, and how do they engage and utilize hip-hop music and culture?" The data presented are drawn from discussion with forty respondents. The sample is relatively small by sociological standards, and the aim of analysis is not to produce a prescriptive or widely generalizable set of results that definitively characterize group behavior. However, the sample size is certainly sufficient for investigating meaning-making processes and provides a series of rich data points that contribute to our understanding of what hip-hop means.

Respondents across racial lines understand hip-hop primarily as a culture and a form of expression or communication. The social status of the narrators who perform hip-hop communication is important to respondents, who generally agree that hip-hop was started by economically disadvantaged African Americans in New York City (further evidence of the prevalence of the myth of black purity in hip-hop). While some black respondents make a special point to identify hip-hop as a culture that began and remains the product of black practitioners, almost none of the white respondents clearly state that contemporary hip-hop is black culture.

Both black and white respondents identify hip-hop as part of what makes them who they are and as a culture that they engage in on a daily basis, primarily through dressing in hip-hop style and listening to hip-hop music. However, black respondents from each class category (cultural elite, stagnant middle class, working class with mobility, and stagnant working class) construct a collective racial hip-hop identity, and their comments suggest that they believe they are connected to other black people in part thanks to hip-hop's focus on black experience and expressions. None of the white respondents connect their appreciation of and experience with hip-hop to a larger collective racial identity (again, consistent across class lines). Race is an important symbolic boundary for black listeners, who use the concept to build a collective identity, and whites, who distance themselves from blackness and to some extent deracialize hip-hop in order to build personal and collective hip-hop identity.

I want to emphasize that I am not suggesting that black people are the only group capable of elaborating collective identity through hip-hop. Those who are fully immersed in hip-hop practice as MCs, DJs, b-boys, or b-girls are highly likely to give strong affirmations of their membership in a hip-hop community. My data suggest hip-hop is a building block of racial identity for black people in a way that it is not for white people. This may be because whites do not think about race as much, while blacks, no matter the topic—cooking, sports, music, etc.—would affirm its racial relevance because of their social experiences as racialized people. But it may also be that there is something about hip-hop that expressly conjures racial identification and recognition.

Listeners relate to hip-hop music both because its narratives communicate something that is generally true about the world and because performers recount experiences or events that mirror listeners' personal lives. A number of black listeners mention race-related experiences or events from personal life that are reflected in hip-hop music. While race is not a similar reference point for white listeners, respondents from both groups and all class categories describe a range of reasons for listening to rap music, and hip-hop is purposely used to achieve different states of body and mind. As a whole, the interview data presented in this chapter bolster our understanding of hip-hop as a social movement and tool for elaborating identity with different forms of correspondence for black and white people. In addition, respondents' definitions of and uses for hip-hop further problematize the notion that hip-hop is nothing more than politically empty, angry, and spectacular posturing.

In the next two chapters, I offer my reading of performances by some of the most widely recognizable acts in hip-hop from 1993 to 2008. My textual analysis introduces the major themes in recent thug-era hip-hop. In addition to making a specific argument about the evolution of black coolness, chapters 2 and 3 provide readers with context to situate respondents' analysis of authenticity and content, which appear in chapters 4 and 5.

TWO

From a Cool Complex to Complex Cool

One of the greatest inventions of the twentieth century is the African-American male—invented because black masculinity represents an amalgam of fears and projections in the American psyche which rarely conveys or contains the trope of truth about the black male's existence.

—Thelma Gordon, "My Brother"[1]

I'm like Che Guevara with bling on
I'm complex.

—Jay-Z, "Public Service Announcement" (2007)

Understanding the "Cool Pose"

Chapter 1 establishes that hip-hop identity is intertwined with racial identity for black respondents, while race is not explicitly discussed as part of white respondents' personal connection to hip-hop. These trends may emerge simply because white respondents do not feel comfortable discussing race, do not think in racial terms, or do not believe race has an effect on their lives. Alternatively, the connection between blackness and hip-hop may have something to do with the form and content of contemporary hip-hop itself. I take this not-so-radical possibility as the premise for my analysis of popular hip-hop music in chapters 2 and 3; there is something about commercially successful American hip-hop that speaks to black American men's experience and identity, and I argue that this phenomenon is inextricably linked to the idea of coolness.

Efforts to disavow black coolness are well intentioned, as the association between blackness and coolness may be used to sustain white privilege through the solidification of mythic white "normalcy." Those who insist on rejecting all notions of black coolness do so on the grounds that any validation of black *coolness* is in fact validation of inherent racial *otherness*. This cool, "soulful" otherness is incorporated into mainstream American culture as a counterweight to the stressful, unrelenting ethic of disciplined labor in postindustrial society. Blacks who ensnare themselves in its pursuit drift further away from the behaviors and life choices necessary for socio-economic stability and political progress (Patterson 1999, xvii–xviii). If someone believes black people are cool, the logic goes, that person thinks white people are ordinary and normal and, perhaps unknowingly, accepts the basis for racism or racist outcomes. No matter how desperately black people attempt to reclaim their otherness by idealizing it as cool, at bottom, self-proclaimed "cool" blacks are self-defeating, self-loathing, or both.

Richard Majors and Janet Bilson's "cool pose" theory of black masculinity highlights denied opportunity and the pain of unrealized masculine aspiration among black men, who cope with these hardships by projecting carefully crafted coolness:

> Blacks have not had consistent access to the same means to fulfill their dreams of masculinity and success. Many have become frustrated, angry, embittered, alienated, and impatient. Some have learned to mistrust the words and actions of the dominant culture . . . [B]lack males, especially those who are young and live in the inner cities of our nation, have adopted and used cool masculinity—or as we prefer to call it, "cool pose"—as a way of surviving in a restrictive society . . . And . . . cool pose propels black males on a collision course with each other and with whites. (1992, 1–2)

Cool pose is a strategy for survival in a hostile environment—a rational adaptation to structural restrictions rather than an inherent biological problem. Tricia Rose (1994), Imani Perry (2004), and others identify related performances within hip-hop, locating this phenomenon within the black folk tradition of "badman" narratives. Rose argues that "the ghetto badman posture-performance is a protective shell against real unyielding and harsh social policies and physical environments" (1994, 12). This notion of oppositional black male identity draws from Signithia Fordham and John Ogbu's (1986) work on the black-white education achievement gap and has been reconsidered and expanded numerous times (Massey and Denton 1993; Elijah Anderson 1999; Waters 1999; Fryer and Levitt 2004; Carter 2005). Oppositional identity theory posits that once African Americans realize that resources are distributed unevenly along racial lines and that American institutions are ill suited to account for or combat significant race-based disadvantages, black Americans, especially black men, are prone to develop a sense of identity that disregards social norms and rewards behaviors that are at odds with mainstream notions of achievement. As Herman Beavers asserts, "Cool pose . . . is 'dialectical.' On one hand it reflects a mistrust of white society and the poses used to communicate control and 'detachment.' On the other hand, this coolness can destroy motivation to learn and acquire the material and cultural skills needed to overcome racism" (1997, 257). Cool pose is a cultural code that both reflects disadvantageous social structure and structures society disadvantageously for those who embody it.

Richard Majors and Janet Mancini Bilson characterize the behavioral adaptations and the mental state of cool posers as

> carefully crafted performances that deliver a single, critical message: pride, strength, and control . . . They [black men] communicate to others through the use of an imposing array of masks, acts, and facades . . . For many blacks, life is a relentless performance for the mainstream audience and often for each other . . . The performance aspect of being cool means that as a black performer leaves his house in the morning, he is "on" and cannot ever completely relax. (1992, 4)

Black manhood is thus conceived as a self-conscious state of perpetual performance. Majors and Bilson graft the representations of black male celebrities in mass media on to the behaviors and belief systems of everyday black men, whom the authors believe to be under a social spotlight similar to that of celebrities such as LeBron James and Lil' Wayne. The trouble with this line of thinking is not that Majors and Bilson emphasize the performative elements of identity but that they seem to understand cool performance as pathological or tragic by definition and that every single performance undertaken by black men is boiled down to the message of "pride, strength, and control."

Though Majors and Bilson do not make use of it, cool pose is linked to Raewyn Connell's theory of hegemonic masculinity (Connell 1987, 1995; Connell and Messerschmidt 2005). Hegemonic masculinity is not a category, nor is it the type of traditional masculinity that dominates all others. Instead, it describes *social relations* wherein one form of masculine identity is celebrated above all others, and men who cannot embody the dominant form are degraded and oppressed yet still desire to obtain it. In the American context, the dominant "traditional" form of masculinity atop the hierarchy is that of the straight, bourgeois, white Christian male. Subordinated men's aspiration to the dominant form is what makes the relations hegemonic, as it aids in their continued oppression. In their quest to embody the dominant form, men of subordinate status employ domination as a strategy themselves and may exhibit a range of identity management techniques, including "(1) being homophobic, (2) devaluing femininity, (3) increasing masculine bravado, and (4) claiming masculine space within the larger feminized area" (Eric Anderson 2005, 339). Black men's performance of imposing coolness might easily utilize any of these four techniques, and in the case of commercially successful hip-hop performance, the first three (homophobia, devaluing femininity, and bravado) are crucial.

The Roots of Cool Pose

The intellectual history of black coolness reveals two distinct though not necessarily opposed explanations for black coolness that provide context for cool pose. The first explanation is that black American coolness is developed out of necessity, as black people take pride in remaining calm, composed, and "unimpressed by the horror the world might daily propose" (Baraka 1963, 213). Coolness in this case is specifically drawn from the experience of black people dealing with racism and exploitation. Life in a racist society is painful, and coping with this pain results in double consciousness, as the treatment one receives as an "other," a nonmember of American society, conflicts with a private understanding of oneself and experience within black communities (Du Bois 1903). This experience is frequently represented in black American writing and scholarship through the invocation of the veil (Du Bois 1903), or the mask; as Paul Laurence Dunbar writes in "We Wear the Mask,"

> Why should the world be over-wise,
> In counting all our tears and sighs?
> Nay, let them only see us while
> We wear the mask. (1896)

When discussed in this way, as a commitment to "live with your head in the lion's mouth . . . overcome 'em with yeses, undermine 'em with grins, agree 'em to death and destruction" (Ellison 1952, 16), wearing the mask is a means of both survival and resistance. Whereas this may have been a necessary strategy for survival among African American men in eras past, Majors and Bilson seem to suggest that it has outlived its utility or morphed into a more hostile performance and now results in unnecessarily injurious social outcomes.

In contrast, Robert Farris Thompson (1974a, 1974b) argues that black coolness is not an outgrowth of racial insult and double consciousness, a strategy for survival, or a weapon of political warfare. Instead, it can be traced to African cultural practices and philosophies. To distinguish long-standing African coolness from its more commonly invoked African American manifestation, he explains:

> The "mask" of [African] coolness is worn not only in time of stress but also of pleasure, in fields of expressive performance and the dance. Control, stability, and composure under the African rubric of the cool seem to constitute elements of an all-embracing aesthetic attitude . . . I have come to term the attitude "an aesthetic of the cool" in the sense of a deeply and complexly motivated, consciously artistic, interweaving of elements serious and pleasurable, of responsibility and play.
>
> Manifest within this philosophy of the cool is the belief that the purer, the cooler a person becomes, the more ancestral he becomes. In other words, mastery of self enables a person to transcend time and elude preoccupation . . . This is not the stony silence of anger. This is the mask of the mind itself. (1974a, 41)

Thompson's coolness carries a more spiritual and mystical meaning and a wider range of expressions than coolness as a mask worn to face racism or as a coping mechanism in the context of social inequality. According to Thompson, the "aesthetic of the cool" prioritizes "patience and collectedness of mind" (1966, 73). It is present in African art, song, dance, and spirituality rather than in black experiences with Western powers that practice exploitation and degradation. The mask of the cool (composure) is but one of five elements that make up cool philosophy, the others being visibility, luminosity of motion, smoothness, and rebirth/reincarnation (Thompson 1974b). This visual emphasis on proudly and persistently shining reappears in hip-hop aesthetics as stylin', a point to which I return later in this chapter.

Cool Pose and Hip-Hop

Majors and Bilson's epistemic commitments more closely align with double consciousness and resistance to racism than with the cool philosophy and aesthetic. The problem is that coolness as resistance to racism has grown into a cultural pathology and borderline neurosis for black American men. If we apply the cool pose model to commercially successful hip-hop, Majors and Bilson's criticism of coolness seems to make sense at first. Commercially successful hip-hop performances prioritize coolness, and this commitment to coolness often relies on oppressive race and gender scripts (social pathology), especially in the case of thug representations.

However, the nature and definition of hip-hop coolness requires additional consideration. Following Timothy Brown (2006), who points out that hip-hop identity is a contradictory site of struggle between progressive and regressive black masculinities, I argue that hip-hop's *complex coolness* is more than a masklike coping mechanism run amok. It is not a facade that always prevents sincerity, and the pursuit and upkeep of cool style does not always preclude the possibility of genuine substance. To the contrary, complex coolness, a descendent of both Thompson's cool aesthetic and Du Bois's undeniably painful double consciousness, represents a new step in cool's evolution. Complex coolness is more transparent than previous manifestations of black coolness. It openly foregrounds and sustains the *conflicts* of black American masculinity rather than concealing them, saturating these struggles in an appealing marinade of pride in one's hip-hop skills and sensibilities. That is, hip-hop's complex coolness is what allows commercially successful representations to simultaneously contain narratives about collective racial identity, political injustice, God and the afterlife, Cadillac Escalades, strip clubs, and drug money.

Thompson describes the cool aesthetic as "complex," but he does so primarily to distinguish his African cool from the Western model (1974b). For Thompson, complexity is revealed primarily in the malleability, flexibility, and ubiquity of "cool" as a signifier and philosophy employed by an astonishingly high number of different African cultural communities. I want to retain Thompson's notion of flexibility, but public hip-hop performances of internal conflict and vulnerability do not quite mesh with the coolness he describes, and Thompson would never say that bragging about exploiting women and driving expensive cars is encompassed by his cool aesthetic. I argue that, regrettably, these themes are central to complex coolness, a coolness that is marked by its dissonance.

That these themes are performed in a market context largely driven by immediate gratification through consumption and many hip-hop performances glorify poisonous market values does not mean this turn toward publicly conflicted, complex cool black masculinity is completely contrived or extraneous. We can safely say that plenty of commercially successful hip-hop performances fail to aid in the struggle for black American political empowerment. But the existence and mainstream visibility of these unfortunate performances does not justify the reduction of all hip-hop into a fundamentally oppositional, dishonorable, or frivolous set of practices. Nor do negative representations of blackness in hip-hop render those who identify with hip-hop politically immature or irrelevant. Hip-hop acts engage political and existential subjectivity during performance, and many hip-hop listeners come to understand themselves through the music.

This new explanation of coolness and its rules of operation should not be read as a romantic celebration of a new postracial and liberated black subject, free to express himself in an era without racial restrictions and anxieties. The black male body, pregnant with historical and contemporary significance as a site of fear and fascination in America, is indispensable for recognizing the significance of these openly conflicted but still cool performances. My argument about complex cool is not that every performer aims to portray himself or herself as complicated or is constantly communicating the message "Look! I'm complex, isn't that cool?" Nor do I mean to imply that every single lyric and gesture has a consciously encoded hidden or alternate meaning that confers complexity and cancels out negative messages. My point is threefold: First, when we consider commercially successful performances as a whole, hip-hop discourse and meaning is multifaceted. Second, even in the context of the restrictive political economy of the record industry, black masculine conflict and vulnerability are exposed in contemporary hip-hop in a way that is not explained by previous theories of black coolness. Lastly, these themes are reliant on signifying, so complexity is not only manifest in the discourse itself but is also produced by the style and character of indirect communication during performance.

I argue for these claims about complex coolness by criticizing the cool pose theory, which I challenge on three main fronts.

1 Black male complex coolness is a collective discursive phenomenon in hip-hop rather than a psychosocial neurosis. Narratives about the "hood" exemplify this collective quality, as rappers build hood and race consciousness by describing personal character traits and collective local experiences as ghetto residents.

2 While they affirm black cultural practices and black collective identity, discourses of black authenticity and coolness in hip-hop do not propel black people on a collision course with white people, nor are they fundamentally oppositional to traditional American standards of status attainment as cool pose theory argues.

3 Black men craft and perform hip-hop narratives of criminality and consumption, which bolster the most objectionable stereotypes of black manhood and often reinforce hegemonic masculinity based on domination.
However, these narratives also express guilt and regret about these pleasures,
fear about one's place in the universe, vulnerability, and love. This point is
taken up in chapter 3.

I do not deny the importance of sexist macho posturing to hip-hop performance, nor do I excuse objectionable behavior associated with the quest
for respect. It should be clear from my analysis that complex coolness does
not qualify as a truly progressive black masculinity, which is defined by
commitment to antiracism, antisexism, and the ethical stance against all
systems of domination (Mutua 2006). However, hip-hop performances
build a publicly conflicted discourse of black masculinity, far more complex and far more forthcoming about vulnerability and connectedness
than cool pose theory allows for.

The Hood Comes First

Since Grandmaster Flash and the Furious Five released "The Message" in
1982, the ecology of urban life has weighed heavily on the minds and
rhymes of the hip-hop community. Rapping "It's like a jungle sometimes / it
makes me wonder how I keep from going under," the Furious Five explain
that living in the dilapidated city is unpleasant and stressful for protagonists who have to deal with disorder, crime, and violence in their neighborhood on a daily basis. Given the rise of the hyperghetto/prison in the
late twentieth and early twenty-first centuries, it is no surprise that 50 Cent
echoes the Furious Five's disgust with the urban "jungle" two decades later,
as he raps, "Different day, same shit, ain't nothing good in the hood / I'd
run away from this bitch and never come back if I could."[2]

As Christopher Smith notes, "In rap's dominant marketing paradigm,
blackness has become contingent, while the ghetto has become necessary . . .
with local knowledge of misery the exportable commodity to be wrought
from otherwise arid soil" (1997, 346–47). The ghetto is a necessary prereq-
uisite for narrators' affirmation of black identity in hip-hop, and knowing
the ghetto is largely about knowing ghetto danger and pain. However, MCs
also insist on claiming the ghetto as home, often taking pride in their residential sections, and representing the ghetto amounts to more than merely
cataloging one's struggle. This relationship between ghetto pain and pride
fits within the paradigm of complex cool, as describing ghetto hardships

rather than masking or muting them is central to proudly representing one's blackness:

> You either workin' or you slangin' cocaine on my block
> You had to hustle, 'cuz that's how we was raised on my block
> . . . .
> On my block, we duck the nigga-haters and the cops
> . . . .
> On my block—it's like the world don't exist, we stay confined to this
>   small little section we livin' in
> On my block, I wouldn't trade it for the world, 'cause I love these
>   ghetto boys and girls. (Scarface 2002)

In these lines Scarface points to the socialization of the ghetto as an isolated space, where limited economic opportunity makes "hustling" the norm.[3] As a whole, "On My Block" takes on a nostalgic tone, as Scarface discusses growing up in Houston and professes his love for his neighborhood and the people in it. Note that the complex coolness embedded in this verse does not spring purely from Scarface's performing the role of tougher-than-thou ghetto war hero. Rather, it is a pride woven through connections to other "ghetto boys and girls," whom he "loves."

Scarface is not alone in his thankfulness for ghetto upbringing; Kanye West, a Chicagoan, echoes Face's sentiments. In "My Way" (2004) he raps:

> I been broke, now I'm good bitch
> I ain't no Kennedy, but I'm hood rich
> So I say, my way, thank you to the ghetto
> Everybody else, thank you very little.

One possible reading here is that West owes his financial improvement to ghetto consumers who supported him as a struggling artist and continue to do so as a commercial success. But West thanks the ghetto not only for its financial support but also for his sense of self and the black artistic traditions and life experiences that he draws from in his work as he does it "his way."

To explain the balance between representations of the ghetto as a site of desperation and struggle with others that affirm spatial pride and love, Murray Forman (2002) introduces the concept of "the hood." The hood can be Scarface's ghetto in Houston or Kanye's ghetto in Chicago. Despite the negative portrayals and difficult material conditions of the ghetto, building a narrative about the hood opens the possibility of new productive and prideful identities. As Forman explains, speaking about one's section and connecting it to other hoods and ghettos challenges or reorganizes the spatial hierarchy that places some residents in spaces of privilege and others in spaces of deprivation (65). He writes:

> The 'hood accommodates the general spatial image of the ghetto, but the term also allows greater flexibility when used by members of the hip-hop generation to describe and delineate locality . . . Thus, where the ghetto has been culturally shackled to a negative symbolic configuration of images and ideas, the 'hood offers a new terminology and discursive frame that can simultaneously address conditions in all 'hoods everywhere, the individuated places, or to particular sites of significance. (65)

The song and video for "'Round Here" (2003), performed by Memphis Bleek, T.I., and Trick Daddy, exemplifies this invocation of the hood as simultaneously universal and local.[4] The video opens with an image of Memphis Bleek standing in front of the Marcy Projects in Brooklyn, where he and his mentor, Jay-Z, grew up. Bleek begins a voice-over without music from the track: "Eight o'clock Monday morning, December 16th, Marcy Projects. It's either you claim your spot, or somebody else will. Boss come through makes sure everything's good, everything's a 'go' 'round here. You know? It's no games." While Bleek narrates, Jay-Z drives up in a Rolls Royce (he's "the boss com[ing] through" who "makes sure everything's good"), rolls down the window, and has a brief, inaudible conversation with Bleek. As the conversation ends and Jay-Z's car pulls away, the music begins.

In this introduction, without any music, Bleek uses signifying to firmly establish himself and his neighborhood. By claiming his spot on the corner, Bleek indexes the working world of the street-level drug dealer, who must establish his post on the block before competitors do.[5] As Nas says, "Sometimes the rap game reminds me of the crack game,"[6] and Bleek's "spot claiming" also refers to his position as Jay-Z's protégé in the rap game, where artists must establish themselves in the battle for space in the hip-hop marketplace. In this case, Bleek establishes himself with two symbols that denote his legitimacy:[7] his closeness with Jay-Z, perhaps the most popular and successful rapper in history, and his grounding in the Marcy Projects as a spatial symbol of the hood.

The video is set in three locations, and each setting aligns with the rapper who delivers the verse. Bleek begins on the sidewalks and streets surrounding his projects. To further root himself in New York, Bleek always wears at least one item, such as a Brooklyn Dodgers coat or hat, with words or symbols associated with the city. During Bleek's verse, three basic settings are used by the director. In the first setting, Bleek appears alone, rapping in front of the apartment buildings, occasionally with a large sports utility vehicle in the background for decoration. The second setting is Bleek with a group of roughly forty extras, all of whom are black and presumably Marcy residents who live in the neighborhood the video is filmed in. The extras sing and dance along with the song, positioned as a cluster standing around Bleek, who is front and center. The third group of pictures comprise solo and group shots of the extras, a number of whom are children. Bleek does not appear with the extras as they strike stationary poses, looking directly into the camera with indifferent if not solemn expressions on their faces, symbolizing the unfiltered reality of day-to-day life in the ghetto.

Bleek's verse ends, and the scene switches from winter in New York to scorching hot Miami, Florida, home of Trick Daddy, who raps the second verse of the song. Bleek, still dressed in New York gear, appears intermittently alongside Trick, who is depicted in scenery that is the Miami analog to Bleek's hood. Like Bleek, Trick is dressed in clothing that celebrates his hometown, primarily consisting of oversized replicas of University of Miami football and basketball jerseys. He raps either seated on steps outside of low-rise and presumably low-income housing or standing in front of a run-down corner store with a faded sign that reads "Fried Chicken." The director uses the same three motifs as in Bleek's verse: Trick rapping alone, Trick rapping with a group of extras in the background behind him, and shots of local extras (including children) standing still, looking unimpressed as they stare down the camera. The only significant scenic diversion from Bleek's verse is that, as Trick rhymes about women more frequently, scantily clad female extras appear in the Miami scene in accordance with the lyrics.

The third verse is rapped by Atlanta native T.I., following the same formula as the preceding verses. Bleek (still in New York garb), stands with T.I. (who dons an Atlanta Braves cap) and a smaller collection of extras in the front yards of small, ill-kept houses. Though present in the New York and Miami scenes, luxury cars appear more frequently as background details, as T.I. often delivers lyrics while leaning against a Cadillac parked on a lawn or in a driveway. Again, we see shots of T.I. rapping alone, T.I. with extras, and extras holding their poses as the camera shoots them in what is supposed to be their natural habitat.

Visuals support lyrics, and the content of each verse overlaps with the others, while maintaining its local flavor. Each rapper embeds himself in his residential locale, casting himself as a powerful person within his environment by rapping about the drug economy, sex with women, smoking marijuana, and owning expensive cars. These representations are more in line with the sort of glorified commercial badman that cool pose critics lament. However, we must also attend to discursive dynamics within the representations that complicate and distinguish the particular brand of coolness being performed. Rappers use the video themes as building blocks of a hood collective in addition to glorifying these excesses for their own sake. By outlining spatial borders and imparting local knowledge, Bleek, Trick Daddy, and T.I. tell us who they are and what it's like in the local and universal hood. Consider the following excerpts:

My hood, my set, my strip, my p's, whatever
We down, we real, we bang forever
Put in game down here, make change down here
Cause I serve them fiends, that raw 'caine down here. (Memphis Bleek)

So many bitches out there, snitchin' 'round here
That's why every summer, bitches be missin' 'round here
I roll with—straight killers, thug niggas, and drug dealers
And if they ridin' wit me, best believe they my niggas. (Trick Daddy)

Them dope boys keep the trap locked and sewn 'round here
It ain't safe for the faker walkin' home 'round here
Hell with who you know, if you ain't known 'round here. (T.I.)

By affirming "my hood, my set, my p's [projects], whatever" Bleek affirms the universal hood. The word *whatever* tells listeners that "whatever" you call it (hood, set, or "p's"), no matter what the dialect in your neighborhood, what makes the space valuable is the people who reside there. Bleek continues, describing the people he lives with as "real" and unafraid of violence ("we bang forever"), and these characteristics are echoed by the other rappers. In each verse, the hood niggas each narrator associates with are described as those who make money through the drug economy and are unafraid of violence. Further, these moneymakers are also rule makers in their sections: as T.I. tells us, "dope boys keep the trap locked and sewn 'round here" (drug dealers control the street), and Trick Daddy implies that those who snitch (cooperate with police) are liable to go missing. The cool pose of pride, strength, and control seems to be of paramount importance for the narrators and their hood peers, and their ability to embody these qualities make Bleek, Trick Daddy, and T.I. similar to other hood residents.

However, narrators' power and respect is not derived solely from their capacities to earn money through drug sales, defy authority, or commit acts of violence but from the social capital they gain from neighborhood associations. T.I. raps, "Hell with who you know, if you ain't known 'round here," and disregards both the individual capacities of an imagined subject to project strength and that subject's connections to other networks, affirming the importance of his local connections to other hood residents as a source of respect. Both Bleek and Trick Daddy confirm this collective source of respect, as Bleek uses both the pronouns *we* and *I* to describe his character, and Trick Daddy tells us exactly who he "rolls with." Pride, strength, and control are thus revealed as collective and communal phenomena rather than individual psychological defense mechanisms.

The character of the social capital that imparts strength and pride to the narrators should not be overlooked, as performers' relationships with fellow hood residents are extremely important. Bleek and Trick Daddy are sure to communicate their loyalty to and appreciation for those they associate themselves with, as Bleek raps, "We down, we real, we bang *forever*" (emphasis added), and Trick echoes, "If they ridin' with me, best believe they my niggas." It is not simply that Bleek and Trick associate with those who reside in their neighborhoods; hood residents are Trick's "niggas," and they are so important to Bleek that he raps that their relationship will endure "forever." These performers claim to be deeply invested in the relationships they have with the hood as a spatial location and a community of people, and in addition to the aforementioned lyrical evidence of this appreciation, the video shows us evidence by featuring everyday people as costars in the visual story of the song. Again, this love and appreciation for those who surround, support, and ground cool posing black men is overlooked in cool pose theory, which emphasizes detachment and self-contained strength and control. Complex cool emphasizes a reciprocal relationship: rappers represent the hood, while the presence of the hood gives rappers pride and makes them seem both powerful and authentic as representatives of a neighborhood constituency.

Hood-making, or building the universal hood through affirmation of local hood experience, applies to *race-making*, or building notions of blackness from specific racialized experiences. Hood residents in Houston, Chicago, Brooklyn, Miami, and Atlanta are subjected to similar but not identical forms of disadvantage and oppression by their ecology, and blacks in each neighborhood do not share a single, rigid, authentic, or essential black experience or set of cultural practices. But by recognizing blackness as the marker for mistreatment and hood connectedness as a source of pride, rappers build a discourse of collective identity and social awareness. Blackness signifies parallel or comparable experiences of oppression among potential allies with similar social goals. In order to protect collective identity and strengthen these connections, commercially successful MCs often employ the rhetoric of authenticity.

From Hood Living to Black Authenticity

Social authenticity, racial or otherwise, is dangerous terrain. Groups cultivate cultural scripts, or "narratives that people use in shaping their life plans and in telling their life stories" (Appiah 1996, 67). As certain narratives become increasingly robust, they grow into more than stories, becoming "truths" about the group in question and part of group members' individual and social definition. A relatively small number of stories rise to prominence and are used as shortcuts to categorization and definition by both group insiders and outsiders. In many cases, these authenticity indicators enable a sense of pride and distinction along lines that challenge the understandings prescribed by social conditions or power relations. But the dark side of this phenomenon is that robust authenticity scripts can be restrictive, resulting in the naturalization of social differences (Appiah 1996, 67). Group members who do not fit scripted roles are often isolated from their social group, defined as suspects and deviants both by those within their collective and by onlookers who impart an "other-otherness" to such pariahs.

Grounding his analysis in black literature and literary criticism, J. Martin Favor (1999) illustrates the connection between discourses of black authenticity and celebration of the black folk experience. Pointing to Henry Louis Gates and Houston Baker as seminal figures in the literary discourse of black authenticity, Favor argues that both Baker and Gates affirm the narrative voice of the folk as a project in antielitism. By affirming the *vernacular* tradition of black narration as a phenomenon worthy of *literary* attention, Gates and Baker challenge notions of black inferiority by placing black folk culture on equal ground with Western literature, affirming the intellectual contributions of a materially disadvantaged but intellectually sophisticated race (Favor 1999, 6). This vernacular distinction is a crucial marker of black authenticity.

As Favor notes, Gates (1988) argues that the "signifying black difference" of black narration is found in the vernacular (Favor 1999, 5). This implies that "difference lies only in the vernacular, and that vernacular is a language spoken most often by persons of the folk, or those with a conscious connection to folk culture" (Favor 1999, 5). Favor also highlights Gates's belief that signifying is learned as part of adolescent education (Gates 1988, 52), and we see that what makes "talking black" a marker of authentic blackness is its naturalness. From the earliest stages of intellectual development, from the time blacks learn to speak, signifying is second nature. Signifying is preconscious, or at least subconscious, for blacks who are connected to "real" black culture, immersed within a black world spoken into being by the black folk themselves.

Hip-hop as black vernacular culture presents a paradox for conceptions of black authenticity rooted in folk naturalness. Unlike the performances designed to confer authenticity upon other genres of music, hip-hop authenticity is often purposefully theatrical and spectacular (Barker and Taylor 2007, 244), recalling the visibility and luminosity of Thompson's cool aesthetic without its spiritual component. The material goods such as cars and jewelry flaunted by many commercially successful hip-hop artists symbolize financial gain through either rapping or street-level hustling. When MCs claim they earn money by rapping, displays of wealth serve as visual proof that listeners are buying their records and therefore that there is a public consensus that the rapper in question is talented or skilled. When rappers claim hustling as the source of their wealth, they signify their connection to "real" black folks in disadvantaged hoods with healthy illegal economies. On one hand, these two performances fit together perfectly, as each represents a claim to the hegemonic masculine ideal rooted in the capacity to acquire economic capital. On the other, they conflict with one another, because everyday black people (the folk) do not have the economic means to purchase luxury goods, and anyone who flaunts his wealth flaunts his distance from true folk experience.

Rappers keep these complex cool performances in balance and cultivate a spectacular authenticity that resonates with the folk thanks to two countervailing forces. First, Thompson's cool African aesthetic is reframed as the black American tradition of "stylin'," best explained by Shane and Graham White (1998). *Stylin'* refers to traditions and performances of black self-expression that trace their history back to West African cultural traditions and present significant challenges to Western notions of stylized self-presentation. White and White argue that, historically, black Americans have been denied dignity and self-expression in public and private life in the Western world, and in response, African Americans cultivate stylin' culture as a means to affirm self-worth. Clothing, paintings, hairstyles, and musical performances proudly exhibit elements counter to traditional Western notions of beauty and taste. Commercially successful rappers often strive for a visual aesthetic and narrative of self that is unabashedly loud and extraordinary, and stylized performances of authentic hip-hop blackness are validated by black folk who grow up in cultures where stylin' is the norm.

The Big Tymers, composed of Mannie Fresh and Baby of Cash Money Records, provide a poignant example of the stylin' and the tension between lavish stylistic tastes and financial straits of everyday black folk on their track "Still Fly"[8] off the album *Hood Rich* (2002). On the chorus for "Stay Fly" Mannie and Baby rap:

> Gator boots with the pimped out Gucci suits
> Ain't got no job, but I stay sharp
> Can't pay my rent, cause all my money's spent
> But that's okay, cause I'm Still Fly
> Got a quarter tank of gas—in my new E class
> But that's alright, cause I'm gon' ride
> Got everything in my momma name
> But I'm hood rich—da dah da dahhh.

Despite the financial realities of joblessness and financial insecurity, the narrators doggedly cultivate their fly[9] image by purchasing and showcasing luxury goods. Again, the behaviors described in the song serve as alternative routes to masculinity for the narrators, who are cut off from traditional paths to male breadwinning. Not only does this excerpt point to the importance of stylin'; it explicitly connects these phenomena to hood culture, as the Big Tymers describe themselves as "hood rich" by virtue of their ability to style rather than how much wealth they posses.

While much of "Still Fly" focuses on Fresh and Baby's extraordinary car collection and the video contains numerous scenes of the two rappers driving and rapping in front of luxury vehicles, comedy abounds. Throughout the video, the Big Tymers and a variety of extras, including other hip-hop celebrities, dance with inane expressions on their faces, in obviously unserious ways. Additionally, the video features a running comic subplot enacted by Fresh and Baby cast as next-door neighbors who compete to see who is best at showing off.

However, spending what little resources one has on luxury goods is no laughing matter to some critics, and the second and more cynical explanation for hip-hop's resolution of the spectacular/authenticity paradox is that the folk are blinded by their belief in the "American Dream" and intoxicated by conspicuous consumption.[10] That is, hood residents do not celebrate flashy clothes and expensive cars because they are embedded in a noble and uniquely expressive black culture; they celebrate luxury items because they are denied traditional paths to positive self-image, and self- and social esteem can only be achieved through purchase and ownership of these goods as a coping strategy. Those who cannot consume luxury items are considered less valuable, both financially and socially, than those who can, and in order to know oneself as someone who is valuable, the consumer, especially the black consumer, must possess and use expensive commodities that signal his or her value to others.[11] Mainstream hip-hop in this context becomes a form of escapism, as commercially successful rappers invite their audience to identify with a ridiculous and largely staged life of luxury that ordinary people will never experience.

Black Authenticity and the American Dream

Rappers who rise from the poorest ghettos to the privileged class are cast as proof that underdogs can triumph in American capitalism and that black people have the capacity and the right to consume the very best and be counted among those who are important. MCs are marketed as representatives of impoverished communities, giving mainstream visibility, audibility, and creative credibility to constituencies that are ignored at best and dishonored at worst. All of this may inspire a false belief and faith in America's yet unrealized promise of equality of opportunity and provide a smoke screen that prevents the folk from recognizing and criticizing the structures that impede their economic and political progress. In addition to theory-driven scholarship on the importance of ideology to contemporary hegemony, a number of empirical studies document the importance of the American Dream myth to blacks in particular. Jennifer Hochschild (1996) notes that working-class and impoverished blacks exhibit a strong belief in the American Dream that each individual has equal opportunity to pursue life, liberty, and happiness. In contrast, many middle-class African Americans are disheartened by a steady stream of race-based oppression regardless of the social contexts they find themselves in, exhibiting less belief in the dream and less hope for the future.

Similarly, James Sidanius and Felicia Pratto demonstrate the importance of "legitimizing myths," defined as "values, attitudes, beliefs, causal attributions, and ideologies that provide moral and intellectual justification for social practices that either increase, maintain, or decrease levels of social inequality among social groups" (2001, 104). For example, Sidanius and Pratto argue that myths such as equality of opportunity partially explain why nearly 60 percent of black Americans believe discrimination is not a factor in their ability to secure quality housing at fair prices, when empirical evidence affirming the historical and continued presence of discrimination and racism within the housing market is unassailable (107). For Sidanius and Pratto, social order is best explained by this phenomenon—the fact that disadvantaged groups adhere to myths that mask their social domination—rather than by oppressive, authoritative power exercised by privileged groups to keep subordinates in their place (44).

In the song and video for "I Can" (2002a),[12] Nas weaves oppositional identity, black authenticity, and adherence to American Dream ideology together with a complex cool product ripe for multiple interpretations. The musical track contains samples from both Ludwig van Beethoven's "Für Elise" and "Impeach the President" by the Honeydrippers. This combination both glorifies and signifies on notions of classical music, recasting sounds that Westerners are taught to recognize as the pinnacle of artistic brilliance within a hip-hop framework. At first producer Saleem Remi's use of "Für Elise" as an homage to Beethoven seems to validate the ideology that celebrates European art at the expense of African, indigenous American, Arab, and Asian art traditions in the service of white supremacy. But by combining Beethoven with the sample from "Impeach the President,"[13] a funk/soul classic released in 1973 in the context of the Watergate scandal, Remi challenges traditional notions of classic(al) music and, by extension, white supremacy.

The third verse of "I Can" intensifies this challenge, as Nas presents a black nationalist rap, contesting notions of African diasporic inferiority by highlighting the artistic and intellectual accomplishments of ancient African civilizations and the colonization and exploitation of black and brown people by militaristic European empires. But as Nas raps, "Before we came to this country/We were kings and queens, never porch monkeys." He wears an oversized black T-shirt with the phrase "I AM THE AMERICAN DREAM" stenciled across the chest in bright yellow letters. In one of the video's final scenes, Nas opens his leather jacket to fully reveal the shirt and glares defiantly into the camera. Once again, he signifies on traditional notions of American identity by contrasting the American Dream with his own image as a young, somewhat discontented black man committed to hip-hop culture and molded from ghetto experience.

The black nationalist lyrics, notable musical samples, and visual desta-bilization of the American Dream myth form a firm ground for reading "I Can" as an oppositional text. But the lyrical content of Nas's first two verses complicates such a reading, as he affirms traditional notions of the Ameri-can Dream without signifying on or questioning its content. Smith insists that "despite its xenophobic vitriol, as with most African American artistic expression, hip-hop's preoccupation with *oppositional* personae is actually a camouflaged means of *negotiation*, a cultural alchemy where apparent isolation is transformed into contingently employed, tactical maneuvers designed to foster inclusion with more mainstream social bodies" (1997, 348). Nas's performance can certainly be read this way, as he urges young people to embrace monogamous male/female romantic partnership, sex-ual chastity, and commitment to education and hard work as the pillars of individual success. "I Can" celebrates puritan American individualism and a relentless work ethic as forces capable of conquering all odds, and the video features Nas leading a collection of children, the vast majority of whom are black, through the streets of a dilapidated urban neighborhood. Nas sings the chorus with the children, who repeat each of the following phrases after him:

> I know I can
> Be what I want to be
> If I work hard at it
> I'll be where I want to be.

Such blatant celebration of Protestant-work-ethic individualism in the con-text of imagined equal opportunity stifles the song's oppositional under-current, even as representations of opposition to traditional Americanism appear throughout the song.

"I Can" is equal parts motivational speech, black nationalist critique, and traditional American anthem. But more important to discussions of black masculinity is its relationship to black authenticity, considering its representations of the hood, the folk, and consumer capitalist success. Like the video for "'Round Here," "I Can" is set in the hood and features scenes of Nas rapping among ordinary black folk, in this case children, who act naturally in the space they call home. The video contains scenes of Nas and his followers standing in front of apartment buildings as well as clips of children playing in vacant lots and dancing on the sidewalks and in the streets. Not only does Nas keep it real by keeping the hood and the folk

close by, he crafts an oppositional narrative that disputes traditional notions of black inferiority, and he characterizes opposition as both cool/
trendy and authentically black. However, achieving professional success
and economic stability in the context of American capitalism is part and
parcel of resistance for Nas, who tells children that they can become "an
architect, doctor, maybe an actress" if they work hard, embrace education,
and remain determined to reach their goals.

Authenticity and Complexity

Where does this leave us with respect to black authenticity? Prudence
Carter writes:

> Resistance to "acting white" for many African American students is about
> maintaining cultural identity, not about embracing or rejecting the domi-
> nant standards of achievement . . . [R]esistance to "acting white" refers to
> their refusal to adhere to the cultural default setting in U.S. society, to what
> is seen as normative or "natural"—the generic American, white, middle-class
> patterns of speech and mannerisms, dress and physical appearance, and
> tastes in music and art forms. (2005, 53)

Many hip-hop narratives affirm traditional norms of American success,
such as asserting masculine dominance and acquiring economic capital.
Insistence on black authenticity in the service of these norms is partially
driven by the notion that there are other ways to communicate and style
oneself besides those prescribed as "normal" (white) by mainstream society. Affirming these different communicative and cultural styles does not
rescue black authenticity narratives from their contradictions. John L. Jackson addresses these contradictions, as well as the possibility for multiple
interpretations of black authentic acts, by redefining these performative
phenomena as exercises in sincerity rather than authenticity. He explains:

> Authenticity presupposes a relation between subjects (who authenticate) and
> objects (dumb, mute, and inorganic) that are interpreted and analyzed from
> the outside, because they cannot simply speak for themselves.
>
> Sincerity, however, sets up a different relationship entirely. A mere object
> could never be sincere, even if it is authentic. Sincerity is a trait of the object's
> maker, or maybe even its authenticator, but never the object itself, at least not
> as we commonly use the term. Instead, sincerity presumes a liaison between
> subjects—not some external adjudicator and a lifeless scroll. (2005, 15)

Black authentic narratives are prevalent in hip-hop not because they congeal to produce a single coherent discourse of authenticity but because performers strive to build sincere connections with the audience. Rappers are not judged purely on the validity or ideology of the texts they craft; they are judged as performers—as subjects—by their audiences. Each hip-hop representation is a reaching out from one subject to another, and sincerity is validated when the narrative connects performer and audience to each other. This is what Richard Peterson means when he describes authenticity as a social construct as "a claim that is made by or for someone, thing, or performance and either accepted or rejected by relevant others" (2005, 1080). The messages and ideologies expressed in "authentic" black hip-hop narratives may be vastly different from each other; no two hands reach for each other in exactly the same way. But once made, the collection of sincere hip-hop connections makes the concept of authenticity meaningful—a seam that holds the hip-hop world together.

Thematically, "real" blackness entails loving and celebrating the hood as a spatial reference point for collective identity while trying to escape it as a material reality. It means staying connected to folk culture while affirming disciplined individualism and actively distancing oneself from ordinary people by purchasing goods that signify extraordinary wealth. Nas implies that authentic blackness necessitates a rejection of racist stereotypes of black identity that cast African Americans as shiftless ghetto dwellers who ignore the law, while many of the MCs discussed in chapter 3 claim living life as a thug is the only way to be real. Authentic blackness is all of these things because each is acknowledged by at least one community of listeners, not all of whom are black.

There are social forces that produce discourses of authentic black masculinity. These forces include the political economy of the music industry, replete with long-held beliefs about audience demand; racial stratification and racism, which spatially and socially isolate disadvantaged black people from the rest of society; hegemonic masculinity and gender norms that reward some gender performances more than others; and cultural beliefs about who has the right to speak for a folk constituency. Power relations are determined not only by these social forces but by the actions of people subject to them. The ways we understand ourselves and the meaning we give to social conditions affect social organization and social action. In commercially successful rap music, the authenticity discourse produced by these forces is employed in an effort to build connections between performers and listeners around the idea of a stable and honorable race/gender identity. But because human subjects both absorb and reconstruct such discourses, human imperfection, contingency, and fluidity always find their way into the sincere connections being built.

When we examine these efforts to connect through authenticity, we see just how complex and conflicted black authenticity truly is. This means that the seeds of authenticity's undoing are always present in its social and performative construction. The possibility that we might understand ourselves and our conditions differently because of cracks and holes in the discourse means that power relations are constantly contested through discursive production. These contests do not always produce socially just or politically desirable outcomes for disadvantaged people, but the fight for such causes, along with others, is ongoing.

In the next chapter, I examine the emergence of the hip-hop thug, a performative trope tied to the idea of black criminality, and a character seemingly obsessed with domination-driven masculinity. Without forgiving any of the thug's transgressions, I build the case for a complex cool understanding of thug life in hip-hop performances.

THREE

Thug Life and Social Death

A spinoff of gangsta rap music, the thug role is a vivid manifestation of that "aggressive insubordination." Thugs perpetuate the myth of a socially sanctioned Black male warrior, who, by mere coincidence, is also sexually charged . . . One of the hallmark characteristics of a thug is his desensitization, his emotional paralysis. In other words, a thug does not feel, except when his territory (i.e., family, physical space, or physical person) is threatened.

—Ronald Jackson, Scripting the Black Masculine Body

Nobody loves me, I'm a thug nigga
I only hang out with the criminals and drug dealers.

—Tupac Shakur, "All about U" (1996a)

Welcome to Thug Life

In addition to advancing a critique of the criminal justice complex, gangsterism in hip-hop is fundamentally concerned with the performer's ability to assume a dangerous persona who is willing to injure and exploit others for personal gratification. This permutation of black masculine performance is the elephant in the room for those who herald hip-hop's narrative diversity and defend the politics of popular hip-hop music. The violent black supercriminal bent on capital accumulation and personal gratification seems to bear no relation to organic black folk culture or traditional American measures of status attainment. What began as a figment of the white racist imagination now thrives as a commoditized sign of immoral rebellion and masculine strength, and black hip-hop performers' willingness to repeat these representations legitimates troubling links between American discourses of race and crime.

This chapter addresses these issues and more as I examine the hip-hop thug. I begin by explaining the structural and discursive setting in which the thug originated, as the interwoven discourses of race and crime in late-twentieth-century America provide the context for this hip-hop phenomenon. After establishing the origins of thug life, I make the case for the thug as a paradoxical figure. On one hand, this performative trope is born from mainstream society's revulsion and characterized by nihilism and mercenary capitalist impulses. On the other, contemporary thug representations are deeply concerned with love and admiration. In pursuing love and admiration, commercially successful thug MCs rely on a number of sexist and objectionable narratives, which must not be excused or overlooked. However, affirmation of thug love within commercially successful rap foregrounds vulnerability and connectedness and advances the case for complex cool black masculinity in hip-hop.

Structure and Culture of Black Criminality

According to the stereotype, the ghetto-poor black male is a heartless criminal, fulfilling his own destructive prophecy as he ruthlessly navigates a desolate concrete jungle. He is not merely *a* problem but *the* problem, responsible for alienating and threatening greater American society while wreaking havoc on families and reinforcing social disorganization within his community. Recent changes in the political economy and the criminal justice and punishment system produce circumstances in which poor black men are disproportionately cited and penalized for legal transgressions. In addition, images and narratives of threatening black masculinity are mass-produced by major American media outlets for commercial gain, resulting in a popular discourse that seems to legitimate the reality of racial inequity in criminal justice outcomes. Structure, culture, and discourse combine to provide the context for criminal narratives in hip-hop.

The Reagan era was marked by a drastic increase in military spending at the expense of a host of other government-funded programs, which combined with rapid deindustrialization to erode the local economies of America's cities. With economic deterioration came social deterioration as living conditions worsened for the largely black urban poor. William Julius Wilson (1987) explains that inner-city ghettos are strongly affected by the decline of urban economies, as the dearth of stable and fruitful jobs results in unprecedented concentration of poverty within these communities. Middle-class African Americans migrated from the city to the suburbs in the 1970s and 1980s, and this exodus created urban ghettos without a strong middle-class presence to socialize those less fortunate and preserve communal faith in institutions of purportedly equal opportunity. Without the guidance and aid of a more privileged class, poor black inner-city communities grew increasingly disorganized and isolated from the values and life patterns of mainstream society. The socially isolated ghetto poor adopt a range of cultural coping strategies as a result of their structural disadvantages, and these self-destructive behaviors further entrench their social, political, and economic desolation.

Loic Wacquant (2001) draws on Wilson's analysis, arguing that black American ghettos have transformed from communal ghettos into the "hyperghetto." The hyperghetto has four distinctive characteristics, two of which, the overlay of class segregation and loss of positive economic function, are first identified in Wilson's work. Additionally, the hyperghetto is distinguished by the ascendance of state institutions rather than communal institutions as instruments of social control and by the "depacification of everyday life" (Wacquant 2001, 107). State control and surveillance of the most fundamental realms of communal life in the ghetto, such as schools, homes, and hospitals, transform the hyperghetto into a strikingly carceral environment. This conflation of ghetto and prison occurs at the level of both structure (institutionalized state surveillance) and culture, as street and carceral symbolic expression fuse into one set of ghetto-carceral cultural patterns of interaction. The structural changes that bred the hyperghetto/prison society create in reality that which always existed in the white supremacist imagination: the immoral black criminal, pathological by nature, fit for imprisonment, and beyond reprieve or rehabilitation.

Wacquant's point about the depacification of everyday life in the hyperghetto/prison is worthy of emphasis. Too often, in well-intentioned efforts to undo a racist discourse of crime, critics and scholars ignore the material and cultural reality of impoverished ghetto residents. Urban hyperghettos can be dangerous places, with massive structural impediments to economic sustainability and mobility, and men and women who live in these neighborhoods may be both executors and victims of terrible crimes. The illegal drug economy and prevalence of weaponry (especially firearms) creates a hypermasculine culture that Elijah Anderson calls the "code of the street," or "set of informal rules governing interpersonal public behavior, particularly violence" (1999, 33). Anderson argues that young people from impoverished urban areas are alienated from the norms and rewards of legitimate society and engaged in a constant quest for respect. Ghetto residents cannot ensure their public safety without respect, and because respect is hard won and easily lost, many of the measures taken to secure it may seem obscene, irrationally violent, or petty to outside observers. Without adequate protection and aid from the state and other legitimate institutions, violence emerges as a viable tactic for both self-preservation and the administration of justice for hyperghetto/prison residents (Kubrin and Weitzer 2003). This culture, based on the projection of masculine toughness and willingness to harm one's neighbor, is an everyday reality for many hyperghetto/prison residents, not simply a figment of the racist imagination.

Criminal Justice Policy and Outcomes

As arrests and convictions mounted during the late 1980s, prison overcrowding emerged as a concern, and state and federal government responded by stimulating the prison industry. During the late 1980s and early 1990s, prison construction and maintenance emerged as a critical growth industry for the local economies of states throughout the country (except in parts of the Midwest and Northwest). The boom occurred in the context of a transitional period for the American economy as workers throughout the United States suffered through an economic recession brought on by the confluence of military downsizing and the continued transition to technological industries (Goldberg 2000). The prison industry emerged as a savior in a multitude of depressed communities and states, providing new employment for suburban and rural populations of unskilled workers. All told, "between 1980 and 1993 [during the Reagan and George H. W. Bush presidencies], federal spending on employment and training programs had been cut in half, while corrections spending had increased by 521%" (Mauer 1999, 68).

From 1985 to 1995, the number of inmates in federal prisons rose by 126 percent (Mauer 1999, 125), and America is now home to more than 2.3 million prisoners, a number that embarrassingly eclipses the prison population of any other developed country in the world. More than 900,000 of these 2.3 million prisoners are African American (Mauer and King 2007), which points to another clear result of the new emphasis on punishment and incarceration: the broadening of the black-white gap in incarceration rates. During the same ten-year period, the incarceration rate of African Americans nearly doubled, from 368 per 100,000 to 725 per 100,000 (Mauer 2003, 4), and African Americans are currently incarcerated at approximately 5.6 times the rate at which whites are incarcerated (Mauer and King 2007).[1]

Black women are severely affected by these trends, as the black female prison population rose by 204 percent from 1985 to 1995, compared with a 143 percent rise for black men (Mauer 1999, 125). But black men remain the most disproportionately represented race-gender category among prisoners, and involvement with the criminal justice system is commonplace among the African American male population. There are currently more black men serving time in federal or state prisons than are enrolled in institutions of higher education. One-third of black men between the ages of twenty and twenty-nine are under some form of state supervision, and a black male born in the year 1991 now has a 29 percent chance of spending time behind bars at some point in his life (Mauer 2003, 200).

Though national crime rates decreased during the period from 1986 to 1996 by some measures (Johnson 2001, 35), the rates of specific crimes, such as violent crimes committed by blacks, remained stable in the 1980s and 1990s (Mauer 1999, 127). Significantly, public opinion has barely been affected by the entrenchment of punishment and imprisonment as the American ethic of crime prevention or selective citations of crime rate decline, and fear of crime remains stable (Johnson 2001, 35). Crime rates seem to be only marginally related to the new obsession with punishment, if at all.

Discourse

The late-twentieth-century "tough on crime" discourse was jump-started by the reactionary "law and order" presidential campaigns of Goldwater and Nixon and carried to the extreme by presidents Reagan, George H. W. Bush, and Clinton (Mauer 1999, 45–48). Getting "tough on crime" cannot be separated from its historical context. As Katherine Beckett (1997) and Bruce Western (2006) argue, the discourse of law and order was mobilized by southern officials looking to thwart and discredit the civil rights movement. Protestors seeking racial justice were characterized as troublemakers who broke the law purely to disturb the peace and spit in the eye of government. The late-twentieth- and early-twenty-first-century crime debate has been rife with racial meaning since its beginning.[2]

There is ample evidence that the American criminal justice complex produces racist outcomes, but some might argue that this evidence is not grounds for convicting the system of racism. Such a conclusion depends on the characterization of the system as an active producer of race-based social inequality, using the social phenomenon of crime as a mechanism to exert the will of the state on poor nonwhite citizens for the purpose of maintaining a racial hierarchy. Katherine Russell provides evidence for this premise, beginning with the harsh reality of racial targeting, harassment, and brutality by the police (1998, 37). Russell also cites scholars who disavow a characterization of the criminal justice system as essentially racist but readily admit that the racial disparity in incarceration rates cannot be empirically explained in terms of disproportionate rates of black offense (30). Thus the system presents itself as an active producer of the social marginality that contributes to criminal behavior within impoverished ghettos.

Alternatively, William Bennett, John Dilulio Jr., and John Walters (1996) argue that there is no substantive evidence that the criminal justice system is racist. From legislature to legal process, equal protection is the law, and therefore racial disparities can only be explained by offense rates. In *Body Count* (1996), Bennett and his coauthors assert that young black males commit crimes at a higher rate than young white males (45) and that the differences in the number of black and white criminal offenses reflect the familial instability and disorganization of the ghetto poor (22). Many researchers concerned with structural inequality readily acknowledge the importance of familial instability as a factor in the development of deviant behavior. But Bennett and other behaviorists diverge from Wilson and others, identifying *moral* poverty as the root cause of criminal behavior among deviant young black men. The authors of *Body Count* highlight the pervasive nihilism of the ghetto poor as the force responsible for robbing today's poor black youth of any sense of right and wrong. The character of their violent crimes and self-destructive lifestyle suggests that young black criminals are not merely insufficiently socialized but completely "unmoralized" as a result of social isolation. According to Bennett, Dilulio, and Walters,

> America is now home to thickening ranks of juvenile "super-predators"— brutally remorseless youngsters who murder, assault, rape, rob, burglarize, deal deadly drugs, join gun-toting gangs, and create serious communal disorders . . . To these mean street youngsters, the words "right" and "wrong" have no fixed moral meaning . . . They live by the meanest code of the meanest streets, a code that reinforces rather than restrains their violent, hair-trigger mentality . . . So for as long as their youthful energies hold out, they will do what comes "naturally": murder, rape, rob, assault, burglarize, deal deadly drugs, and get high. (28)

These coauthors argue that the cure for America's plague of "super-predators" has three ingredients. As an initial step, society must not for the sake of "tolerance and open-mindedness" condone immoral acts but instead acknowledge its recent moral displacement and fight to reinstill morality in America's social fabric (197). Second, parenthood must be resurrected as a privilege reserved for only those who can afford the temporal and psychological costs of raising children (201). Finally, society as a whole must "remember God," as the spiritual component of moral poverty is the most vital, given that this struggle will be "won or lost in the human heart" (207).[3]

Ultimately, *Body Count* collapses under its own weight as the authors immerse themselves in a race-*based*—and arguably *racist*—discourse to assert the power of cultural, moral, and perhaps biological deficiency. Bennett and company disavow the importance of institutionalized racism and poverty in the criminal justice system and the development of a "new breed" of violent criminals. There is no denying that the hyperghetto/prison is commonly the scene of violent and disturbing acts or that black men are frequently the executors. However, the phenomenon is described in the quotation above using language that implicitly substantiates racist ideologies and completely ignores structural factors.

One example of such language is the trope of the black predator, which has a long history in the white supremacist discourse of black deviancy. *Predator* takes on multiple meanings in historical context, but its strongest roots as a descriptive paradigm of black masculinity are embedded in racist fears of black men as physical beasts and *sexual* predators bent on violating white women. This image of black men has been visually conjured at various moments in the history of American popular culture, perhaps most famously in D. W. Griffith's 1915 film *Birth of a Nation* and more recently during the media extravaganza that was O. J. Simpson's 1994 murder trial.[4]

Another example is the authors' reference to the "code of the meanest streets" as the governing dictum of "super-predator" life. At no point in their description of the "super-predator" do the authors explicitly identify the criminal as black, but the "code of the meanest streets" alludes to the same code delineated in Anderson's *Code of the Street*, which focuses on poor African American life and the culture of respect in the inner-city. Finally, Bennett and his colleagues evoke blackness as a central component of the "super-predator" identity by characterizing the behavior as "natural" in the "new breed" of criminals, inviting readers to irresponsibly connect criminal acts with a predisposition somehow rooted in racial biology.

The "super-predator" as presented in *Body Count* has heavily racial connotations, and the image of the criminal in the American popular consciousness is a black man. Perceptions of African Americans as threatening to one's economic resources is a strong predictor of white people's punitive attitudes (King and Wheelock 2007), and when white people imagine policies and punishments suitable for violent offenders, they often imagine offenders as black rather than white (Peffley and Hurwitz 2002). Anticrime political campaigns, such as the Willie Horton campaign launched by former president George H. W. Bush, are proven to prime fears based on race rather than crime, even when politicians frame the issues in racially neutral terms (D. Johnson 2001; Mendelberg 2001). Russell notes that at the time she was researching *The Color of Crime*, a search for "white crime" on the LexisNexis database found roughly fifty articles, many of which discussed white crime in relation to black crime, but a search for "black crime" generated a list of over a thousand articles (1998, 115).[5]

Media representations of black urban communities, and black men specifically, are equally important. As Patricia Hill Collins explains, "The authentic Black culture so commoditized in the media, creates images of criminality that explains the failures of racial integration by placing the blame on the unassimilability of African Americans themselves. The joblessness, poor schools, racially segregated neighborhoods, and unequal public services that characterize American society vanish, and social class hierarchies in the United States, as well as patterns of social mobility within them, become explained solely by issues of individual values, motivation, and morals" (2004, 178). Collins asserts that "authentic" black culture is constructed and commoditized by mass media as the opposite of that of inauthentic, "respectable" blacks, who gain acceptance to white spaces because they have separated themselves from black communities. The proliferation of "black crime" discourse functions as justification for racial hierarchy and social inequality, obscuring the root causes of poverty and placing blame for blacks' collective failure to attain respectable cultural and economic status on black culture and behavior alone.

The effect of media representations of "black crime" is worth accentuating. In their landmark study on black images in the media, Robert Entman and Andrew Rojecki find that, in contrast to whites, black criminals are rarely identified by name on local newscasts, solidifying their image as a "single undifferentiated group of offenders" (2000, 83), and whites are drastically overrepresented as victims of crime[6] rather than perpetrators (81). Black people are also shown in physical custody (such as handcuffs or bodily restraint) far more often than whites, and black criminals appear in street or jail clothing more frequently as well (83). And as newscasts code black figures as criminally inclined, urban, and poor, they consistently omit stories documenting racial discrimination and other significant causes of black poverty, which abets white denial of racism and inhibits political programs designed to destroy racial inequality (105).

Conservative discourse on America's crime problem blames black Americans for the economic deterioration of urban centers and the continuous disorganization of black families (Thernstrom and Thernstrom 1999), and mass media contribute to the misconception that blackness or black people cause crime. But this causal relationship does not exist as social reality, according to more rigorous empirical study. African Americans are not particularly prone to violent crime, nor do black communities tolerate crime more readily than white communities. Relevant variables for analyzing and predicting instances of criminal behavior are age, class, social organization (including but not limited to family structure), and neighborhood collective efficacy (Sampson and Groves 1989; Sampson and Wilson 1998; Sampson and Raudenbush 1999; Morenoff, Sampson, and Raudenbush 2001). Social ecology, not simply race, produces criminal outcomes. There is, however, an undercurrent of cynicism in some African American communities about the police and court system (Sampson and Bartusch 1998), as institutions of law and justice have historically combined to disproportionately penalize black offenders while failing to protect innocent black citizens from harm (Kennedy 1997).

The historical relationship between race and crime is distorted when characterized as the "black crime problem," but such characterizations are met with insufficient resistance. Left-leaning progressives and liberals with structural critiques of criminal justice outcomes are marginalized in mainstream politics for fear that the public will reject such explanations as mere apologies for wrongful and punishable criminal behavior. Meanwhile, black American advocacy groups seem paralyzed by the link between race and crime, afraid to acknowledge and challenge the myth of black criminality (Wacquant 2001). Rappers, however, are not afraid to talk back, producing narratives that both challenge and bolster some of the most basic assumptions about black deviance by speaking from the subject position of the imagined and embellished criminal.

From Gangsta Rap to Thug Life

Eithne Quinn locates the genesis of "gangsta rap" as a phrase and genre in 1989 when N.W.A. (Niggaz with Attitude) hit the newly launched *Billboard* rap singles chart (2005, 10). Quinn urges us not to view gangsta rap as a static musical category but "as part of an ongoing history," explaining that a "process-oriented logic nicely captures the intersecting recent and longer-term historical trajectories of the gangsta story, in which age-old expressive repertoires collided with new technologies, industrial possibilities, and social and political conditions to create a new production trend" (191). Other scholars conceive of gangsta rap as a marketing pose and commitment to image management for the purpose of exploiting the audience's fascination with sex and violence (Watkins 1998, 185) and as a social critique and style of musical performance characterized by hard-hitting semiautobiographical "urban reality rap" popularized by West Coast acts but related to the delivery and style of East Coast rappers KRS-One and Schoolly D (Kelley 1994, 118).

There is value in each of these understandings of gangsta rap—as a style of music, a social critique, an ongoing process, a marketing strategy, and a by-product of music industry trends. The key turn for the purposes of this project is locating the *thug* within the gangsta tradition. Economic marginalization, descriptions of illicit activity, and racist criminalization of black youth have been major themes from the beginning of gangsta, and while rap music has always been autobiographical in some respects, the stakes of autobiographical narrative authenticity were raised when gangsta rap started selling and became easily identified as a genre. When G-Funk (Gangsta Funk) burst on the scene in the early 1990s and smoothed out gangsta's rough edges, rugged masculine authenticity had to be reaffirmed as a complement to gangsta's progression toward easy-listening. With the advent and commercial success of G-Funk, the gangsta genre split into a tradition with two distinct but related protagonists, each of whom refocused audiences' attention on the *identity* of the performer rather than the style or category of music. One of these characters is the G-Funk gangsta, who is often sonically identified by Dr. Dre's trademark Parliament Funkadelic samples and keyboard synthesizers and visibly identified by his daily routine, coolly cruising down the Los Angeles freeway with gin and juice in his cup on his way to a party. When first conceptualized, the thug allowed an extension of the gangsta concept to non-G-Funk rappers and a solidification of threatening black masculine authenticity as a trope to connect with consumers. I am not suggesting that these two types are opposed, clearly bounded, and irreconcilable but only that the thug trope allowed for a sonic and spatial expansion of gangsterism beyond the West Coast.

As Todd Boyd (2007) notes, the word *thug* has come to stand in for *nigger* as an epithet for criminally inclined black men. "Thug" can be spoken in the public sphere without rebuke (Boyd 2007) because it is ostensibly racially neutral, making it a far better fit for our current racial epoch, in which implicit (rather than explicit) appeals to racial prejudice reign supreme (Mendelberg 2001). One of many discursive strategies employed by black American speech communities to resist racist insult and mistreatment is to reclaim and transform the meaning of words in order to evade the surveillance of nonblack onlookers or to affirm black self-worth. The paradigmatic example of this practice, discussed in detail in chapter 5 of this book, is the word *nigger*, which is transformed to "nigga" and frequently employed as a term of endearment. Similarly, commercially successful rap acts since the mid-1990s have embraced the word *thug* as an unapologetic affirmation of their experiences as black men, marginalized and insulted by mainstream America and socialized in violent and economically depressed American ghettos.

The reclamation of *thug* by popular rappers is not accidental or random. It occurs in the context of the success of the gangsta genre in the music industry, at a time when the racist discourse of black criminality was updated and reinforced by policies that neglected poor black and brown communities and locked up their inhabitants. Simply put, reclamation and redefinition of a word is driven by the social, political, and economic conditions of those who use it and not by chance, unfettered individual choice, or artistic ingenuity divorced from social context.

Thug Life and Social Death

Criminalized African Americans live in danger of what Orlando Patterson (1982) calls "social death." Patterson uses this concept to unpack social relations in slave societies, and it is doubtful that he would willingly apply this framework to present conditions of African American life in the hyperghetto/prison. Regardless, his analysis is useful as we seek to understand the liminal position of the partially real and partially imagined black criminal in twenty-first-century America. Patterson's conception of social death relies on two notions of exile. In the intrusive mode, the slave is socially dead because he is an outsider or intruder. By contrast, social death in the extrusive mode points to the slave's status as "one who had been deprived of all claims of community" and "became the enemy because he had fallen" (44).

Both arguments are used in the construction of white supremacist ideologies. Early American racist discourse constructs African Americans as biologically different because they are African and, as such, incompatible with American culture. African slaves were brought here against their will, and their outsider status is inherent, rooted in their blood. Since the fall of Jim Crow, however, we have seen a shift toward laissez-faire racism (Bobo 1997) and the extrusive mode, where racist ideologies tell us that African Americans have fallen from what should have been a reasonable degree of grace gained through the civil rights movement. With equal rights, so the discourse goes, black people have every opportunity to be good citizens and realize a portion of the American Dream, but their cultural deficiencies—specifically laziness, violence, and sexual deviance—have made them "the enemy," with no valid claims to American citizenry given their behavior.

As Patterson explains, "The essence of slavery is that the slave, in his social death, lives on the margin between community and chaos, life and death, the sacred and the secular. Already dead, he lives outside the manna of the gods and can cross the boundaries with social and supernatural impunity" (1982, 51). While poor African Americans in the hyperghetto/carceral state are not slaves and contemporary American society is not a caste or slave society, like the slave, the imagined black criminal from the hyperghetto/prison lives on the margins of legitimate society. At best, he is weakly attached to the labor market. His civil rights are frequently violated or denied by police who stop, search, and brutalize without just cause and by employers, educators, realtors, and everyday civilians who discriminate based on demeanors or aesthetics that supposedly signal danger. Hip-hop thug discourse catalogs these experiences. Thugs learn that laws are not applied to them as they are to others, so living "outside the manna of the gods," the hip-hop thug makes his own moral and political laws, borrowing from both acceptable (love-driven and hopeful) and despicable (violent, exploitative, and nihilistic) models of the universe.

While the politics of respectability argues that being poor and black does not make someone a criminal, thug discourse thumbs its nose at the establishment and plainly says, "If simply being me, born poor and black in the ghetto, is criminal and wrong, I don't want to be right." Thug narratives embrace the criminal label and stretch its meaning. Living in the margins as an outside observer and actor, thug narrators recite criticisms of freedom, justice, and morality, crossing the boundaries between mainstream and gangster norms and managing a tumultuous love affair with an American public that is repulsed and enamored.

Tupac: Original Thug

Though he was not the only rapper to fashion himself a thug in the 1990s, Tupac Shakur was the most influential.[7] Shakur's career and his relationship to thug life should be understood as a nonlinear progression. Much of Shakur's early work on *2Pacalypse Now* (1991) and *Strictly 4 My N.I.G.G.A.Z.*

(1993) deals with the unjust criminalization and resultant anger, depression, and nihilism of black ghetto residents. He does not regularly refer to himself as a "thug" on record until he forms the group Thug Life[8] in 1993, but when he starts claiming "thug life," the character of that life is rooted in his depictions of black ghetto discontent. Despite crafting a number of politically oppositional raps early in his career, his antiestablishment gangsta image was crystallized closer to the end of his career (Shakur died in 1996) when his raps were far less critical of the state and less frequently focused on black consciousness building. This change in focus coincided with his signing with Death Row Records, and his metamorphosis reflects similar changes within gangsta rap as a genre, which emphasized social protest and criticism at its genesis and moved toward image crafting as it gained commercial appeal (Quinn 2005, 176). The concept of the thug underwent a similar transformation, from signifying disgust, rebellion, and nihilism to evoking coolness and power.

It is common knowledge among hip-hop fans that Tupac described the phrase "thug life" as an acronym for "This Hate U Gave Lil' Infants Fuck Everybody." In an MTV interview he explained:

> I mean like I'm not scared to say how I feel. Part of being [a thug] is to stand up for your responsibilities and say this is what I do even though I know people are going to hate me and say, "it's so politically un-correct," and "how could you make black people look like that? Do you know how buffoonish you all look with money and girls and all that?" That's what I want to do. I want to be real with myself. (quoted in Dyson 2001, 113)

Thug subjectivity is rooted not only in outsider and rebel status but in the fact that *existence as a thug is based on the premise and knowledge that you are hated*. Tupac acknowledges, "I know people are going to hate me," and the "hate" in the acronym THUG LIFE is "Hate U Gave"—hate given by another to the thug, not hate born within and projected by the thug himself.

This knowledge of one's status not only as an outsider but as the target of hatred produces multiple responses. In the excerpt above, Shakur explains that this hatred inspires him to "be real," and Michael Dyson (2001) rightly notes that Shakur's effort to build a "real" nihilistic life that matched his spectacularly thuggish raps had tragic consequences. In addition to making self-destructive personal life choices, Tupac's desire to be real often meant owning up to his own vulnerability, loneliness, and pain, as we hear in songs like "So Many Tears" (1995), "When Thugz Cry" (2001), and countless others. These two sides of Tupac's thug life, the imposing gangsta and the tortured soul, were reinforced by his film career, as he played gangsta characters in films like *Above the Rim* (1996) and *Juice* (1992) but also starred as an earnest romantic in *Poetic Justice* (1993). Tupac's self-styling as a ruthless yet vulnerable thug, to be feared and redeemed, is critical to the evolution of thug desirability. Shakur set the precedent for hip-hop thugs' balancing multiple and seemingly contradictory versions of heteronormative masculinity while clinging to the trope of authenticity, a complex cool performance reprised by a number of modern-day hip-hop thug celebrities.

Offend and Conquer

In choosing thug life over social death, thug MCs are likely to offend audiences that do not want to hear what they have to say. When evoking a criminal identity, the artist often makes the intent to offend explicit, and the offense may come in the form of vulgar language, claims about his manhood, or violent life experience. Describing the genesis of "tough on crime" rhetoric, Bernard Harcourt (2001) documents a crucial rhetorical move by political conservatives, characterizing criminals as doing *harm* to the public, not merely offending public standards. Critics of civil disobedience during the civil rights movement argued that (black) protestors were not just disturbing but in fact harmful to society. This change in the criminal from deviant to agent of harm illustrates the delicate line many contemporary rappers tread as they claim their thug identities and describe their lifestyles. Poor black Americans are frequently characterized as lazy, undeserving, violent, and uncivilized; that is, one's identity as either poor or black (or both) inherently defines one as offensive to other populations and American morality. Natural status as the offender is often a given for thug performers, but many rappers embellish this offense through tales of violence as proof of their manly mettle in conflict or their ability to overcome hardship.

On "Renegade" (2001), Eminem and Jay-Z proclaim that they

> Never been afraid to say
> What's on my mind at, any given time of day
> 'Cause I'm a RENEGADE!

Jay's raps include a defense of his role as storyteller, telling listeners:

I give you the news
With a twist it's just his ghetto point-of-view
The renegade
You been afraid.

Both Eminem and Jay-Z affirm their positions as social critics over the course of the song, arguing that their point of view is bound to offend because of where they come from. Jay-Z's rhyme shows how easy it is to make the slip from offense to harm when he exposes his critics as "afraid." In occupying the role of rebel and bringing an oppositional narrative to American ears, Jay-Z conceives of himself as someone who inspires fear. In a song fundamentally about the power of offense, the potential to harm and the fear it engenders are the other shoe waiting to drop.

T.I. (Clifford Harris Jr.) also takes this step toward harm and fear. His 2006 album *King* was the best-selling rap album of the year, selling over 1.5 million copies domestically (Sanneh 2007b). While he raps about a range of subjects, including partying, courtship, death, and mourning, T.I. crafts an image of himself as a thuggish threat to be feared and respected on the song "Undertaker." The music is heavily driven by keyboard samples, and one of the most salient sounds on the track is a sample that resembles a church organ. The title and content of "Undertaker" (the chorus repeatedly boasts, "We bury niggas!") invite listeners to connect the song to funerals and burials and envision the performers as agents capable of bringing death to others. In the opening verse T.I. raps:

Ready for the gun play, prepared for a fistfight
Roll up on your bitch, ask her, "What that pussy hittin' like?"
First she acting funny, in a minute she gon' get right

. . . .

Nigga spit rounds
Turn your stomach to spaghetti when it hit the ground

. . . .

I pimp hard through all the pages in the calendar
Bitch, it's pimp squad, all action no cameras.

While this excerpt cannot simply be read as a truthful representation of T.I.'s genuine willingness to end someone's life, the lyrics form a picture of a problematically thuggish and fearsome character.

First, T.I. emphasizes his capacity to harm other men through physical violence, warning listeners that he is ready for either fistfights or gunplay and describing the gory scene of his victim's carnage as spilled spaghetti. Domination-driven masculinity and the potential to inflict harm are further affirmed through the portrayal of women as sex objects without agency and the construction of weak men as feminine. T.I.'s two-line courtship of another man's "bitch" begins his gendered description of power with multiple layers, as he communicates his attraction by asking the woman, "What that pussy hittin' like?" After this blunt verbal courtship and violent characterization of sex as "pussy hittin'," he assures listeners that even if the woman he desires is initially offended, "in a minute she gon' get right" and assume her proper role as the object of his pursuit who will accede to his advances.

This conquest is harmful to the absent male adversary whose property (the "bitch") is seized. T.I. then describes himself as the opposite of a weak man, or "pussy nigga," in that he is ready to commit acts of violence by "spit[ting] rounds," or firing his gun. To close his celebration of ruthless masculinity and feminine degradation, the narrator assures listeners that his construction of self is "all action, no cameras." The scenes he depicts are not staged or disingenuously acted for the "camera"; they are the way the rapper "really" lives. Jay-Z echoes this metaphor for authenticity on "Public Service Announcement" (2003), when he raps, "Let me tell you dudes what I'll do to protect this / Shoot at you actors like movie directors." Actors are those who are not real enough to take Jay-Z's possessions or his place atop the rap industry hierarchy, and he warns that he is willing to protect himself from weaker, less authentic men with violence (a claim few serious rap fans would believe, given Jay-Z's lofty status as a hip-hop icon).[9]

Nihilism: Ride or Die

Thuggish hip-hop authenticity is not merely about claiming the capacity to commit criminal acts and dominate others; it is about claiming this capacity with full knowledge of the consequences of such behavior, legal and otherwise. Again, Shakur's work is instructive. In a live session performed at a concert with Notorious B.I.G., Tupac raps:

> Mobbin' like a motherfucker, livin' like I wanna
> And ain't no stoppin' at the red lights, I'm sideways
> Thug life motherfucker crime pays!
> Let the cops put they lights on, chase me nigga
> Zigzaggin' through the freeway, race me nigga

In a high-speed chase with the law
The realest motherfucker that you ever saw.[10]

Shakur's refusal to bow to the police and insistence that "crime pays" confer authenticity on multiple levels. First, the refusal implies connection to other black people who distrust the police for the explicitly racial reasons already discussed, and second, Shakur's contempt for authority affirms his own rugged individualism as a rebel without a cause. His disregard for public and personal safety tells listeners that he is not ashamed to live however he wants; he has given himself over to reckless abandon, and he is not afraid to expose this risky, fearless side of himself as who he really is. But this particular use of authenticity as a barrier is puzzling because Tupac describes an unquestionably nihilistic scene. This raises the question, Why bother to erect authenticity as a barrier between you and the fakers if your life is dark or meaningless? Why bother to protect a social space where the ethos is not only "fuck the establishment" and "fuck the police" but, as Tupac says, "Fuck the world"?

Phillip Harper writes, "All debates over and claims to 'authentic' African-American identity are largely animated by a profound anxiety about the status specifically of African-American *masculinity*" (1996, ix). As hip-hop narrators engage nihilism, they speak about vulnerability, spirituality, and love among men, none of which are traditionally masculine topics that impart power to the narrator in the context of hegemonic masculinity. The barrier of authenticity is erected as a protective wall, keeping fake men out and preventing them from witnessing and empathizing with thug vulnerability. In erecting this barrier, thug narratives invert the value of painful lived experiences and hyperghetto social death. Trouble is transformed from a source of trauma to a badge of honor that earns thugs the right to be vulnerable, spiritual, and loving, as they simultaneously distance themselves from "weak" men who exhibit the same qualities. Tracing this process begins with confronting nihilism.

Cornel West explains that nihilism is a response to "meaninglessness, hopelessness, and (most important) lovelessness" (1993, 14) and that the "nihilistic threat" is the "major enemy" of black survival in modern America. Nick De Genova asserts that West errs in reducing the African American condition to a matter of spirituality instead of focusing on the "objective structures of exploitation or oppression" that restrict black life (1995, 92). De Genova argues that nihilism must be viewed, at least in part, as a productive, revolutionary force in black politics. At its worst, nihilism is "something far more complex than its flatly antiromantic portrayal in

West's redemptive and evangelical political posturing" (98). Nihilism in rap is therapeutic for poor young people of color who swim in the postindustrial urban stream of social isolation and self-destruction (116). The art gives this population a voice, serving as affirmation that they are not alone as they confront their social death on a daily basis. For these reasons, nihilism should be seen as a force ripe with possibility, as those who claim it have nothing left to lose. For De Genova, the nihilist impetus is a far more likely engine for social revolution than West's yearning for prophetic love and democratic socialism; it raucously rejects the rules of unjust authority.

Hip-hop nihilism as manifest in thug discourse is often angry and depressed. Narrators choose thug life over social death and struggle with their problems between cries of "Fuck the world." Despite its anger, hip-hop gangster nihilism is not loveless or wholly purposeless. Tupac provides us with a deeper look into the nihilistic mind of the hip-hop thug in the song "My Block" (1995):

> It appears that I've been marked for death
> My heartless breast, the underlying cause of my arrest, my life is stressed
> And no rest forever weary
> My eyes stay teary for all the brothers that are buried in the cemetery
> Shit is scary, how black on black crime legendary, but at times unnecessary
> I'm gettin' worried
> Teardrops and closed caskets, the three-strikes law is drastic
> And certain death for us ghetto bastards
> What can we do when we're arrested, but open fire
> Life in the pen ain't for me, cause I'd rather die
> But don't cry through your despair
> I wonder if the Lord still cares for us niggas on welfare
> And who cares if we survive
> The only time they notice a nigga is when he's clutchin' on a four-five
> My neighborhood ain't the same
> 'Cause all these little babies goin' crazy or they sufferin' in the game
> And I swear it's like a trap
> But I ain't given up on the hood it's all good when I go back
> Hos show me love, niggas give me props
> Forever hop 'cause it don't stop, on my block.[11]

In this verse, Shakur considers a variety of positions from the "black crime" and nihilism debates. The cause of his arrest could be his "heartless breast," which echoes the conservative, or individual volition, discourse re-

garding the problem of black crime. But the rest of the verse clearly eradi-
cates the notion that he is incapable of emotion or empathy, as Shakur
describes the pain and regret he experiences as one of the ghetto forsaken.
Black-on-black crime is described as "legendary," and the lyric communicates the sense that the phenomenon of black-on-black crime occupies a
mythic space in the public imagination, as the preceding analysis of American race/crime discourse suggests. The only times poor blacks are noticed,
the only times they are recognizable to America at large, are those times
when they are "clutchin' on a four five [.45-caliber pistol]," threatening the
peace. Criminal law is cast as an active force that injures poor blacks, as
Shakur tells us that it prescribes "certain death for us ghetto bastards." As
a response to the persecution perpetrated by the criminal justice complex,
Tupac tells listeners that opening fire seems a reasonable choice when one
considers the alternative of life in the penitentiary.

Shakur admits that material conditions detract from his mental health
and emotional stability as he fights the depression that comes from closeness to social and physical death. He even asks if God, who is supposed
to love all creation, "still cares for us niggas on welfare," advancing West's
claim that the absence of love destroys the moral fabric of black communal life. This story is undeniably dependent on the construction of race,
as Shakur uses "niggas" and "brothers" to describe those he struggles with
and those he has lost. The ghetto features prominently in the story, as the
neighborhood personified is "goin' crazy," reproducing conditions that
yield pathological socialization from generation to generation, as even
babies are "sufferin' in the game." Despite the pain, the verse ends with
an affirmation of love for the hood, and the explanation that what allows
him to keep from "giving up" is the love he receives from hood residents.
Though he is depressed and he acknowledges the violent, self-destructive
impulses that result from his structural and cultural location, Shakur complicates the image of the nihilistic criminal monster. He cares for people
both living and dead and, despite a God that has forsaken him, manages
to maintain both hope and love as he claims the space of the hyperghetto/
prison as home.

The work of Shakur, a self-proclaimed thug-poet and posthumous folk
hero, is treated with great care by hip-hop scholars who acknowledge that
he is a unique and complicated subject, capable of subverting paradigms
of race, class, gender, nihilism, and other sociophilosophical phenomena.
Shakur is canonized as a one-of-a-kind figure and an exception to the rule
of gangster rap. However, thug life is frequently portrayed as part of more
complex narratives that reveal interdependent beliefs about love, loss, mo-

rality, and the individual will to survive and triumph. Shakur is far from the only thug to be a poet, and contemporary rappers have added layers to the thug image to the delight and disgust of rap fans and critics.

Get Rich or Die Tryin'

For structural reasons already discussed, the illegal drug economy exploded in poor black urban communities toward the end of the twentieth century, and street-level drug dealers became influential agents of socialization and neighborhood icons in American ghettos.[12] As Kanye West, a hip-hop icon who has never claimed thug life, raps, "As a shorty I looked up to the dope man / Only the dope man I knew that wasn't broke man" (West 2004, "We Don't Care"). Tommie Shelby argues that late capitalist societies encourage us all to get rich, and when those societies fail to provide equal opportunities to pursue this goal, we can hardly call the turn to crime an unreasonable or unforeseeable choice for those without access to opportunity (2007, 148). Many rappers have come to use the narrative of the street hustler, always working and surviving by any means necessary, as a story easily transferable to their lives in the music industry. As a tactic to confirm their authenticity as authentic ghetto subjects, many performers insist that drug dealing was their profession prior to making it as an artist. But there is more depth to the narrative of the drug-dealing hustler than affirmation of one's status as a mercenary capitalist, as performances reveal struggles with regret, depression, and vulnerability as a result of the drug trade.

On "Go Head" (Ruff Ryders 2000), Styles P of the Lox laments:

> Fill my clip to the tip kinda hopin' you trip
> Push my whip to the limit kinda hopin' it flip
> I feel sorry for the crackheads, but happy for myself
> So I got mixed feelings 'bout this hustling shit.

The passage begins in typically thuggish fashion as the narrator carries his loaded weapon, almost hoping that an opponent will test him, thus presenting the opportunity to quench his thirst for violence. Read in isolation, "Fill my [gun] clip to the tip kinda hopin' you trip [act out or challenge me]" could be understood as a typical exercise in hegemonic masculinity, where Styles aims to realize his manhood through dominating someone else. But Styles modifies the meaning of this outwardly destructive impulse by juxtaposing it with his capacity for inward self-destruction. He drives his car ("whip") as fast as possible, "kinda hopin'" that it flips over with him in it, just as he almost hopes that an enemy provokes him into firing his gun. Whether Styles or someone else is the victim of nihilistic violence, the verse suggests that these desires spring from the torment of the drug dealer, who regrettably profits from his customers' pain.

On a separate collaborative effort with Styles entitled "I'm Not You" (2002), Pusha T of the Clipse echoes Styles's sentiments. Pusha tells listeners:

> Yes it pains me to see them need this
> All of them lost souls, and I'm their Jesus
> Deepest regret and sympathies to the streets
> I seen 'em pay for they fix when they kids couldn't eat
> And with this in mind, I still didn't quit
> And that's how I know that I ain't shit.

Despite the potential to earn copious sums of money and acquire respect through violence and intimidation, drug dealing is a dangerous game, not only because one's personal safety is under constant threat but also because one's sense of self-worth is constantly strained by a vocation that helps drug abusers poison themselves.

The benefit of enduring these threats is that if a performer can emerge from the drug trade with body, mind, and finances intact, his success speaks to his ability to overcome mammoth odds and positions him as a legendary thug capitalist figure. In the early twenty-first century, 50 Cent (Curtis Jackson) stands as perhaps the finest example of the phenomenon of the rapper who constructs his mythology from his experiences as a drug dealer. Over the course of his career, Jackson survived bouts between himself and drug-trade competitors, and though his body was scarred by multiple gunshot wounds, his bravado remains intact. He parlayed tales of his gangster past into legendary commercial hip-hop success, winning eleven American Music Award nominations in five years and garnering international sales that made him the body and face of rap music and commoditized thug life.

Jackson's first studio album, *Power of the Dollar*, was released by Columbia Records in 2000 and earned him a small following of hip-hop fans, but he became an international success after he signed with Interscope Records and fell under the direction of producers Dr. Dre and Eminem. 50 Cent's breakout LP with Interscope, *Get Rich or Die Tryin'* (2003), is certified six times platinum by the Recording Industry Association of America (RIAA). His career peaked in 2005 with his follow-up album, *The Massacre* (certified five times platinum) and the release of a semibiographical motion picture, *Get Rich or Die Tryin'* (released and distributed by Paramount).[13] Jackson's music sales have dipped in recent years—*Curtis* (2007) had sold only 1.3 million copies a year after its release (Caulfield 2008), and *Before I Self Destruct* (2009) posted a lackluster opening week after reports that the album had leaked on the Internet (G. Kaufman 2009)—but his star power remains intact.

Jackson strikes muscled and menacing poses on his album covers and in magazine photo shoots, and he frequently raps about his capacity to make money, dominate men, and sexually engage and exploit women. At the 2003 WQHT Hot 97 Summer Jam concert in East Rutherford, New Jersey, 50's performance included a "public service announcement" that served as a verbal attack on hip-hop rival Ja Rule, designed to undermine Ja's authenticity. The video presentation of the concert opens with 50 Cent sitting in front of a computer monitor, looking directly into the camera, as he begins, "Ladies and gentlemen, it has been brought to my attention that you guys don't know what a bitch ass nigga looks like. Take a look at this." The film cuts to a clip from one of Ja Rule's videos, "I Cry" (2000), which features a close-up shot of Ja Rule's face with tears streaming down his cheeks. Jackson continues with a voice-over condemning Ja Rule and appealing to the audience as 50 proclaims, "I know that's not hip-hop. You know that's not hip-hop." Jackson then reappears on the screen and closes the video, declaring, "So there you have it, ladies and gentlemen. Next time you're flipping through your radio, or through your TV, you'll know how to identify a bitch ass nigga."[14]

This performance of sexist, domination-driven masculinity is especially troubling because it reaffirms black hypermasculine invulnerability as an endemic aspect of hip-hop. Excerpts from Jackson's work appearing later in this chapter illustrate the importance of vulnerability and existential uncertainty as components of 50 Cent's complex cool self-construction as a thug. But Jackson suppresses these elements of his persona and sticks to the performance of domination-driven masculinity in the context of his battle with Ja Rule as a strategy to discredit his opponent and strengthen his own fan base. Tough talk alone is insufficient for building and preserving a hip-hop following, but the need to be loved by the public is a deep undercurrent running through these performances.

"I Get Money" celebrates 50's corporate success with lyrics about his good fortune as a major investor in Vitamin Water stock and typically festive rhymes about expensive cars and women as disposable sex partners. In the closing lines of "I Get Money" 50 proclaims:

When I come out of court
Yeah I pop the cork
I keep it gangsta, I'll have you outlined in chalk
In the hood if you ask 'bout me
They'll tell you I'm 'bout my bread
Around the world if you ask 'bout me
They'll tell you they love the kid.

These lyrics suggest that 50 has made it. He is powerful enough to conquer any and all who stand in the way of his success and too "gangsta" to be threatened by the criminal justice system or street adversaries who attempt to impede him. With a reputation that extends from local hoods, where he is known and respected as a money earner, to global hoods, where he is loved and respected as an entertainer, 50 insists he is everyone's favorite thug. He relishes the fact that his fans "love the kid," and despite their propensity to insult and offend, thugs' desire for both romantic and platonic love presents itself as a major theme in their narratives.

Bonnie and Clyde Romance

Tupac's "real talk" about being a hated thug galvanized deep, diverse, and abiding love among his admirers, including romantic love (Dyson 2001, 107). Shakur was clearly aware that he commanded women's attention, but in his raps he does not interpret this attention, or women's willingness to grant him sexual pleasure, as incompatible with hate. To the contrary, lyrics suggest deep suspicion of female admirers, who he believes are primarily concerned with exploiting his wealth and celebrity rather than caring for him. This is the original paradigm of thug desirability: though thugs are reviled by polite society, their outlaw status makes them sexually desirable to women, but the exchange of sexual pleasure between thugs and women is fundamentally exploitative. However, there are an increasing number of commercially successful rap artists who advance a less oppositional version of thug romance.

One of many examples of contemporary rappers' refashioning Tupac's performances is Jay-Z's remake of Shakur's "Me and My Girlfriend" (1996) as "'03 Bonnie and Clyde" (2002). At first glance, the differences between the two songs are apparent. In Tupac's version, his girlfriend is a metaphor for his gun, a loyal partner whom he cherishes above all else. Jay-Z signifies on Tupac's song, replacing the gun with his wife (then girlfriend), Beyonce Knowles, and celebrating their triumph. The original rendition seems centered on violence. Tupac uses wordplay to describe his gun as a power-ful female counterpart capable of paralyzing other men. He is aided on the track by an unnamed female vocalist who personifies the weapon he describes, firing rounds of verbal threats at Tupac's imagined adversaries. These verbal interludes, intended to be understood as the gun's speech, are reckless fits of shouting with no regard for flow rather than carefully crafted raps. Tupac describes his gun as an indispensable partner in this "life of sin" and affirms their dedication to each other no matter how perilous the circumstances.

In the Jay-Z and Beyonce remake, the female counterpart is represented by Jay-Z's girlfriend rather than a gun, and Beyonce's adjustments transform the affect of the song, striking a far less lonely and nihilistic tone. Unlike the female protagonist in the Tupac version, Jay-Z's romantic partner is not an active thug on the track, as Beyonce sings sweetly rather than shouting threats, promising to give her life and celebrating the couple's future hap-piness. Throughout "'03 Bonnie and Clyde," Jay-Z brags about how well he and his girlfriend complement each other and asserts that nobody can stop them from living a life of luxury. In contrast, Tupac's life is anything but comfortable in "Me and My Girlfriend," as he describes the dire circum-stances in which he and his partner reside and their joint journey into a life of hustling and crime.

These are significant differences, but in both cases the Bonnie and Clyde raps express the need for companionship, and in both cases romance is articulated with a thuggish grit and "do what we want to do" disposition. Both Jay-Z and Tupac express genuine longing, desire, and appreciation for fulfillment through their companion rather than simply lust for an object. The difference is that Tupac's desire for a loyal human counterpart goes unfulfilled and is displaced on his weapon. As a result, the tone in which he rap-sings the chorus is drenched in melancholy, as he is resigned to the fact of his loneliness. Jay-Z is more fortunate in love, and his companion reinforces his commitment to her by validating their triumph as a couple with buoyant vocals.

The "partners in crime" narrative is not only a crucial site for the ex-amination of commercially viable thug love and romance, but it provides opportunities to explore the limited representations women are allowed to embody. In contrast to the "tricks" and "hos" who are to be treated with sus-picion as disposable sex objects, women who are thugs' partners in crime are "down ass chicks," valuable not only for their sex appeal but for their loyalty and emotional support. In many instances, thug romance narratives emphasize not only romantic loyalty but loyalty in the face of violence, arrest, and imprisonment. A down ass chick does not snitch, nor does she, as Shakur raps, "give nobody no coochie while I be locked upstate" (1996a, "I Ain't Mad at Cha"). This "ride or die" romanticism represents a real danger to women who belong to communities of color, given the inequities of the criminal justice complex and the rates at which young people of color are arrested and incarcerated. In the world beyond entertainment, the potential for romantic loyalty to encompass compliance with criminal activity and disregard for the sexual health risks associated with incarcerated populations is exacerbated under these circumstances (Pough 2004, 191). The "pitfalls of racial reasoning" (West 1993, 21) result in a closing of the ranks and commitment to heteronormativity. This strategy mandates that women sacrifice personal agency, aspirations, and physical, emotional, and political health for the sake of "the [ethnoracial] cause," which is often a pernicious mixture of male supremacy and ethnocentrism (West 1993).[15]

Hip-hop thug representations of women tend to fall into one of two categories: women are either tricks/hos, or they are down ass chicks. Kathryn Gines notes the presence of this paradigm in hip-hop representations and the ways in which it controls and restricts women's sexuality. She explains:

> To avoid being labeled a whore, Black women must go to the opposite extreme of becoming "pure" virgins. But the problem is that at both extremes, whether the virgin or the whore, women have no authentic sexual voice. They are forced to either be the *hypersexual whore* (which becomes an excuse for the label of "bitch" and "ho") or the *pure virgin* (who is expected to be intimidated by or even fearful of sex, avoiding it altogether). (2005, 99)

The roots of the virgin/whore paradigm are thought to be located in Judeo-Christian traditions, as sexually powerful female characters often represent the embodiment of sin in legends and allegories about the dangers of giving in to temptation (Allen 1983; Wyman and Dionisopoulos 2000, 209). Hip-hop is far from the only musical (or artistic) tradition where these tropes are found, as constructions of femininity across popular music fall into a paradoxical pattern wherein women are simultaneously cast as impossibly innocent and childlike yet sexually available (Dibben 1999, 336). In hip-hop, however, the paradigm veers slightly away from traditional notions of the virgin and the whore. The "whore" position is essentially unchanged, as the dishonorable, gold-digging hip-hop trick appears in performances from Lil' Jon and the East Side Boyz to Kanye West. By contrast, the down ass chick, who occupies the honorable "virgin" position in the model, is not only sexualized but expected to be such a talented lover that she is worthy and capable of locking down a sexually potent thug in an enduring relationship. Despite this acknowledgment of the down ass chick's sexual aptitude, women's agency is restricted, and complexity is ignored at both ends of the spectrum; commercially successful hip-hop thug representations offer very little middle ground between the two extremes of what a woman can be.

Shorty Wanna Thug (No Homo)

Though the range of options is markedly different, restrictions apply to constructions of masculinity as well. As mentioned in chapter 2, masculine subjects who occupy a hierarchical location other than the ideal (straight, white, Christian, bourgeois) may adopt a range of coping strategies, including displaying bravado, highlighting male distinctiveness in feminized space, and degrading both women and gay men (Eric Anderson 2005, 339). In his smash hit "Lollipop" (2008), Lil' Wayne finds himself in a sexualized and feminized performative space thanks to his new musical style—a more harmonious and seductive vocal sound facilitated by Auto-Tune. Many of Lil' Wayne's representations of women simply situate female admirers as sex objects in the "ho" mold, to be exploited and conquered, as is evident in commercially successful songs such as "Drop It Like It's Hot" (1999) and "Fireman" (2005). On "Lollipop," he is unable to ruthlessly degrade women, as the song celebrates the object of his affection in seductive style. "Lollipop" is a euphemism for oral sex, an act that might potentially be performed on Wayne by either a male or female partner. In order to eliminate ambiguity, Wayne describes encounters with an attractive female admirer and issues the homophobic qualifier "no homo" (short for homosexual), which he speaks quickly at the beginning of the track. This caveat exemplifies masculine anxiety and the compulsion to negate queer sexuality as a defense mechanism.

No homo is a phrase with roots far deeper than Lil' Wayne, as a derivative of the black colloquialism pause.[16] Both pause and no homo are spoken jokingly as words that neuter any unintentional homoerotic reference within a conversation. In an interview published by Vibe magazine, Wayne uses the phrase in response to a question about being referred to as a "ho" by 50 Cent:

WAYNE: The word whore, that's a nigga who be smashing a lot, like fucking a lot.

INTERVIEWER: Don't you call yourself that in a song?

WAYNE: Yeah, I said I'm a whore. I'm a whore. Whatever. And I live it to the full-
est. I'm like Trey Songz, no homo. (Checkoway 2007)

As Wayne compares himself to rhythm and blues singer Trey Songz, with whom he has collaborated, he is careful to include "no homo," indicating that he does not have sexual feelings for Trey. This implies that any time a man constructs himself as an overtly sexual being or shows admiration for one of his male peers, he must firmly reassert his own straightness to avoid suspicion. Though these two examples suffice, a review of Wayne's recent music catalog reveals countless other "no homo" proclamations, testament to the compulsory nature of this symptom of masculine anxiety.[17]

Within various hip-hop communities, the "no homo" phenomenon developed into a signifying game, as hip-hop fans on the Internet and in the material world began playing on and implicitly critiquing the phrase for its bigotry and the paranoia it reveals. When something is written or spoken that could possibly be construed as "gay," the signifying and satirical writer or speaker might emphatically or repeatedly say "no homo" as a parenthetical joke, poking fun at others (like Wayne) who use it seriously. Despite this occasional deconstruction and critique of the phrase through exaggerated repetition, *no homo* remains relevant as a flagrant marker of homophobia because there remains plenty of discursive space for its nonfarcical existence within mainstream hip-hop communities and no space in mainstream hip-hop for affirmation of nonstraight male sexual identity.

Conversely, Wayne's celebration of heterosexual desire and conquest is central to his persona, as is evident from his proclamation that he is "a whore." Elaborating on his respect for Trey Songz, he explains:

Every picture of this nigga, he got his fucking shirt off! He's looking at the camera like he's looking at a hoe. I said, ya know what? Trey Songz don't give a fuck—he be like, Fuck ya'll nig*as! I'm eating, bwoy! Fuck how you think I look in this picture, your hoe love this picture! It's her screensaver nig*a! When you call your hoe, my song play, fool! Holla! Trey Songz I fuck with you, you heard me? (Checkoway 2007)

If one reads Wayne's admission that he admires Trey as a veiled expression of the need for love, this excerpt imparts a need to feel loved by women, who are objects of his desire. Wayne denounces men who condemn his self-construction as a sexual and romantic figure, dismissing male disapproval as jealousy—a necessary price to pay for female admiration. Ironically, this affirmation of female love and dismissal of male approval is simultaneously, if unconsciously, an attempt to gain male approval through portraying oneself as a sexually potent and therefore dominant and respectable man. Just as Wayne admits that he reveres ("fuck[s] with") Trey for his unabashed sex appeal, it follows that Wayne's celebration of his "ho" lifestyle will result in his garnering admiration from other men. Some men will despise Wayne out of jealousy and envy, but others will respect his hustle, just as he respects Trey's. So while Wayne's statements draw our attention to the disdain he may be subject to for constructing himself as a ladies' man, he knows from his own experience that fans' and onlookers' love is an equally guaranteed outcome of his self-construction as a sex symbol.

The commercial success of "Lollipop" as well as "Every Girl" (2009)[18] (with its chorus "I just want to fuck every girl in the world") is proof that sexualized thug performances are celebrated and appreciated by a huge number of fans, not all of whom are women. Beyond its capacity to draw love from its audience, "Lollipop" is significant because its performance infuses the word *thug* with considerable elasticity. As Static Major sings the infectious chorus, which begins, "Shorty wanna thug," the meaning of "thug" bends in multiple directions, as a noun that identifies the protagonist (*a* thug) and as a verb (*to* thug). The word *wanna* in "Shorty wanna thug" transforms the phrase into either "Shorty wants *a* thug as intimate partner," or "Shorty wants *to* do what she wants to do." Under the first interpretation, the thug is a desirable figure, and under the second, thuggin' is a more inclusive, distinctly enjoyable activity. In chapter 2, I cite Smith (1997), who argues that "oppositional" hip-hop performances can actually be read as means of "negotiation" and a desire to achieve inclusion in the mainstream. I want to take this argument one step further and argue that these performances are evidence of desire not only for acceptance but for love.

Love is thus understood in three distinct but related ways. First, we see evidence of thugs' need for love in their quest for women's love, whether this love manifests itself as testimony to thugs' sex appeal or their ability to achieve partnership with a "down ass chick," as argued above. Second, celebrations of thug life take on an increasingly elastic and inclusive character, such that thuggin' reveals itself as an activity or lifestyle celebrated and admired by fans and onlookers of both genders; as 50 Cent says, "Around the world if you ask 'bout me, / They'll tell you they love the kid." The third form of love, explained below, is a platonic bond among thug brothers, used to ward off existential angst and the perils of thug life.

Thug Love and the Pearly Gates

Like that of other narrators, 50 Cent's thug status is derived in part from hood experience. On "In My Hood" (2005), 50 assures other men that he is capable of harming them and affirms his desire for heterosexual conquest and luxury goods. However, the lyrics also deal with the constant paranoia of the hood subject, whose safety and well-being are under constant threat from others who live by the code of the street.[19] The chorus laments:

> In my hood niggas is grimy
> I stay on point, I roll with my gat
> In my hood niggas might buck [shoot] at me
> So I keep somethin' around to buck back.

An alternative reading of such narratives posits that they are spoken in self-defense rather than selfish affirmation of pleasure and power.

Such a reading certainly recalls descriptions of the cool pose as an individualized defense mechanism for black men who feel they are under constant attack and scrutiny. But in cool pose theory, the pain and vulnerability of black male experience is cloaked by the pose itself, and though the pose is theorized as evidence of their hidden presence, feelings of sadness, guilt, shame, and concern are concealed from onlookers and listeners. Many of 50 Cent's performances incorporate considerable self-reflection and a thuggish vulnerability that cool pose cannot account for.

On "U Not Like Me" (2003), 50 rhetorically locates himself in the criminal tradition, announcing his entry into the commercial rap world by warning competitors, "You got fat while we starved, it's my turn / I done felt how the shells burn and still won't learn." The first phrase, "You got fat while we starved, it's my turn," is the same line spoken by Christopher Walken's character mob boss Frank White in the gangster movie classic *King of New York* (1990).[20] The second line refers to 50's surviving a drug-related shootout prior to the album's release and seems to affirm his insistence on leading a dangerous, nihilistic lifestyle despite the lesson he should have learned by coming so close to death.

Jackson continues with references to God and the afterlife as he describes the disjuncture between his life experiences and traditional versions of morality. He raps:

> I done been to the pearly gates, they sent me back
> The good die young, I ain't eligible for that
> I shot niggas, I been shot, sold crack in the street
> My attitude is gangster, so I stay in some beef.

This excerpt calls to mind Tupac's description of his own "heartless breast." By 50's own admission, he is not "good" enough for heaven, just as Tupac worries that the source of his trouble may be personal moral failing. Rationalizing his survival of a near-death experience as a product of the gatekeeper's disappointment in him rather than a blessing from God, Jackson is sent back to the streets. He remains a product of the past, trapped by previous moral transgressions. His violent experiences not only result in self-criticism but keep him close to threat and confrontation.

Jackson knows heaven is not for him, and this experiential knowledge as one of the forsaken enables further critique of faith. Elsewhere in "U Not Like Me" he raps:

> Momma said everything happens to us is part of God's plan
> So at night when I talk to him, I got my gun in my hand
> Don't think I'm crazy 'cuz I don't fear man
> 'Cuz I fear when I kill a man, God won't understand.

There is a rift between 50 and a God who cannot possibly understand his plight. Jackson fears that there will be eternal existential consequences, not because what he has done is truly wrong but because the moral standards by which he is judged are inappropriate. If the ticket to heaven is a clean moral slate, 50 will be denied admission. In light of his fear of God's misunderstanding and his lack of fear for dangerous interpersonal confrontations, he urges listeners not to think he is crazy. This assertion of his sanity stands as a rejection of completely irrational, self-destructive, self-abhorring nihilism. Jackson ponders existential questions as he struggles with his personal moral status and refuses the label of shallow, purposeless renegade.[21]

Jackson's concerns about God and the afterlife reiterate those expressed by Tupac, who asks:

> Where do niggas go when we die?
> Ain't no heaven for a thug nigga
> That's why we go to thug mansion
> That's the only place where thugs get in free and you gotta be a G.
>   (2002, "Thugz Mansion")

Shakur affirms his black male identity, aligning himself with all "niggas" who resist death. Whether death refers to biological death or serves as a metaphor for oppression and marginalization (social death), the potential for collective reconciliation with death is linked to his identity as a nigga living thug life. There is "no heaven for a thug nigga" because to get to heaven one must accept standards of culture and behavior that are out of sync with the structural and moral location of the criminalized ghetto subject.

"Where do niggas go when we die?" is a question Shakur often asks in rhyme, in songs like "Thugz Mansion" (2002) and "I Wonder If Heaven Got a Ghetto" (1997). The question is a critique of American utopianism. Shakur asks, "If this (the modern American hyperghetto/prison) is the promised land, blessed by God, can I expect heaven to be similar?" When faced with the possibility that the existential best-case scenario might merely be a reflection of the indignity and injustice of life as a truly disadvantaged black American, Shakur imagines another place, Thugz Mansion, where he and his "niggas" can live and rest in peace.

Tupac and 50 Cent do not blindly romanticize or valorize the ghetto, because life in the ghetto is troublesome. But while hip-hop discourse confirms that the hood is a troubling space, performers refuse to leave it because doing so constitutes poor marketing strategy according to industry logic and because so many thug performers come to understand themselves through life in the ghetto. Tupac cannot be "the rose that grew from concrete" without describing the concrete and keeping it present in his raps. To fail to return to the ghetto in memory is to forget who he is, not merely as a black person but as a human being who gained social awareness through constant negotiation of virtue and vice and who came to grips with the immediacy of death in his place of residence. Thus when he asks if heaven has a ghetto, he asks, "Can I know myself?" Or "Can I be me and make it to heaven?"

Despite the odds against them as criminalized hyperghetto/prison residents, polluted by hegemonic, domination-driven masculinity and locked in a battle with nihilism, hip-hop thug narrators retain hope and affirm love. Jay-Z's 1999 single "Money, Cash, Hoes," featuring DMX, seems an unlikely text in which to look to for evidence of thug love, as Jay proclaims:

> Only wife of mine is a life of crime
> And since life's a bitch with miniskirts and big chest
> How can I not flirt with death?

In addition to echoing other narrators' affirmation of criminality and nihilism, the track is rife with other familiar thug references, such as glorification of consumption and self-affirmation through interpersonal domination. The chorus, which amplifies the most accessible message of the song, consists of Jay-Z and DMX performing a call-and-response chant, with Jay-Z calling, "Money, cash, hoes / Money, cash, hoes," and DMX responding, "What!" or "Come on!" between calls.

However, DMX tempers the song's message as he speaks the final lyrics on the track at the end of his verse. He raps:

> Just 'cause I love my niggas
> I shed blood for my niggas
> Let a nigga holler, "Where my nigga?"
> All I'mma hear is "Right here, my nigga."

While 50 Cent describes his willingness to execute violence as a means of self-defense, fitting squarely into the code of the street, DMX sheds blood because of his loyalty to his niggas, highlighting the manly loyalty expressed by Memphis Bleek, T.I., and Trick Daddy in describing their connection to and reliance on those around them in "'Round Here." This is an ethic echoed by Jadakiss of the Lox, who raps, "More or less I'll forever be a thug / Shed my blood, for everything I love."[22] Similarly, on "All about U" (1996a), a track about the pleasures and perils of meaningless sex with female fans, Tupac raps, "I love niggas 'cause we comin' from the same place." These performances offer a basic affirmation of loyalty and love driven by experience as a racialized and criminalized ghetto resident who relies on others for security and community in a world where physical danger and isolation are constant threats.

Perhaps this expression of love can be dismissed, or demystified and restated, as a tragic mutation of militaristic loyalty—a loyalty strictly for the sake of survival, without any genuine ethic of sacrifice or caretaking. Perhaps hip-hop thug-nigga narrators don't love each other but only use each other to secure protection, respect, or material goods. Such a dismissal relies on a utilitarian reinterpretation of thug love: if I protect you and you protect me, each of us will reap material benefits. But in a discursive world where narrators communicate a profound intimacy with death, the shadow of death casts light on another version of thug love, one that extends beyond our present material world. As Dyson explains:

> By detailing the horrors that enclosed the lives of their fallen friends, rap music helps to chronicle the social pathologies that grow inside the body politic and that claim black and brown lives with unacceptable regularity. But the

gesture of examination is also one of self-protection: It secures the place of recent ancestors in the urban cosmology by giving them their just due. In so doing, survivors extend their lives, blessed by the memory of late comrades who interceded with the powers that be on their behalf. (2001, 228)

Note the three elements here. First, Dyson connects narratives about the death of fallen comrades to the material reality and social pathologies of hyperghetto/prison violence. In hip-hop, this violence is doubly manifest, as a textual theme in the lyrics of so many of its narrators and as the subject of a hip-hop discourse that extends beyond the music, focused on those young, black, male hip-hop icons such as Tupac, Notorious B.I.G., and Jam Master Jay who met their deaths early through violent means. Second, rapping about death builds an "urban cosmology" for thug narrators, who orient themselves through the dead in their physical and spiritual worlds. As Dyson says, this orientation is self-protective for the narrators because it helps them order the universe and place themselves within it. I would suggest that in addition to being self-protective, it is empathetic and evidence of a caretaking ethic among those who rap about death. Through shouting out the names of the deceased, rappers care for the dead, placing them among the stars and aiding them in their afterlife.

Finally, Dyson asserts that this mourning process extends the lives of thug performers, because maintaining connection with the dead constitutes a blessing. So the dead reciprocate the care provided by their still-living friends, blessing them as they continue on earth. All of these connections are made possible by the notion that the hood links thug niggas to each other through a deep and loving bond, strong enough to endure the trials and tribulations of both life and afterlife. Patterson describes the power of social death, which allows for "cross[ing] boundaries with social and supernatural impunity" (1982, 51), and we can understand these hip-hop themes as affirmations of transcendent love that throw the boundary between life and death into disarray.

Skeptics may point to narrators' pervasive nihilism as a textual theme that invalidates or contradicts any arguments about love. But to the contrary, purposeless battles, experience with violence, and closeness to death provide a necessary context for this expression of love. For example, on "Hate It or Love It" (2004), a track featuring 50 Cent and his rap crew, G-Unit, Young Buck raps, "Let me show you what a thug 'bout, born to die / I took the bullets out of 50, put them in my four five."[23] A skeptical reading of this hip-hop thug narrative defines the narrator as nihilistic and so committed to detached coolness that he is unfazed by the obvious danger that confronts him. Young Buck's refusal to take 50's injury as a warning sign and his willingness to immediately continue on a self-destructive path is emphasized by his eagerness to load his gun with the bullets lodged in his fallen friend. A thug is "born to die," and Buck clearly does not care whether he or his comrades survive.[24]

However, an alternate reading, following the complex cool path to thug understanding laid by Dyson, casts Buck's treatment of 50's injury as a display of honor and caretaking. Rather than leaving the bullets inside his friend and leaving him behind, Buck "examines" the mangled black body, as Dyson says, and takes a piece of his dead friend (the bullets) with him as he lives on. The bullets that were lodged inside 50's body represent his thug spirit and serve as both a physical and spiritual form of protection for Buck. Buck's care for 50 and tribute to his death is paid back by the spirit of the dead, which blesses Buck on earth as he moves on. Buck's disregard for death as a threat grows not solely from his own nihilism but from his commitment to honoring and staying connected to fellow thugs, regardless of whether they reside in this world or the next.

Thug love challenges nihilism and heartless black manhood, blurring the line between life and death and imparting hope to those who give and receive it. On their 2006 collaboration "Pearly Gates," 50 Cent and Mobb Deep address Tupac's question of whether thugs can make it to heaven, replying in the affirmative. The chorus, rapped by 50, pleads:

> Homey, if I go to hell and you make it to heaven
> Just get me to the gate, and I'll talk my way in
> I got a gift, I'm special, with the flow I'm good
> Shit, I talked my way up out the hood.

In these lines 50 exemplifies hip-hop thug narrator conscience. Like Tupac, he knows he is not good enough to make it to heaven on moral merit as traditionally conceived. Instead of changing his behavior, he influences the standards for admission in two distinct ways. First, he relies on his connection to his thug brother, his "homey" (note the spatial connotation: a homey is a friend from the same the same hood). Though both 50 and his partner are dead, both physically and socially in the context of this verse, death fails to sever the bond between them and does not prohibit them from caring for each other.

Second, once 50 arrives at heaven's gate thanks to his homey's efforts, he believes he will be saved because he is "special." The rapper's sense of himself as one of the blessed is grounded in his life experience as someone who survived the hyperghetto/prison, proving his manly, thuggish tough-ness. But instead of merely affirming his capacity for physical ruthlessness as the key ingredient for hood survival, 50 points to his signifying skill and artistic capacity, which confer authenticity in this case, as proof positive that there must truly be something special about him; after all, he "talked [his] way up out the hood." Despite being damned by structures, cultures, discourses, and perhaps even gods that criminalize them and cast them aside, thug narrators are saved through hip-hop and their love for each other, rapping themselves in a hideous and beautiful black masculinity of strife and promise.

Summary of Chapters Two and Three

I'm a thug, but I swear, for three days I cried.

—Notorious B.I.G., "Miss You" (1997)

Chapters 2 and 3 present my answer to one of the major research questions of this book: "How should we understand black men's hip-hop performances, many of which contain degrading content and themes pertinent to theories and stereotypes of black pathology?" In chapters 4 and 5 I provide space for respondents to answer this question, presenting interview data that specifically address issues of taste, authenticity, and moral panic in hip-hop.

In summary, my analysis in chapters 2 and 3 demonstrates that hip-hop performances do not qualify as cool pose because (1) performances affirm a collective black male identity that emphasizes connections to others as a source of strength rather than a neurotic projection of the invincible individualized supercool self; (2) performers advance narratives of black authenticity as means to establish the boundaries of their social worlds, but the black hip-hop authentic ethos contains a wide range of context-dependent messages and is not fundamentally oppositional to mainstream notions of success or status attainment; and (3) hip-hop thug narratives communicate vulnerability, existential anxiety, and desire for, and expressions of, love, which are antithetical to cool pose posturing.

Performers selected for textual analysis are drawn largely from discussions with my respondents, who mention them frequently, as detailed in the appendix. Each artist has achieved considerable commercial success. As such, these artists stand among the most public and popular hip-hop figures and are most often chastised for aspiring to nihilist, narcissist, sexist, and upsetting representations of blackness. My readings simultaneously acknowledge these troubling representations while highlighting additional discursive themes we might not expect these artists to address. The conflict and contradiction inherent in these representations suggest not only that hip-hop cannot be understood using the cool pose framework but that the framework itself is flawed. Homi Bhabha writes:

> An important feature of colonial discourse is its dependence on the concept of "fixity" in the ideological construction of otherness. Fixity, as the sign of cultural/historical/racial difference in the discourse of colonialism, is a paradoxical mode of representation: it connotes rigidity and an unchanging order as well as disorder, degeneracy and daemonic repetition. Likewise the stereotype, which is its major discursive strategy, is a form of knowledge and identification that vacillates between what is always "in place," already known, and something that must be anxiously repeated. (1994, 2)

Cool pose theory is not a stereotype, but it is dependent on the fixity explained by Bhabha. The goals and outcomes of cool pose are fixed; no matter the context or form the pose takes, the aim is pride, strength, and control, and cool pose inevitably sets black men on a collision course with each other and with whites. In addition, cool pose is a perfect example of the "daemonic repetition" that Bhabha identifies; according to the theory, black men feel they are always "on," compulsively snapping into pose mode the moment they step out into the world. This is why cool pose, or any other theory that explains the essence of black masculinity in fixed terms, is dangerous: it precludes the possibility of contingent and contradictory performances, and it ignores the multiplicitous subjectivity of each black man, insisting on a single true individuated subjectivity. Hip-hop narratives about thug life may simultaneously express pain, love, hedonism, and mercenary aggression, and while it is absolutely necessary to criticize the problematic elements of these narratives, there is no cause to dismiss any one element in favor of another when building a case about hip-hop's significance. Whether a theory of blackness insists that black men are truly hypersexual brutes (the racist Western stereotype), truly morally and spiritually superior African kings (an Afrocentric counternarrative), or truly "normal" Americans trapped beneath the pose facade (the modern psychosocial diagnosis), the idea of the true, fixed self is the first false move.[1]

That said, hip-hop is at least in part about being cool. Many performances in commercially successful rap music are designed to portray personas as imposing and proud masculine figures worthy of respect and admiration. In the American racial context, rappers' blackness imbues these performances with a sense of defiance, as the pride and strength being communicated are read as a superpowerful pride and strength capable of neutralizing one's racially derived dishonor and social disadvantage or capitalizing on the dangerous nature of blackness. Hip-hop is decorated with trophies of consumer culture and bodily representations that connote sexual power, and the desire to embody this coolness and celebrate a figure capable of procuring gratification contributes to hip-hop's appeal.

However, the most regularly cited definitions of coolness, as either defiant and detached self-composure, aspiration to holistic spiritual luminosity, or blind desire to compensate for masculine shortcomings, do not adequately explain representations of black masculinity in hip-hop. Rappers' cool performances do not embody pure mystical smoothness, nor do they suffocate black masculine complexity, even with market pressures to produce easily digestible musical commodities with broad appeal. Further, the fact that hip-hop is cool, in the sense that it is popular and appealing, does not automatically make hip-hop politically irrelevant to, or poisonous for, black people.

This is why we need a new understanding of contemporary black coolness, one that acknowledges the importance of previous models, from Du Bois's veil and Dunbar's mask to Thompson's African aesthetic of the cool. The *complex cool* exemplified by the performances discussed in chapters 2 and 3 is distinguished by its transparency, in that the conflicts and imperfections of black masculinity are publicly performed, though they flow through channels of indirect communication. A careful reading of commercially successful rap performances gives one the feeling that (1) MCs celebrate stylin', drawing attention to their luminous, self-possessed, visual bodily aesthetic (in the spirit of Thompson); (2) they make outrageous and disturbing claims to exaggerated forms of domination-driven masculinity involving capacity for violence, wealth, and sexual potency (in the spirit of Majors and Bilson); and (3) they are often self-conscious and forthright about pain, vulnerability, and desire for love and admiration, themes that resound in concert with the more troubling elements of coolness.

Beyond merely explaining complex cool, I want to suggest that it is significant as evidence of multifaceted black identity in spite of the ways blackness is restricted by the options provided by the entertainment industry. Even though black men's access to public airwaves is circumscribed by the roles they are expected to play, alert consumers will hear and see black experiences that do not jibe with expectations and stereotypes.

Stuart Hall and his colleagues warn us that there is no purely subcultural/symbolic solution to large-scale problems of economic marginalization and inequality (Clarke et al. 1989), and therefore the symbolic work accomplished by hip-hop practitioners and fans is insufficient for structural change. Put differently, this reading of black masculinity is not going to magically solve all of the problems that contribute to black men's degradation or that of other groups subject to material suffering through intersecting systems of race, gender, and class oppression. But as a first step toward political progress, these readings are important because they do not romanticize, mythologize, or pathologize black masculinity in hip-hop. Unfortunately, the treatment of black male performances as powerful, complicated, and imperfect *human* endeavors is something we still cannot take for granted in the American pop cultural landscape. As a complement, my analysis echoes that of others who rightly note the problems with celebrating the products of domination-driven masculinity—namely sexism, homophobia, and the reification of race/gender/class hierarchy. Whatever the productive political criticisms of hip-hop performances and hip-hop communities may be, the problems associated with hegemonic masculinity and patriarchy must be recognized and addressed. Perhaps unexpectedly, the potential to make headway on these issues is already present within the same set of performances, as the need for love, care, empathy, and interpersonal connection is clearly manifest on even the most thugged-out albums.

In chapters 2 and 3, discourses on race, space, class, and gender inform my understanding of contemporary hip-hop. In the chapters that follow, I make room for alternative readings and allow respondents to talk back, not only to hip-hop critics, but to me.

FOUR

Hip-Hop Authenticity in Black and White

While some aspects of black expressive cultures certainly help inner city residents deal with and even resist ghetto conditions, most of the literature ignores what these cultural forms mean for the practitioners. Few scholars acknowledge that what might also be at stake here are aesthetics, style, and pleasure. Nor do they recognize black urban culture's hybridity and internal differences.

—Robin D. G. Kelley, "Looking for the Real Nigga"

I like realness. I don't like all the fake, sugar up, candy-coated. I like realness in a person.

—Sean (b2)

On the Real

At the end of chapter 2, I follow John L. Jackson (2005) and suggest that hip-hop authenticity is better understood as sincerity—that is, repeated efforts on behalf of performers to build connections among themselves and with their audiences. But agreement among academics that authenticity is socially constructed and contingent does not tell us what authenticity means to everyday hip-hop listeners. We have a responsibility to investigate authenticity's reception and interpretation by its audience, and if black or hip-hop authenticity is more commonly understood as a race-based oppositional disposition and commitment to domination-driven masculinity, and hip-hop is a primary means for its transmission, that would be a finding worth documenting. Moreover, my textual analysis cannot fully communicate how ubiquitous "keepin' it real" has become in hip-hop, a culture with a "religion and ideology of authenticity" (Perkins 1996, 20). Speaking with respondents gives us a sense not only of what authenticity means but how meaningful it truly is.

This chapter focuses on aesthetics in hip-hop, as respondents describe how they evaluate hip-hop, what makes good rap music, and how they understand authenticity as a hip-hop theme. Based on the importance of authenticity in art worlds, the role of racial authenticity specifically within rap music, and the ways in which real-life racial experience informs respondents' definitions of hip-hop, it is reasonable expect that the two racial groups in this study would produce different patterns of qualitative data. Data show that while sociocultural location undoubtedly influences respondents' mental maps of what makes hip-hop good, bad, real, and fake, the ranges and patterns that present themselves in data do not simply reflect the popular discourse about hip-hop's racial purity and pollution. I begin with a brief word on the sociology of taste.

Musical Taste and Authenticity

Pierre Bourdieu (1984) argues that people do not freely choose the objects and consumables they find aesthetically pleasing, as our preferences are dictated and reinforced by social class position. As members of high society maintain their own culture by transmitting elitist modes of taste among themselves, they restrict the network of people with whom they can have meaningful interaction, as only those with similar standards share the interests and modes of communication necessary for gratifying social exchange. Cultural capital (command of taste) thus influences social capital (social connections) and preserves economic capital, as the material privileges and opportunities afforded by wealth remain enclosed in the domain of the wealthy, passed on through social bonds and institutional advantages.

Bourdieu's theory of taste is often criticized and empirically challenged. Zygmunt Bauman (1989), James Twitchell (1999), and John Fiske (2000) emphasize the imaginative, creative, and individualizing potential we exercise as we consume. Diana Crane (1992) argues that generalizations about high culture and popular culture are insufficient for understanding social inequality because the structure and nature of artistic cultures have changed since the 1960s, when Bourdieu conducted his study. Richard A. Peterson and Paul DiMaggio (1975) introduce the idea of "culture classes," or groups of people who share similar taste and consumption preferences across social class, while Peterson and Albert Simkus (1992) and Peterson and Roger M. Kern (1996) find that "highbrow" taste is increasingly eclectic, marked by an "omnivorous" consumption of all sorts of music, rather than disdain for the popular and snobbish defense of elite aesthetics. A final criticism of Bourdieu is that he fundamentally misunderstands what music is and how it can and should be studied. Antoine Hennion emphasizes music "as a doing, a 'performative' use inextricably entangled with other non-music practices" and laments that the sociology of music is inappropriately reduced to "a mere double of a sociology of art, taken as the analysis of modes of production, diffusion and reception of a given object" (2001, 3).

Though Bourdieu's social analysis is outdated, positivist subjectivity has been battered, and the possibilities of consumption as a symbolic process have multiplied, he remains relevant because his central claim is intuitive and sensible: social location influences taste, and studying these patterns is worthwhile. Bourdieu argues that the high culture (pure) aesthetic is driven by an "elective distance" from material struggle (1984, 5). Consumers of privilege are trained to examine the formal qualities of a work because they have the leisure time necessary to learn about these dimensions of art. Conversely, the working-class aesthetic prioritizes agreement between the message of art and real life, and therefore concerns about the narratives within artistic representations are paramount. Bourdieu highlights the importance of narrative authenticity, the idea that what is represented in art must be connected to real life, as a requirement for working-class appreciation. This model might easily be extended or transferred, as one would expect people in different racial and ethnic categories not only to judge music differently but to hold vastly different understandings of "the real" based on life experiences.

In addition to narrative authenticity, questions of authenticity apply to artists themselves. The representation and the creator of the representation are simultaneously judged when amateur and professional aestheticians evaluate the quality of a work. As Howard S. Becker writes, "Artists' reputations are a sum of the values we assign to the works they have produced . . . The reputation of the artist and the work reinforce one another: we value more a work done by an artist we respect, just as we respect more an artist whose work we have admired" (1982, 23). Becker illustrates the extent to which ostensibly objective aesthetic judgments are truly subjective, socially constructed, and based on connections between the artist and consumer, echoing the work of Peterson (2005) and John L. Jackson (2005) described in chapter 2. In hip-hop culture, the desire for this connection is explicitly articulated by the artists themselves, as they repeatedly proclaim the authenticity of their personal narratives and skills as badges that signal their right to respect. Authenticity matters in all art worlds,[1] but hip-hop is unique in its incorporation of "real talk" within the artistic commodities; the message of authenticity dominates entire songs, albums, and careers.

Evaluating Hip-Hop

As discussed in chapter 1, songs that respondents like often have a positive affective impact, and good hip-hop, for many respondents, is hip-hop that *sounds* good. Both beats and vocals are discussed as sonic elements that contribute to a song or artist's quality, but in many instances where respondents discuss sonic quality, they discuss the music rather than the voice on the track.

> No matter how skilled any MC is at delivering lines, I can't get into it unless it's got a really compelling beat, or some sort of really well-done track. That's what appeals to me first, and then I think in order for it to be a really great record, the vocal style has to play off that, and mesh with it, and be good in its own right too. But I definitely start from the bottom up in terms of the music. (Kenny, w1)

> To me, I like beats too, heavy beats, a lot of bass. (Damien, w4)

> I like a good producer. Good beats is like, kind of what goes with the music. Like for gangster rap, or whatever, they talk about shooting each other, you got, like, a funeral sound. (Fred, w3)

> Someone like Method Man, I'm always going to feel that he's a good lyricist. But the thing that would make his album either good or bad or just alright is the beats . . . Sometimes there are beats where some people like them and some people don't, but when you got beats that are universally not liked, it's not going to work out. Because you got songs out there that just have good beats, and don't have good lyrics, and people love them. The beat, to me, is always going to supersede the lyrics. (George, b3)

I followed George's comments about the beat superseding the lyrics by asking him, "What makes a good beat, or are there any rappers or producers who seem to always have good beats?" He replied by naming a number of his favorite producers and identifying Dr. Dre and Pharrell as his favorites, which led me to ask about any similarities those producers share that make them appealing. But George could not identify traits or characteristics of the producers or the beats that made them good, instead stating that they have unique styles. This inability to specify exactly which musical qualities he prefers may arise because respondents like George do not think of music in terms of its elements and do not conceptualize music in terms of meter, harmony, and melody. Alternatively, pointing to specific musicians, such as Dr. Dre, rather than musical elements may speak to the conflation of "objective" aesthetic qualities with subjective feelings about the artists themselves, just as Becker, Peterson, and John L. Jackson suggest.

Like George, Nolan does not discuss meter, melody, or harmony when talking about the music he prefers, but he clearly describes the affective impact of good beats as he explains what he likes.

NOLAN (B3): There's certain beats for me, they just attract you and you can really feel them. They just get into you and you really vibe with them. Most of these artists, they use a lot of samples, like soul samples, either speed them up or slow them down, stuff like that.

MICHAEL: What does that mean, "The beats get in you," and "vibe"? What does that mean?

NOLAN: This might sound a little cliché, but it's like you become a part of the beat. I don't rap, but if I rapped [*pauses*] they make you want to rap. You listen to a song, when it first comes on and the beat rides out, it gets in you and makes you want to rap. It's just something that comes over to you. Automatically I can tell if I like the song by the beat.

Sean describes a similar affective process.

MICHAEL: What would make a good album?

SEAN (B2): I think beats. You got to have beats, that's number one. You got to have good producers, sound mixers.

MICHAEL: Who are some producers that are examples of that?

SEAN: Some producers that I know are Dr. Dre, Puff Daddy, couple of other guys. Those two guys are really mainstream, and they're really on top.

MICHAEL: What makes a beat good?

SEAN: You can hear it. I can't tell you, you'll hear it. You start shaking your head, get your body moving. You'll know when it's a good beat.

The beat matters to listeners Sean, Nolan, and many other respondents, including George (b3), Kenny (w1), Paul (w1), and Damien (w4), identify the sound of the music as a trait they prioritize in their evaluation processes. Most respondents who discuss beats have difficulty describing the musical elements of the beats they enjoy, but data from Nolan and Sean, in combination with data from chapter 1, establish the importance of bodily affect in forming musical tastes. This affirmation of affect complicates traditional sociological notions of taste, especially Nolan's claim that "it's like you become a part of the beat . . . it gets in you and makes you want to rap," which transforms the listener into part of the music, as Hennion (2001) would have it. However, music as an enveloping, transformative, affective force is a relatively small slice of respondents' statements about what makes good hip-hop.

The preceding comments make it clear that the music in hip-hop songs matters to respondents' evaluations, but when asked about hip-hop tastes, respondents discuss MC skills with more depth and clarity than they do musical sounds. Respondents evaluate narrative (the content of the song), rap technique or ability (often referred to as "flow" in canonical hip-hop literature),[2] and authenticity (honesty and sincerity). When respondents praise or criticize the content itself, aside from questions of technical skill and authenticity, they do so on the grounds that rappers communicate negative messages (see Damien and Marc below), messages celebrating displays of wealth (Chris and Tim), or no message at all (Kevin and Jason).

I like more of a positive message that doesn't just talk about killing each other or selling drugs. (Damien, w4)

One thing that he [50 Cent] says is like, "You're a window-shopper, you're a wankster"—all this stuff is degrading people. Like, some people aren't on the same level, didn't come from the streets, didn't hustle, don't want to sell drugs . . . He says he gangbangs, he shoots, he kills, he robs, he does whatever he has to do to survive. You can do that, buddy, but I won't listen to you, because I don't feel that way of life, I don't feel that style, and he's just garbage. (Marc, w1)

Another thing I don't like is people just wasting time on the radio talking about jewelry, and what they have, and this and that. Which is fine if they had nothing and then all of a sudden they had it from talking about those things, but anyone making money from talking about getting money is kind of ironic. It doesn't make any sense to me, and I don't like that kind of music. (Chris, w4)

MICHAEL: What makes a good MC to you?
TIM (B2): First I would say is probably the lyrics that they rap about would

have to make sense, would have to give the audience [*pauses*], would have something to do with what people can relate to. That's kind of why I don't like the way hip-hop has taken a turn now, because before it was stuff that you can relate to, as far as, you remember those days growing up in the projects. Now hip-hop is mostly about, you know, "bling," who has a car, who has the biggest chain, stuff like that, that the common man can't really gear to.

MICHAEL: So what makes that song bad?

KEVIN (W3): It could be them rhyming about useless things, going on and on.

JASON (B1): Like Dem Franchise Boys, those dumb songs they come out with.

MICHAEL: What makes them dumb?

JASON: It's simple, it's not worth being a song.

MICHAEL: Why not?

JASON: I mean, yeah, I give it to them for thinking about it and stuff, but it just seems a little stupid, honestly.

MICHAEL: What about it gives you that reaction? If on the one hand, you can say "I give it to them, they made a song," then on the other hand, what about that song elicits a negative reaction from you?

JASON: It's meaningless.

Note that these statements represent all four class categories and both black and white respondents. Though the sample comprises only forty respondents, these data suggest that hip-hop listeners form a taste community or, recalling Peterson and DiMaggio, a "culture class," with some aesthetic commonalities that sustain themselves across race and class divisions, even if there are important differences in their understandings of hip-hop identity.

Flowing and Signifying

Tricia Rose (1994) identifies flow, layering, and rupture as three aesthetic principles that link each element of hip-hop together. For example, seamless flow of layered polyphonic and sampled heavy beats ruptured by DJs' cutting and scratching is complemented by rappers' ability to flow with the music, punctuate the track with vocals, and add layers to their lyrics' meaning through signifying. Despite the convincing manner in which Rose argues for flow, layering, and rupture as the foundation of hip-hop aesthetics, respondents do not immediately invoke these principles as an authoritative and bounded rubric for discussing hip-hop preferences. However, closer examination of the interviews shows that flow and layering in particular are clear aesthetic considerations for hip-hop listeners.

Respondents take narratives into consideration, but they need to see further evidence of rap skills in order for an MC to get respect.

> I don't know if you've ever tried rapping or freestyling, but to freestyle something coherent, that's clever, witty, makes sense, and makes people think, like, "How did he do that?" The other part of the art form is being able to put your experiences, to be able to tell a story in a clever, witty, rhyming way, at the same time without sounding cheesy. That's the art form of it. (Andre, b4)

> NATE (B1): The reason why I say hip-hop heads would listen to different artists is because they're better than the rest, they're better lyrically. So lyrically is the number one eye-opener and difference. Like M.O.P., they're the hardest rappers out, but they're not very good at all.
>
> MICHAEL: I want to work on that a little bit. When you say somebody is lyrically better, can you explain that, like, what makes for good lyrics?
>
> NATE: Anybody could string a bunch of rhymes together, but putting it so it makes sense, do it cleverly, metaphors, not just like "If I say metaphors, I'm hot." That's why everybody thinks they could rap. But just putting it all together, storytelling, actually having merit.

> MICHAEL: What does it mean that they're "coming from the heart"?
>
> RYAN (B4): They put time into their work, what they have to say, how they're saying it.

"Flow" is manifest here in the form of unity and coherence; a talented rapper has to be able to put it all together in a way that makes sense. Ryan's statement is the essence of the idea; hip-hop listeners care about what is said but also *how* rappers say it. According to Bourdieu's understanding of taste, low-status cultural consumers should not be concerned with the technical elements of the performance. Interview data show that both black and white and both wealthy and disadvantaged hip-hop listeners place tremendous emphasis on rapping technique. More specifically, data confirm the importance of signifying, defined as wordplay and indirect communication, to hip-hop taste and evaluation across race and class. This finding is especially significant in light of the racial dimensions of signifying discussed in the introduction. One might expect black respondents to recognize and reward signifying and layered meaning more than white respondents because signifying is a black vernacular tradition, but this pattern simply does not emerge from the data collected from these rap music aficionados. The first four excerpts below (from Eric, Chris, Brandon, Richard) demonstrate white respondents' appreciation for signifying, and the second four come from black respondents (Greg, Ben, Ryan, and Neil). Each is followed by a brief explanation of the signifying referred to.

MICHAEL: Can you give an example of that skill you're talking about?

ERIC (w1): What is it, like, "I'm catching AIDS, 'cuz these niggas be on my nuts too hard." Just like, funny little lines like that. It's kind of a boasting little thing, and obviously you can't get AIDS from someone [*pauses*]—I don't have to explain that, but that's kind of a little example.

Eric appreciates this instance of signifying both because the narrator engages in playing the dozens with his imagined rhetorical opponent and because the meaning of the insult is indirectly derived. He states that he takes pleasure in this performance specifically because it is "funny," and this recognition of humor within hypermacho and supposedly threatening raps is something that is often overlooked. The phrase "on my nuts" means that other men ("niggas") are such fans of the narrator that they would be willing to pleasure him sexually. How much they love or envy the narrator is embellished by the idea that their appreciation of his skill is so intense that it gives the narrator a disease. As Eric notes, reading the sentence without these indirect references renders the boast unintelligible.

MICHAEL: What are you looking for that makes it good? Are there certain things that the songs you like have in common?

CHRIS (w4): What I like is probably something real simple. An MC will say something, like if it's something new and they bring back something old that's not really that widely known, that you think only a few heads will really even understand it. Stuff that you have to listen to it six times before you even caught it, and if you catch it the first time you think that either it's a coincidence or they really know what they're talking about. That's what I like. I like to figure stuff out like that.

Here is a classic example of signifying explained as communication intended for a specific audience. Chris reinforces the idea that understanding what is said necessitates having listened to enough hip-hop in the past to decode references made in the present. He believes the intended audience is strictly a hip-hop audience, and by virtue of his understanding the message, Chris receives the added bonus of placing himself among the informed. Getting from one layer of meaning to the next requires hip-hop knowledge.

> You know the song "This Is Why I'm Hot"? The beat is sick. Simple, but you can't help but bob your head to it. The dude, I can't even remember his name, he's alright, but whatever. He did the one with the reggae version. But then there's another one with Talib Kweli, called "Niggas Lie a Lot." I just thought that was so perfect, because Talib Kweli would never usually go that style, his voice and his flow. He goes and he talks shit about people who are on beats like this, using their style. It's like, "Ohhhhh! Buddy, you just shut these kids up!" It's just perfect. (Brandon, w3)

Talib Kweli is a successful hip-hop artist, but he is consistently critical of mainstream representations of hip-hop blackness and thug life, as his lyrics suggest that he views these representations as both disingenuous and politically harmful for blacks. "Niggas Lie a Lot" could be read in any number of ways, but by identifying Talib Kweli's song as a remix of the original smash hit by MIMS, "This Is Why I'm Hot," Brandon makes it clear exactly which "niggas" Kweli is referring to. Signifying on a commercially successful song by creating a song with a title that rhymes with the original and questions the validity of its claims and, by extension, the claims of all commercially successful rappers, Kweli takes rappers who are consumed with self-promotion and material excess to task. Kweli's willingness to step outside of his usual rapping style makes this effort particularly enjoyable.

> So in this song, he's [Lil' Wayne] doing this crazy thing, kind of robotic, he goes,
>
> > No, I'm sick
> > I vom-it
> > Got-it?
> > One egg short of the om-let
> > Tell 'em ketch-up/ I'm mayonnaise.

And, this is going to sound kind of crazy, but in the middle of it, he just goes, "Ummmm," and it's basically kind of a slap in the face, where he's like, "I can literally plan when I'm going to say 'ummmm' in my rap." And it seems like he's freestyling or kind of flowing, and that's like a head-nod to other freestyling, where people try to think of what they're going to say, but he's so ahead of it that he's like, "I will consciously pretend that I am, just to show that I'm not." So that was a thing that blew my mind. (Richard, w1)

Richard highlights at least two instances of signifying in his quotation from Lil' Wayne. First, Wayne's taunting competitors who can't "ketch-up" with his rhyme skills serves as a typical boast reliant on play between the context of the narrative, which is about food, and the outside context, the competitive field of rap music. Second, Wayne uses delivery itself to signal his lyrical superiority, by purposely hesitating to mimic someone less apt than he. In order to understand this second signal as Richard does, the audience member must be familiar enough with rap music to recognize Wayne's "head-nod" to standard claims of hip-hop rhetorical skill.

MICHAEL: What makes somebody a good hip-hop artist or rapper?
GREG (B4): My opinion, it's more lyrical, more punch lines, more crafty, not just plain and straightforward. Like, play with it kind of. More crafty with your rhymes and delivery to the beat.
MICHAEL: What do you mean more lyrical?
GREG: Like, punch lines, you know what I mean. Like, I rap, I'll say something like

> Get your perception clear
> Look who you steppin' near
> I keep the hawk on me daily, like underwear
> Pardon, I'm a beast
> I be grindin' in the streets
> You swear I be with Shaq
> How I'm movin' with the heat.

You know what I mean? Shaq, Miami Heat, but I'm really saying, the heat, the gun. It's clever, you know what I mean? It's witty.

First, Greg's verse relies on slang, as he uses words like "hawk" and "heat" to refer to a gun. His reference to Shaquille O'Neal, who played professional basketball for the Miami Heat, doubles the signifying stakes, as the intended audience must have knowledge of both street slang and sports to get the meaning. In addition, Greg's characterizing good hip-hop as "play" is equally crucial to the signifying process. As Henry Louis Gates Jr. (1988), Robin Kelley (1998), and numerous others point out, black vernacular signifying is often a game for those who partake, and playing the game requires knowing what should and should not be taken seriously. Greg's boast is rooted in a domination-driven masculinity wherein he casts himself as capable of harming someone else, but the primary purpose of the verse is to prove his skill as a word-player rather than to intimidate those who hear it.

BEN (B4): That argument always comes up too, who's better, Jay-Z, Nas? In my opinion, Nas outweighed him.

MICHAEL: Why?

BEN: Nas was just more clever with what he was saying. He was pulling out points, like Nas seem like he did research on him. He just kept going, he used his own words against him. Like he [Jay-Z] was saying, "I will not lose," and Nas put it in a hook [chorus] and made it more clever.

To identify Nas as the victor in this battle, Ben refers to a previous battle song, or "dis track," performed by Jay-Z. Nas knows that his intended audience has already heard Jay-Z's dis track, and by incorporating pieces of Jay-Z's song into his own, Nas clearly indicates who he is speaking to. While we cannot derive explicit intentions and motivations of specific artists from examples like this, the frequency with which these instances occur certainly speaks to tacit understanding between producers and consumers that they share the same hip-hop world.

RYAN (B4): My favorite rapper of all time is Big L. I usually listen to the old stuff more than the new stuff.

MICHAEL: What about Big L did you like?

RYAN: He just had everything. Character, lyricism, good music, made good songs, like the way he put the words together. I listen to Pac, I listen to Big. Right now I listen to everybody just to see where they're coming from and see how they do it. Even if I don't get the albums, I listen to everything when it comes out.

MICHAEL: Can you give an example of a song or lyrics that makes those guys good?

RYAN:

> Big L is that nigga that catch wreck
> On any cassette deck
> I'm so ahead of my time
> My parents haven't met yet.

That right there, it's just one line. It's witty, something that makes you think about it.

This lyrical excerpt hardly needs decoding, and while it is signifying in the service of self-promotion, unlike other examples, Big L does not rely on putting someone else down to build himself up. In a trend that mirrors his selection of a quotation, Ryan is hesitant to identify rappers who are of poor quality when describing his personal taste throughout the interview, preferring instead to emphasize his penchant for listening to as much hip-hop as possible.

MICHAEL: Can you give me an example of a track you like off the first album?

NEIL (B4): It was the intro track, probably a three and a half minute song, or something like that. The way the beat stops and goes. He's talking about counting money or something like that, but if you read between the lines, you know he's talking about selling drugs. The concept is, you know the sound those money counting machines make? That's running in the back-ground, and the way he's spitting on the track, it's like, okay, this is good.

Neil first notes that the lyrics themselves allow him to "read between the lines" and understand the narrative as drug related—later in the in-terview he specifically mentions the narrator's calling crack cocaine "Diet Coke" as a reference he enjoys. But understanding the song and its play also necessitates hearing the sound samples within the musical track, and once again the listener's comprehension is indirect because it does not flow purely from the text itself.

There is much discussion of signifying in the data, and this selection of quotations is presented because in these passages respondents explicitly connect signifying with their evaluative processes. In each case, signifying is mentioned not merely as a phenomenon in rap music but as something that makes it pleasurable to the listener. What cannot be communicated by quoting the excerpts is the passion and joy with which respondents explain signifying, especially in the instances when they repeat lines from songs as examples of what good rap means to them. Just as they get a good feeling from listening to a beat that lifts their spirits or makes them want to move their bodies, the young men clearly gain positive bodily affect from the play of lyricism.

In addition, the prevalence of a domination-driven masculinity wherein MCs signify on other imagined male ("nigga" is a masculine pronoun) ad-versaries points to a dog-eat-dog path to hip-hop respect that negates wom-en's presence through their absence. Gender is absent from respondents' explanations of why they enjoy signifying in hip-hop, but interpretation of the data presented above would be incomplete without highlighting the influence of hegemonic masculinity, which provides a theoretical frame for modern-day hip-hop boasting as important as the frame provided by black vernacular tradition and play.

Bourdieu's thesis about separation between high and low culture is challenged by the celebration of indirect communication and layered meaning, because respondents from all classes prioritize signifying, which is a technique rather than a narrative. However, data also provide limited support for the notion that class influences taste in instances where respondents discuss linguistic mechanics as part of their aesthetic evaluations. All of the following observations are made by cultural elites.

> You got to rhyme, you have to rhyme. I don't care if it's just like—I'm not sure how much you know about the whole rhyming mechanism—but like, so, there's like *aa* rhyming, where you know, the cat chased the rat to get to the hat, but *aba* is like roses are red, violets are blue, you know, it's something that has a rise and a fall to it. I don't like it when someone, like, says, "Oh, I'm flossing in my big car so I can go to the mall." It's like, "What? That's not a rap, is it? You're not trying to rhyme are you?" I just don't like that. (Darryl, b1)

> And the way they [the Clipse] do it—really intricate rhymes. Impressive, again . . . I like the way the record is structured. Because they're rhyming about, you know, coke dealing, and then the last song is "Nightmares," and it's this really interesting thing because they undo all of the stuff they were saying. I mean not totally. But they say all this shit and then they're like, "I'm having nightmares," and you're like, "Oh, so you know." And it kind of justifies the rest of the record somehow, they kind of get it. The tropes are so well trodden that it's kind of violence in an action film. I mean you see eighty guys get shot and fall off a cliff, you're like, whatever. But you see four guys get shot [*pauses*]—there are ways of driving home what's been said and then there's rehashing. And I think the Clipse don't rehash. (Richard, w1)

MICHAEL: So musically, what makes a good beat?

KENNY (w1): In hip-hop people are working with the same collection of elements to produce any track or any sound. So I notice first off whether they've managed to rearrange those different sound sources or tools at their disposal from something that's different from what I've heard before. Because when you're working with a limited pallet, it's very easy to just re-create what other people have done. So if someone is able to take one of those elements, whether it's a turntable, or whether it's a key-board, or whether it's just an acoustic piano that they've sampled, and use it in a way that I haven't heard it before, that really appeals to me.

And later,

A lot of MCs are clearly very articulate people who get lost in their own vocal power. They have really good vocabularies and a good sense of descriptive ability, and they don't really have a sense of how that fits into their proj-ect. So you get these overly complicated sets of rhymes where they just have enough rope to hang themselves, and they do. So part of what's important is having those tools at your disposal, having that poetic sensibility, and having that vocabulary, and that ability to describe things as you see them in elegant ways, and knowing *exactly* how to deploy that, so it doesn't seem too much or too little. It's that sense of restraint, where you know you can deploy that eloquence, and you do at just the right level and just the right rhythm, and just the right time.[3] (Kenny, w1)

Darryl, a self-described wealthy black respondent from a privileged sub-urban community, attends a music college. He affirms the importance of rhyming as a hip-hop technique not merely by saying, "I like rhymes," but by explaining specific theory of rhyming. It is clear that he understands himself to be someone with advanced knowledge of music, as he pauses in an effort to prevent presumption, prefacing details about rhyming with "I'm not sure how much you know about the whole rhyming mecha-nism." Rappers who do not meet these rhyming criteria are unworthy of his attention, affirming the importance of his high cultural training as a musician.

Richard, an upper-middle-class white respondent, is an English major at an elite university in the Boston metropolitan area. When he praises the Clipse, he talks about narrative "structure," "tropes," and rhetorical strat-egy. Richard finds the structure of a record, rather than simply its narrative, vital to its quality, because the structure informs the narrative. As the Clipse move from a disturbing depiction of the world of drug dealing to a discus-sion of the vulnerable and painful underbelly of that lifestyle, the tenor of the narrative changes from frivolity and sensationalism to self-awareness. Richard believes that the Clipse have this awareness—that they "know," to use his word—because of the way the record is organized.

Finally, Kenny, a white respondent who also attends a prestigious university and hails from a privileged middle-class community, discusses form and technique in both the music and vocals. Though he no longer plays music on a regular basis, Kenny played the drums for much of his seventeen years before college and counts himself a serious fan of jazz in addition to hip-hop. First, he states that all musicians work from a limited pallet, and because of those limitations, originality or uniqueness holds considerable aesthetic value. His discussion of vocals is two-pronged, as he begins on a more literary path, discussing the importance of managing one's impressive vocabulary and descriptive talents. Kenny then reaffirms his emphasis on music as a complement to the words, stating that a quality rapper proves his ability to exercise vernacular restraint with careful consideration of both rhythm and time (that is, MCs have to flow).

Mapping Hip-Hop Authenticity

In the discussion of black authenticity in chapter 2 we saw that Peterson (2005) and John L. Jackson (2005) consider authenticity not something located in one object or another but instead a socially constructed quality arising from performers' ability to manufacture a sincere connection with audience members. To this point, I would add that this process has political consequences. Peterson notes that "the changing meaning of authenticity is not random, but is renegotiated in a continual political struggle in which the goal of each contending interest is to naturalize a particular construction of authenticity" (1997, 220). This emphasis on naturalness directly connects with the importance of ghetto imagery to music videos. Recall the centrality of not only everyday people but ghetto children specifically to the videos for Nas's "I Can" (2002a) and Memphis Bleek's "'Round Here" (2003) discussed in chapter 2. Children, who lack the means to access social and spatial worlds other than those they are born into, are ideal symbols of the naturalness of black ghetto life, undisturbed and self-contained.

If one misguided litmus test for musical authenticity is driven by mythology surrounding those who naturally produce it, another misguided test emphasizes the degree to which music is commercialized. Simon Frith argues against the notion that commercially successful music is inauthentic by definition: "The 'industrialization of music' can't be understood as something that happens *to* music but describes a process in which music itself is made—a process, that is, that fuses (and confuses) capital, technical, and musical arguments" (1987, 94). Authenticity is not simply invalidated through recognition of commercial development and industrial processes.

To the contrary, our understanding of authenticity is *enabled* by those processes. As Frith explains, "It was technological developments that made our present understanding of musical 'authenticity' possible. Recording devices enabled previously unreproducible aspects of performance . . . to be reproduced exactly, and so enabled Afro-American music to replace European art and folk musics at the heart of Western popular culture" (1987, 113). For Frith, elements such as improvisation and spontaneity, which confer black authenticity in musical contexts, had to be recorded and widely heard to emerge as standards for black authenticity. A widely shared and powerful understanding of authenticity requires mass production of music; industrialization and commerce are essential for building consensus about the authentic and enabling a high volume of sincere connections between performer and audience.

Given that hip-hop is so widely commoditized and mythologized as a representative and natural black cultural phenomenon, it is no surprise that many hip-hop scholars enumerate the elements relevant to hip-hop authenticity. Imani Perry provides a framework that encompasses all the crucial elements of the idea of authenticity as constructed in American hip-hop in a passage that echoes Becker's thoughts on how authenticity matters to simultaneous evaluation of art and artist:

> The MC usually occupies a self-proclaimed location as representative of his or her community or group—the everyman or everywoman of his or her hood. As a representative, he or she encourages a kind of sociological interpretation of the music, best expressed by the concept of "the real." "This is the documentary story of my world," we are told. There exists in rap music an identity-based teleological stance. The work of the artist is not intended to be apparent so much as the lyricism is supposed to testify to organic brilliance. (2004, 39)

And:

> The "real" is also an authenticating device responding to the removal of rap music from the organic relationship with the communities creating it . . . [I]t is an explicitly ideological stand against selling one's soul to the devils of capitalism or assimilation as one sells the art form and lives life. (2004, 87)

The "real" carries multiple meanings and serves multiple functions for Perry, who expands on the themes discussed in chapter 2. Authenticity conveys connection to black urban populations and resistance to assimi-

lation by commercial capitalism on the grounds that selling out constitutes a betrayal of one's experience. These meanings enable authenticity to
function as a rhetorical tool for closing the ranks of the hip-hop community and as a schema that allows hip-hoppers to evaluate those who perform (a "real" MC's "organic brilliance" is revealed when he raps about his
hood). Aesthetic and political claims are endemically linked in hip-hop
according to Perry, and the discourse of authenticity allows this link to sustain itself.

Kembrew McLeod investigates these themes empirically, using data gath-
ered from hip-hop magazines, artists, songs, and Internet discussion groups.
In total, McLeod identifies six semantic dimensions along which hip-
hop community members offer support claims for authenticity. His table of
these dimensions is reproduced here.

Semantic Dimensions	Real	Fake
Social-psychological	Staying true to yourself	Following mass trends
Racial	Black	White
Political-economic	The underground	Commercial
Gender-sexual	Hard	Soft
Socio-locational	The street	The suburbs
Cultural	The old school	The mainstream

Source: Reproduced from McLeod (1999).

One of the most notable elements of McLeod's rubric is that some combination of commercial success and mass appeal appears as the opposite of
"real" in three semantic dimensions: "following mass trends" is the opposite of "staying true"; "commercial" is the opposite of "the underground";
and "the mainstream" is the opposite of "old school." The frequency with
which anticommercial sentiment is invoked in discussions of authenticity
with respondents of both races and all class categories is staggering. The
commercial-versus-real distinction is important not just because it sets barriers between different types of music but because it influences the behavior and artistic choices of rappers who are motivated by money. The following quotations represent understandings of authenticity that are most
reliant on distinctions based on commercialism and wealth.

> MICHAEL: Why would that [keeping it real] be something important to
> them?
> JASON (B1): Money changes people, and if you have money and you're still
> the same person, it's a lot better than having money and changing.

MICHAEL: Can you pick up on talking about what makes Paul Wall fake?

ALLEN (B1): He just looks like he has more jewelry than people who have made a name for themselves and have been famous. He's shining more than Diddy. It just seems like he puts all this stuff on so he can try to look, like, gangster or something, and it's just stupid.

If you look at the radio, it's a money thing right now. You're not getting that real hip-hop that comes from the heart. (Ryan, b4)

MICHAEL: Why is it important to you that someone be real on a record?

FRED (W3): Because it's what people can relate to. Real people relate. Real recognizes real and they have an appreciation for it. If you're just out there mainstreaming, you're just about your money, you're not about the game. You're not about hip-hop anymore after that.

They're not talking about real life experiences, they're talking about things, pretty much maybe they can still relate to it, like how much money they have, how much money they can throw around, whatever. Whereas before they were talking about things that your everyday individual could relate to. Struggling, trying to pay rent. (Zack, w1)

If the topic of authenticity does not come up without prompting in interviews, I ask the following questions: (1) When a rapper says "keeping it real," what is he trying to communicate? (2) What does the phrase "keep it real" mean to you? (3) Why do you think we hear "keep it real" so much in hip-hop? For respondents who speak about authenticity in terms of commercialism or wealth the distinction between the real and the commercial is present in all of their answers, which can be summarized in three general statements: (1) rappers say "keep it real" to show they value things other than money, (2) respondents share this value and approve of this understanding, and (3) we hear authenticity in hip-hop because there are many fake rappers who are harmful to the culture. Again, contradictions are present, but none of the respondents, even those who are not explicitly hostile to celebrating wealth, understand keeping it real as chasing riches and commercial exposure, either as a theme in hip-hop performance or as their personal belief.

This is a somewhat surprising finding, considering that these respondents are recruited primarily at sites where commercially successful hip-hop is being consumed, and much of the hip-hop that is played on the radio and at concerts like Summer Jam (one of my recruiting sites) that explicitly highlight expensive jewelry, cars, and clothes. It is important to note the contradictions embedded in these evaluations—a rapper's talking about money is not grounds for dismissing him as fake. For example, Jay-Z was the most popular artist discussed across all interviews, garnering eighteen unprompted references from responses and overwhelmingly positive appraisals of his talent and skill. Jay-Z often celebrates and displays his material wealth and preaches the "stay paid and stay fly" hip-hop ethic on a number of records, but he is not considered inauthentic by respondents. The fact that "inauthentic" themes are manifest in Jay-Z's songs does not impede his ability to build sincere, subjective connections with listeners, remaining "authentic" in their eyes.

These sorts of contradictions do not invalidate interview data on authenticity. In the context of respondents' stated preferences, data show that listeners' authenticating processes are flawed, context specific, and subjective, as Peterson (2005) and John L. Jackson (2005) suggest. However, these data remain useful because they tell us about the authenticity discourse produced by respondents and reveal the power of authenticity as a concept that emphasizes fixity over continuous social construction and disguises subjectivity as objectivity for the purpose of evaluating cultural products.

Is It Really Real?

Discussions centered on authenticity reveal that the claims of rappers who "keep it real" are worthy of tremendous skepticism and, in some cases, disdain.

> You don't know who's telling fairy tales, or what not, or who's real . . . It's like, "I'm the realest," "No, I'm the realest," "No, I'm the realest." It's a cliché. Every rapper is going to say it. (Neil, b4)

> DAVID (b4): Me, if I was in the rap game, I wouldn't pose as nothing, I'd be myself. You feel me? They say things like they did when they never did.
> MICHAEL: Why do they do that?
> DAVID: Because of the market, whatever people listen to. They don't got anything else to rap about.

> KEVIN (w4): I don't believe half of them actually mean what they say.
> MICHAEL: Why would they say it if they don't mean it?

KEVIN: Make money.

MICHAEL: Why would that help them make money?

KEVIN: People think it's cool.

These phrases might have held—they definitely held meaning to me in the past—before they became like exploited and reused. When Chamillionaire says, "Keep it real," what the fuck is that guy talking about? Terminology and catch phrases that are being sold out as much as the music itself is. (Pete, w1)

David, Kevin, and Neil are each from the working-class-without-mobility category, and Pete is more privileged. All four respondents mention market forces as a factor in authenticity discourse. When hip-hop artists proclaim their authenticity, listeners believe they do so because the phrase "keep it real" is valued by their audience—another affirmation of authenticity as the effort to achieve a connection between performer and audience. Respondents lament the popularity of "keep it real" as an over-used catch phrase while simultaneously valuing a version of authenticity that actively rejects commercialism and wealth. Hip-hoppers want the real thing, but the minute they are told it is real by performers, they become skeptical of its authenticity, which again speaks to the inadequacy and distortive nature of authenticity discourse.

Another take on keeping it real recalls the psychological-social element of McLeod's rubric, as numerous respondents extol the importance of "being yourself."

Keeping it real is kind of a funny statement. What "keep it real" means basically is keeping yourself the way you always are, never getting mad or out of character. (Russell, w1)

I think it's just slang, "keeping it real." I think everybody would want to keep it real, they might just say it different. That person might want to keep it real to themselves, it's just a hip-hop thing. (Ryan, b4)

SEAN (b2): It's a way of life, keeping it real. Why settle for anything less? Don't back down from anything. That's how I put it. If you're anything less than yourself, you're not you. You're not the person you say you are.

MICHAEL: What makes that a bad thing?

SEAN: Character-wise. You're just out of character basically. You say you're one thing, then the next minute you're totally something else.

Be true to yourself, be true to your community. You can keep it real by not doing anything in a fight. You can keep it real by shooting somebody in the face a hundred times and walking away. When I say "keeping it real," it means be true to yourself, not listening to corporate America, somebody wearing a tie, telling you you have to do something. "Keeping it real" means being true to yourself. (Marc, w1)

BILL (B4): I think rappers really don't mean anything by it. I think rappers just say it. Because half of these rappers aren't real, you know what I'm saying? Half of these rappers just do it to get the money. That's not real, but to them that's the realest thing. They're not.

MICHAEL: So what is real?

BILL: Real, I put it like this. Real could be that dude standing on the corner from six to six, as long as he knows what he's doing is right to what it needs to be, in the future. Real could be that dude at Harvard University busting his ass, because he knows that's what he has to do to get where he needs to be. We're talking different aspects to different people. As long as you know who you are, and you don't act any different, that's real.

MICHAEL: Do you think that most people understand it the way that you do?

BILL: Nah. Real, it depends, are you talking about most people in an urban area?

MICHAEL: All different people.

BILL: Okay. Most urban kids, they think real is somebody that's out there selling drugs or something or got a gun or something. Talk about the rich areas, they think real is when somebody freaking becomes a lawyer or something. Or talk about somebody who's on some traveling-the-world shit, adventurous. They think real is traveling out the country, seeing the world.

These responses span the spectrum of social class. Respondents who explain authenticity as being oneself are quick to point out that being oneself means different things to different people. The final quotation from the group above, from Bill, hints at the elephant in the room of hip-hop authenticity discourse: racial identity.[4] When respondents discuss racial authenticity, their statements do not simply augment McLeod's research on semantic dimensions. According to McLeod's model, hip-hop discourse equates white identity with other indicators of fakeness, such as rejecting one's true self and obsessing over commercial success and wealth. As we have already seen, there is strong anticommercial sentiment from respondents of all backgrounds—celebrating wealth and mainstream success is

considered inauthentic and harmful to hip-hop. No analogous understanding of white identity emerges from the interview data. Neither black
nor white respondents advance a narrative of white resentment that blames
white people for poisoning "pure" black hip-hop, and they do not discuss
their aesthetic preferences in racial terms. However, respondents do believe
that being oneself means embracing one's racial and ethnic identity, and
they express multiple concerns about hip-hop's influence on listeners' ability to manage their racial selves.

> What "keeping it real" means basically, don't tell anyone lies to be someone
> cool. Don't go out and spend your paycheck on clothes that you wouldn't
> normally buy just so you can fit in with a different crowd. Don't start talk-
> ing differently around a different group of people or a different nationality
> of people just so you can be cool with them. Be yourself, that's pretty much
> what it means. (Darryl, b1)

ANTHONY (w3): A lot of people are good examples of that, like white people here trying to be black people. Trying to act like that, trying to talk
  like that, trying to dress like that. For them, it's a good thing to say, "Keep
  it real." I listen to hip-hop music, I like it, but not because I'm trying to
  be black. I'm who I am. People get confused when I tell them I'm not
  white. I'm really not white, I'm Serbian, from Serbia. I cannot even identify myself as a Serbian now, because 99 percent of Serbians don't think
  like me.
MICHAEL: What would motivate a white person to act black?
ANTHONY: Because right now you can see the things a lot of music is rapping about. Fancy cars, they're rapping about attractive girls, so for them,
  hip-hop is being rich. They think it's cool to have a car. That's not real
  hip-hop. I'm 100 percent that white people wouldn't try to be black if all
  of rap music was about struggle.

DWAYNE (b3): It's estimated that like 80 percent of people that buy hip-hop
  records are suburban white kids, because they got the spending power to,
  that's where the spending power is concentrated. Part of it, we're selling
  this culture to the mainstream that don't necessarily understand where it
  comes from. So they misunderstand it, and they feel like "I got to carry a
  gun," and that's not real, that's dangerous.
MICHAEL: Are the misunderstandings something that suburban white kids
  are more prone to than other people, or is it that anybody can misunderstand it? Is it more misunderstood by one group than another?

DWAYNE: . . . It's certain parts of hoods that you could understand why holding a gun is keeping it real. That young man don't know no better, got
no father figure, been raised by thugs and so he abides by thug rules . . .
So to him, keeping it real, holding that gun is different on that block.
There's no police protection, so you got to protect yourself. Whereas
some kid that lives in Newton, Massachusetts, I don't know what he need
that for.

All three respondents believe that one's racial and ethnic background
limits the choices available for being oneself. The subject position of each
of the respondents quoted above is also noteworthy, as neither Darryl,
Anthony, nor Dwayne self-identifies as white. These race-based concerns
about authenticity are completely absent from white respondents' discussion of the "keep it real" phenomenon. One explanation for this is that the
white respondents are self-conscious about their hip-hop identification as
white people and wish to disassociate themselves from whiteness by re-
fusing to talk about race. Another explanation is that white respondents
display a lack of awareness about their own whiteness, similar to the ways
in which whiteness fails to influence their definitions of hip-hop given in
chapter 1. As noted in the introduction, both of these potential explanations speak to the power of whiteness as a normative, invisible, privilege-
conferring identity marker (or nonmarker). Anthony, who attends college
in the Boston metropolitan area, was raised in an impoverished neighborhood Serbia. Though he understands that most people in America consider
him white, he does not self-identify as such. As a racial outsider, he finds
white aspiration to black identity upsetting on multiple levels. First, it of-
fends him because people are not being themselves, and second, it speaks
to the erosion of hip-hop from a protest culture and social movement by
and for poor people to an industry that celebrates material excess and immediate gratification. Anthony's statement is the most forceful criticism of
white people's attempting to "act black" through hip-hop, and in order to
advance this criticism, he explicitly renounces his white identity, relying on
class and nationality instead.

In contrast, Dwayne is African American and spent his childhood in a
deeply impoverished black urban ghetto, where he and his peers experienced much of the street crime and neighborhood disorder that impede
civil socialization in such communities. He speaks from personal experience, affirming the existence of the code of the street in hyperghetto/prison
neighborhoods like the one he was raised in. Given that this culture is a
reality for hip-hop consumers in neighborhoods like his, he understands

the proliferation of thuggish black masculinity as the "real" in hip-hop. The problem for Dwayne is that this version of authenticity does not apply to white consumers who reside in more privileged neighborhoods and do not need a gun to protect themselves on a daily basis. Industry dynamics certainly inform Dwayne's perspective, but he stops short of blaming white consumers for the current tenor of most commercially successful hip-hop. As he explains, black people are "selling the culture to a mainstream that don't necessarily understand where it comes from." Though he does not say so explicitly, Dwayne may believe that the products being sold, in this case, hypermasculine, thuggish hip-hop performances, are not based in reality and are driven almost entirely by white demand. Conversely, he may believe that the narratives grow naturally from real-life black experiences and would exist as products in the marketplace even without a white consumer base. Either way, Dwayne's explanation does not explicitly blame white people for demanding the elements of hip-hop that they do, even if they can't understand it. Nor does Dwayne identify commercially successful hip-hop as racist propaganda.

Considering the comments from Darryl, Anthony, and Dwayne in concert, the narrative about the importance of racial authenticity is a bit paradoxical. Some respondents believe many white consumers engage hip-hop for inauthentic reasons, and respondents may condemn such behavior. However, they stop short of tracing hip-hop's obsession with authenticity to the phenomenon of white consumption and cooptation, and they do not argue that inauthentic hip-hop performances are primarily driven by white demand or corporate control. Further, there is no effort to tie these patterns of demand and consumption to larger systems of racial inequality and white supremacy.

Thuggish Blackness

The domination-driven version of thuggish masculinity described by Dwayne may be authentic for impoverished ghetto residents, including those who eventually become commercially successful hip-hop performers. However, when respondents who reside in more privileged neighborhoods discuss the authenticity of thuggish narratives in hip-hop, they take these representations with a grain of salt.

> A lot of them try to say that they're so-called thugs or gangsters or whatever you want to call it, and a lot of them have never been in a gangster situation. (Tim, b2)

BRIAN (B3): I'm not going to lie to you. You see where I live [Brian is work-ing class, but lives in a primarily middle-class neighborhood]. But if I was rapping and you never seen me, it's "I dropped out of high school, I got baby mamas, I used to sell drugs." That's what it's about. Tough, so you can sell records.

MICHAEL: Why does that sell records? Why do people want to hear you talk about that?

BRIAN: That's hip-hop, you got to be tough. You're not street, they're not go-ing to buy your album. Why you think everybody like 50 [Cent]? Because he got shot nine times, that's why.

You hear "keep it real," you hear "real talk," but when you listen to what some of the people say, they're just trying to get that credit. Well, are you really keeping it real because you're out there talking about selling ten-dol-lar bags of crack? Are you really out there on that corner selling ten-dollar bags of crack? I doubt it very much, because everybody would know you. (Roy, w2)

Gun busting, that's not real, you probably don't even own a gun . . . I wish I had the quote, but real people don't say it, real people do real things. The realest person in here is probably the person that didn't say anything. People walking around like, "I'm tough, I'm gangster, I'll shoot you in the head." That's not gangster, that's just talk. Those people give hip-hop a bad name. (Nate, b1)

This is an area where intersecting race and class identities bear signifi-cantly on my findings. Thuggish authenticity is important to the respon-dents above because it speaks to the character of the artist in question and because one's authenticity influences aesthetic evaluations: fake thuggery diminishes the quality of the art. However, the stakes of hypermasculine, thuggish authenticity are especially high for black listeners who live in dis-advantaged neighborhoods with symptoms of social disorganization. Each of the three quotations from black respondents who have lived in disad-vantaged neighborhoods below raises serious concerns about the influence of thuggish hip-hop authenticity on their communities.

Hood cred' [credibility] is about not having feeling. I mean really a lot of people try to detach themselves from reality and try not to show emotion. Being a gangster or somebody in the hood is somebody who's cold. Cold to women, cold to his friends, not cold to his friends, but somebody who has the ability to be self-made. And being self-made is not a bad thing, but to just be self-made where nothing else matters to you . . . Black people, we are who we are, and that's a great thing, but now rap has given us license to be that all the time, versus having a time and place for everything. (Andre, b4)

> NOLAN (B3): Let's say I was a rapper; for me to talk about going to school, doing my homework, saying no to drugs even though my friends are doing it, for me to talk about what I'm actually doing, that's keeping it real . . . I think that's what's wrong with the culture and with our group of people now, to do the good things is corny . . .
>
> MICHAEL: What do you mean when you say "our group of people"?
>
> NOLAN: I'm talking about minorities, my community, African Americans.

Who else is really bad? I think 50 Cent too. He's so gifted, he's a leader, he's very entertaining to watch, and I feel like he's using his gift wrong. I mean when I heard "Get Rich or Die Tryin'," I think it's a great album, I love it, but see, I can differentiate what's real and what's fake. But a lot of up-and-coming kids can't. So you hear, "Murder, murder, I'll blow your head off," and it's sad. Because even for a second, I feel that power, like "'Yeah!" But then you snap out of it, this is just music. But a lot of these rappers don't do a good job, saying, "This is just entertainment, it's not real. I'm not really on the block selling crack, I'm not really killing people." (Steven, b4)

And later:

I think now it's just the hood of America has taken over . . . When you're growing up in the hood, it's about who could be the hardest. You can't smile. It's not about who has the brightest smile. You want to prove yourself, you got to be the hardest, the coolest, to earn your stripes. (Steven, b4)

These are the strongest statements about the effect of hip-hop thug performance on notions of black authenticity. Each comes from a black respondent from a community where such representations are reflected in real life—none of the white respondents or black respondents from middle-class neighborhoods speak directly about the impact of thuggish hip-hop authenticity claims on black people's lives. Importantly, Andre, Nolan, and Steven have each moved beyond their economically disadvantaged and racially segregated neighborhoods in some way. Andre enrolled in college hundreds of miles from the neighborhood he grew up in, and while he did not complete his degree, he remains in his college's town, working as a security guard and part-time DJ. Nolan is a college graduate who aspires to attend law school and returned to work in his neighborhood, despite all of its problems, after earning his degree. Steven's mother moved him and his siblings out of the ghetto when he was twelve, and though he retains some social connections to his old neighborhood, his day-to-day life is completely different than it would have been had he remained. He too enrolled in college but terminated his studies before earning a degree. All three respondents have exercised social mobility to a greater degree than most young black men from their neighborhoods.

Each of these young men speaks to the oppositional ghetto culture he has seen firsthand, and each believes that hip-hop plays a role in the proliferation of that culture. Andre speaks about the pressure that ghetto residents feel to "be cold," which he directly connects to the pressure to be "self-made." One proves his coldness in a number of ways, but the gendered performance of coldness emerges as a central concern for Andre, who is speaking about men and mentions relations with women twice in his description of what it takes to earn hood credibility. The pressure to be self-made is pressure to gain status, but without the traditional pathways to status attainment, black men self-make themselves through more objectionable means. Describing these behaviors as "cold" is eerily similar to the "cool" that Majors, Bilson, and others identify as the crucial theme in managing stigmatized identity.[5] Andre explains, "Black people, we are who we are, and that's a great thing, but now rap has given us license to be that all the time, versus having a time and place for everything." As data in chapter 1 indicate, hip-hop is a symbol of blackness, but according to Andre, its significance is that the most objectionable themes in hip-hop become the dominant mode of self-presentation interaction for blacks who have lost the ability to code switch, or modify their behavior based on social context.

In contrast, recall this quotation from Roy about his hip-hop dress code in chapter 1: "If I have to go somewhere that I have to be dressed differently, it's not like I go to a wedding in jeans and a T-shirt. I dress appropriately for the situation." Roy, who is white, tells us that he is most comfortable dressing in a style that signals his membership in the hip-hop community and affirms hip-hop as part of his identity, but he presents himself differently depending on the social context. This distinction between Roy, a code-switching, upper-middle-class white hip-hop fan, and the hood culture described by Andre is precisely the argument made by Patterson in his editorial "A Poverty of the Mind" (2006). He writes, "Hip-hop, professional basketball and homeboy fashions are as American as cherry pie. Young white Americans are very much into these things, but selectively; they know when it is time to turn off Fifty Cent and get out the SAT prep book. For young black men, however, that culture is all there is—or so they think."

I argue that it is incorrect to characterize hip-hop as the constant, undiluted performance of cool pose by young black men. As both my readings and numerous comments from respondents suggest, hip-hop contains a variety of narrative themes and representations of black manhood. Further, its affective and self-regulative capacities as a social technology for accessing a range of different emotions and managing the self cannot be ignored. Patterson's argument about the importance of hip-hop to black men relative to other groups is certainly bolstered by the comments of Andre, whose point is slightly different. Rap music does not embody authentic black oppositional culture at every turn, but black men who are socialized in disadvantaged communities with strong oppositional cultures may find validation in hip-hop. Black men who frequently assume oppositional postures may use hip-hop in different ways than listeners who do not.

Nolan begins by describing authenticity as a true representation of one's life. For him, "keeping it real" is telling me where he comes from and that he has returned to his community in an attempt to make it a better place. Rappers according to Nolan do not keep it real because they lie about their lives and lifestyles, presenting a materially wealthy and thuggish front regardless of whether they engage in thuggery. This misrepresentation of self is important not only because performers fail to keep it real to themselves but because they fail to keep it real to their audience, specifically to black people. Nolan derides rappers who glorify selling drugs and explains how selling poison to one's neighbors sets a cycle of disorganization and violence into motion. He is disgusted that many of his neighborhood peers understand such activities as "cool" and connect this outlaw coolness to disdain for more traditional norms of achievement, specifically educational success; this explanation is the backbone of black oppositional identity theory (Fordham and Ogbu 1986; Horvat and Lewis 2003; Reese 2004; Carter 2005). This description of black/hip-hop authenticity adds to our understanding of why authenticity is important. Many respondents adhere to a psychosocial understanding of hip-hop authenticity because staying true to oneself is an indicator of good character, and keeping it real makes someone trustworthy and sensible. Nolan affirms this psychosocial authenticity because it speaks not only to the performer's *character* but also to his *politics*. Failure to keep it real constitutes disregard for one's obligation to the black community, and many present-day rappers fail to recognize the political importance of this social obligation.

Steven builds on Nolan's argument as part of his conflicted statement about black authenticity in hip-hop. He begins by criticizing 50 Cent for "using his gift wrong" but admits that 50 is a high-quality entertainer and that he enjoys 50's music and feels a sense of "power" when he listens to it. Though he disapproves of the messages in the music, Steven affirms its affective power and states that he "love[s] it," sometimes in spite of its content. After admitting this guilty pleasure, Steven separates himself from "kids" who might not "snap out of it [the feeling of power]" the way he does and don't realize that it's "just music." Steven does not explain why he is capable of snapping out of it when others are not, and the only distinction he makes between himself and those who take the music too seriously is age. Rather than reflecting on what allows him to interpret the music the way he does, he casts blame upon 50 Cent and other artists who fail to distinguish between reality and entertainment.

Authenticity is especially important to blacks, as Steven argues that entertainers have become role models for young black people from the hood.[6] He then goes on to describe the sort of imposing masculine self-presentation that dominates both hip-hop and hood culture, contrasting the current-day "mean" version of black masculinity with a version from generations ago that was more pleasant and "fun." This shift is dangerous to black politics because it destroys black unity and influences the socialization of young people in black communities. When asked to explain the transformation, Steven does not blame white people or the corporations that commodify and promote objectionable representations of blackness, instead lamenting that "the hood of America has taken over."

Summary

This chapter presents data on aesthetics and authenticity directly tied to the vast research in these fields within cultural sociology. The first major finding is that there is a robust set of standards for what makes a good MC, and listeners' evaluations of rap music are not clearly organized along race and class lines. Instead, a culture community of hip-hop fans emerges, and these aestheticians prioritize lyrical content, technique (flow), and signifying (layered meaning) as the principles that are important to rap music. Black and white respondents at all class levels report that being a skilled signifier is especially vital to being considered a good MC. This is an important point, because signifying is a black vernacular tradition and a critical component of the popular narrative about white distance from and cooptation of hip-hop. Whether black or white, the listeners in my sample, who express love for hip-hop and engage it on an everyday basis, are familiar with and appreciative of hip-hop's signifying tradition.

Second, interviews provide contradictory data about authenticity, another widely affirmed aesthetic principle. Respondents believe authenticity is an important trait for an MC, but they are skeptical of authenticity claims. In describing inauthentic hip-hop performances, respondents in all social categories express discontent with MCs' celebration of material wealth; obsession with making and flaunting money is among the most inauthentic traits a rapper can possess. However, though many respondents' favorite rappers harp on these themes, they are still considered skilled and "real" MCs. This contradiction does not mean that respondents are hypocrites; rather, it illustrates that authenticity is not rooted in the objects themselves (song lyrics, for example) and that the theoretical path laid by Peterson, John L. Jackson, and others who affirm subjective, socially constructed authenticities yields the most useful analysis.

Although respondents' efforts to describe authenticity as a fixed, consistent concept may be flawed, the data that result from their efforts to pin down authenticity remain valuable when we consider race and class dynamics. When describing inauthentic and "bad" hip-hop, commercialism and mainstream appeal emerge as central concerns for hip-hop listeners. If a hip-hop performer is primarily motivated by money, mainstream exposure, or the opportunity to showcase his wealth, he is inauthentic, and his art is considered low quality. This anticommercial, anti-"bling" sentiment is the most consistent theme in respondents' discussion of authenticity, which corresponds with McLeod's rubric of the real in hip-hop. McLeod's research also suggests that racial identity should emerge as a corresponding boundary, with whiteness corresponding to hip-hop fakeness and blackness to authenticity. While commercialism is vital to hip-hop authenticity discourse among respondents, the racial narrative about white cooptation of the culture is conspicuously absent. Strong anticommercial sentiment emerges as a clear aesthetic principle for respondents, while antiwhite sentiment does not.

Considering my textual analysis, the findings presented in chapter 1, and the work of numerous hip-hop scholars, the relative unimportance of black authenticity discourse as a key element in respondents' explanations of what makes good hip-hop is a surprising finding. Though it is impossible to know exactly why these data appear, three explanations come to mind. First, white respondents are far less willing to discuss race than black respondents. This corresponds not only with data in chapter 1 but with my comments on white power and white privilege in the introduction high-lighting the invisibility of whiteness and the role of the color-blind ethic in the maintenance of white supremacy.

Second, many of the men I talked with are over the age of twenty and have witnessed hip-hop's expansion as a commercial phenomenon. Jennifer Lena (2006) makes special note of the ways in which authenticity themes tilted toward hustling and street life in the mid- and late 1990s as a result of corporate investment in hip-hop. While they were introduced to hip-hop in the 1990s, after the transition from hip-hop as public practice to hip-hop as commodity, many respondents are sure to remember a time before 50 Cent's *Get Rich or Die Tryin'* shattered the record for album sales during the first week of release, instantly elevating him to global icon status. Bearing witness to hip-hop's commercial expansion may have made respondents especially attentive to this notion of authenticity and fed their disapproval of contemporary "fake" hip-hop that does not remind them of what hip-hop was when they began to follow it.

Third, my social status and self-presentation as an interviewer may have influenced respondents' discussion, or lack thereof, of black authenticity. During recruitment, I introduced myself as a researcher from Harvard University, immediately establishing a spatial and class identity at odds with traditional notions of authentic blackness. During both recruitment and the interviews themselves, I did not dress in clothing that would be considered classic hip-hop style, nor did I speak using vocabulary and delivery that would immediately mark my familiarity with black vernacular—another key marker of authentic blackness. Finally, while I bear a number of phenotypic characteristics that mark me as black in the American racial context, my skin tone places me on the lighter side of the spectrum, a physical marker that might be read as bourgeois or racially impure, given both black and popular historical discourses of black authenticity. It is impossible to account for each of the insider/outsider methodological factors that influence qualitative data collection and dangerous to allow these suspicions about researcher/respondent relations to become explanations for data sets. Still, it is fair to wonder whether I was consistently marked as not truly black by many of the men I spoke with and whether this marking influenced their discussion of black authenticity, or lack thereof.

This does not mean, however, that none of the respondents relate their understandings of hip-hop to discourses of racial authenticity. To the contrary, a number of black respondents from working-class social backgrounds discuss the prevalence of objectionable representations of black masculinity in hip-hop and believe that the code-of-the-street, hood-thug hip-hop stereotype is inauthentic and harmful to blacks. However, these respondents fail to link the proliferation of such representations to white corporate control of hip-hop or to white supremacist hegemony, and they express more disappointment with members of the black community for allowing them to flourish. Though one of the white men speaks explicitly about racial authenticity, further solidifying the racial boundary between blackness and whiteness observed in chapter 1, none of the white respondents discuss black authenticity the way black respondents do, nor do white respondents discuss the potential harm of hip-hop representations of black masculinity to black people.

Black respondents' unwillingness or inability to connect the proliferation of corporately supported representations of dishonorable blackness is symptomatic of a larger trend among all respondents: a nearly complete failure to discuss the political economy of the music industry. Respondents detest commercially successful rappers' inauthentic performances and lament the fact that rappers incorporate inauthentic elements because they sell. But this disappointment and disgust can lead to unsophisticated interpretations of the authenticity debate that simply blame black people for regrettable representations of blackness, as blacks seem to jump at the opportunity to perform in this manner and to consume such representations. Severe limitations are imposed on commercially successful artists' creative control by the incentive structure of the music industry and various mechanisms that discourage risk and prevent nontraditional race/gender/sexuality scripts from gaining popular visibility and acceptance. While there is a general sense that corporate and commercial forces are harmful to hip-hop, there is little evidence that respondents understand what these forces are or that they may be connected to white supremacy or patriarchy.

Gender dynamics are often unspoken but vital to considerations of aesthetics and authenticity. Comments about the centrality of toughness and coldness to authenticity narratives appear in many interviews, and respondents describe different reasons and levels of approval for the presence of such narratives in hip-hop. Young men affirm the ability to boast according to the rules of domination-driven, hegemonic masculinity as an indicator of lyrical skill and as something that contributes to the quality of hip-hop. Respondents' comments about women and girls are almost entirely excluded from the data presented above and are instead presented in chapter 5 as part of a broader discussion about masculinity and the position of women in hip-hop.

FIVE

Parental Advisory: Explicit Lyrics

Is it OK to call me a nigger and your wife a bitch? If I object to that then I'm a conservative? That is ridiculous!

—Wynton Marsalis[1]

My understanding of "thug life" is it stands for "This Hate U Gave Little Infants Fuck Everybody." And "nigga" being "Never Ignorant Getting Goals Accomplished." Of course, that's not how everybody understands it, but that was his [Tupac's] point.

—Dwayne (b3)

Hip-Hop and Moral Panic

In 1985, Tipper Gore and three other wives of politicians started the Parents Music Resource Center (PMRC) to combat sexually explicit lyrics in music. This group eventually came to be responsible for pressuring the music industry into putting "parental advisory" stickers on explicit records, visually warning parents and guardians about the damage that toxic music might inflict on their children. Originally, the main PMRC targets were heavy metal acts, but by 1990, the year in which Gore's letter criticizing gangster rapper Ice T appeared in the *Washington Post*, rap artists became public enemy number one. Thanks in no small part to these efforts, hip-hop became a frequent target for politicians looking to score points by appealing to mainstream moral sensibilities. At a Rainbow Coalition convention during his 1992 presidential campaign, Bill Clinton publicly criticized activist and hip-hop producer Sister Souljah (also a convention guest) for her controversial if tongue-in-cheek suggestion that black people stop attacking one another and direct their violence at whites instead.[2] Also in 1992, Dan Quayle chided TimeWarner for the release of a song called "Cop

Killer," performed by the black rock band Body Count, featuring Ice T.[3] By 1994, congressional subcommittee hearings on rap had brought these issues to a legislative crescendo, producing two main outcomes. First, artists would be forced to record a "clean" version of their objectionable songs for radio play, and second, television networks would be subject to increasing pressure to regulate and change music video programming (Keyes 2002, 106).

Roughly one decade removed from the congressional subcommittee hearings, moral panic about hip-hop language reassumed its place as a lead story on prominent American digital and print news outlets. On April 4, 2007, radio host Don Imus jokingly referred to the Rutgers University women's basketball team as "nappy-headed hos" on his nationally syndicated talk radio program; he was condemned, shamed, and ultimately fired. Imus issued multiple apologies and met with the Rutgers women and their coach, who graciously and publicly accepted his effort to make amends. However, the "nappy-headed hos" comment had legs beyond those that carried Imus out the door of his CBS studio, as it sparked a firestorm of public discourse about the culpability of black people, and hip-hop culture specifically, for pushing such language into mainstream spaces. Imus, like so many people indelibly affected by hip-hop's corporate pop-cultural reign, was mimicking black/hip-hop vernacular in the service of comedy. If rappers had not made "dissing hos" such a popular pastime, the logic goes, Imus never would have joked the way he did.

Shortly after the Imus scandal, Oprah Winfrey held a televised town-hall meeting on her talk show, entitled "After Imus: Now What?" The feature addressed the double standard whereby black hip-hop artists are absolved from blame, while Imus and his white contemporaries are skewered. Def Jam Records founder Russell Simmons appeared on Oprah's show and released a public statement validating its premise, suggesting that the recording and broadcasting industries ban the words *bitch*, *ho*, and *nigger* from rap music. In an open-letter response, slam poet extraordinaire Saul Williams argues:

> Our love affair with gangsterism and the denigration of women is not rooted in hip-hop; rather it is rooted in the very core of our personal faith and religions. The gangsters that rule hip-hop are the same gangsters that rule our nation. 50 Cent and George Bush have the same birthday (July 6th). For a hip-hop artist to say "I do what I wanna do / Don't care if I get caught / The DA could play this motherf——in' tape in court / I'll kill you / I ain't playin',"

epitomizes the confidence and braggadocio we expect and admire from a rapper who claims to represent the lowest denominator. When a world leader with the spirit of a cowboy (the true original gangster of the West: raping, stealing land, and pillaging, as we clapped and cheered) takes the position of doing what he wants to do, regardless of whether the UN or American public would take him to court, then we have witnessed true gangsterism and violent negligence. (Williams 2007)

As Kelefa Sanneh of the *New York Times* astutely points out, "This is not a debate about freedom of speech; most people agree that rappers have the right to say just about anything. This is, rather, a debate about hip-hop's vexed position in the American mainstream" (2007a).

Hip-hop culture is routinely criticized for sexist and antisocial themes and refrains. Many, including Williams, argue that these intolerable representations have their origins in mainstream American cultural institutions. Further, the robustness of these themes in popular culture is dependent on financial and promotional backing of major corporations that often play both sides. For instance, Warner Music Group owns Atlantic Records, of which Interscope Records and Death Row Records are subsidiaries. The Interscope/Death Row partnership made part-time rapper, part-time pornographer, and reality show star Snoop Dogg[4] a household name and is viewed by many as the industry birthplace of commercially successful gangster rap. TimeWarner also owns *Essence* magazine, which became the major sponsor of the "Take Back the Music" campaign. "Take Back the Music" began in 2005 on the heels of a black-student-led protest of Nelly's degrading and misogynistic music and video performances.[5] TimeWarner strives to profit on both sides, promoting artists who are unapologetic in their use of sex and female objectification as a marketing tool, and using a TimeWarner company to brand and facilitate antisexist activism.

Whether we focus on or ignore the complicated relationship between hip-hop culture and corporate/mainstream America, commercially successful hip-hop performances often contain objectionable portrayals of manhood and womanhood laced with racially controversial symbolism and language. Everyone who comes into regular contact with hip-hop, from *New York Times* columnists to everyday observers without a national platform, reckons with the moral panic that engulfs it. This chapter addresses three topics from the moral panic debate using interview data drawn from conversations with my respondents: women in hip-hop, the "n-word," and gangsterism and criminality.

Bitches Ain't Shit

At the center of hip-hop's gender problem are the numerous performances wherein women are rhetorically objectified, degraded, and insulted. Frequently cast as objects for sexual consumption and the justified targets of male scorn by commercially successful hip-hop artists, "bitches," "groupies," "gold diggers," and "hos" are to be used and cast aside without the benefit of care, concern, or financial compensation. This ethic of disrespect and disposal is often cultivated as the flip side of the "thug love" and male loyalty described in chapter 3.

As with all issues of interpretation of the content of rap music, attention must be paid to the signifying tradition when discussing hip-hop lyrics, and the possibility that hip-hop's serious unseriousness with respect to sexism is misread by audiences that do not get the joke must be allowed for. The much-publicized public trial of 2 Live Crew during the early 1990s serves as a flashpoint for this discussion and is one of the most cited moments in the history of hip-hop gender politics. The group's album *Nasty as I Wanna Be* was declared obscene by a federal judge in Florida in 1990, and when the group performed at a concert in Broward Country, they were prosecuted.[6] Henry Louis Gates Jr. was presented at the trial as an expert witness on signifying in defense of the rap act. Gates argued that the graphic and often insulting sexual acts described on many of 2 Live Crew's songs could never be taken literally by those who understand signifying and that they were intentionally crafted as oppositional exaggerations of black sexual stereotypes. Gates's testimony led to one of the most widely read black feminist editorials on the subject of women and hip-hop, penned by Kimberle Crenshaw, who writes:

> Rather than exploding stereotypes as Gates suggests, I believe that they were simply using readily available sexual images in trying to be funny. Trading in racial stereotypes and sexual hyperbole are well-rehearsed strategies for getting some laughs. 2 Live Crew departs from this tradition only in its attempt to up the ante through more outrageous boasts and more explicit manifestations of misogyny. Neither the intent to be funny, nor Gates's loftier explanations, negate the subordinating qualities of such humor. (1991)

The names and faces of the critics and criticized have changed since the 2 Live Crew trial, but when it comes to misogyny and antiwoman content in hip-hop music the issues remain the same. Those who defend hip-hop often do so on the grounds that rap artists provide convenient targets for a racist moral panic machine that looks the other way when white superstars conduct themselves in similarly reprehensible ways. Implicit in this defense is Gates's idea that most critics are in no position to offer their opinions on the matter, as rap artists play a vernacular game with which they are unfamiliar. This is why the contributions of women of color, black feminists, and hip-hop feminists are central to this particular permutation of hip-hop's gender problem: thinkers like Crenshaw recognize that these discussions occur in the context of politics of racial hegemony. Their criticism comes from a position of cultural authority that attends to the racist dimensions of conservative moral panic without letting sexism and black vernacular violence against women off the hook.

It is important to note that within the rap music universe, women have never taken their abuse lightly. In recent years, however, the form that commercially successful female MCs' rhetorical resistance frequently takes is an adoption of the hegemonic masculine ethos of sexual exploitation. Whereas MC Lyte or Queen Latifah may have demanded respect on the grounds that reducing them to exclusively sexual vessels constitutes a denial of their humanity, many of today's most famous female MCs, such as Lil' Kim and Foxy Brown, demand respect by reducing men to sexual pawns whom they control and exploit for erotic and monetary gain. The evolution of hip-hop sexual exploitation narratives crafted by black women MCs coincides with an explosion of visual representations of women of color as "video hos" who decorate the videos of so many commercially successful rap acts (Emerson 2002; Pough 2003; Sharpley-Whiting 2007). These scantily clad music video dancers serve as symbols of artists' power and testament to the extent to which representations of sex as exploitation and trade have come to dominate the hip-hop landscape.

Respondents are included in this study because they engage commercially successful hip-hop on a regular basis, so by definition the sample does not include men whose outrage about sexism in hip-hop leads them to disown or boycott music that includes objectionable representations of women. However, affinity for hip-hop must not be read as men's support for misogyny, and a number of respondents point out that while they enjoy some music that contains degrading content, they also enjoy songs that celebrate women for traits other than their sexual potential.[7] Respondents from each socioeconomic and racial group express remorse about sexism and misogyny, while others admit to enjoying women's sexual objectification with various levels of guilt. One of the more robust explanations for the prevalence of unflattering representations of women in hip-hop is that there are different types of women, and when hip-hop acts portray women as "bitches" and "hos" they are referring to women who fit a specific description.

> I get their story, they deal with some bitches. There's a difference, though, between a woman and a bitch. Luke Tupac said, a female is like, a hard worker, independent. But a bitch is somebody that's just nagging you, not independent, want to sit around and smoke weed all day, and then want to play you for your money, use your money to support they habit . . . Tupac made it clear, there's a difference between a bitch and a female. (Greg, b4)

> WALLY (w1): There's a song by Jeru the Damaja, like "I'm not talking about the queens, but the bitches." So he makes a distinction. I don't know like if people agree with that or not.
> MICHAEL: What about you personally, do you find that distinction makes sense to you?
> WALLY: Well, actually I think Jay-Z breaks it down perfectly. He has a song called "Bitches vs. Sisters," and he's like, "Bitches want this, sisters want this," he breaks it down. Obviously, I'm a guy; I know women that I would consider bitches.

> Some rappers, they down women, they call them bitches, because there's some of them that are like that. Where I grew up, some women were grimy, acting shysty, you know? You have a Benz and they'll try to entice you so they could have one. So when rappers are talking about different classes of women, it's because they've probably been through that . . . There's different ones, you just got to know which ones are which. (Ben, b4)

> Women have been inherited into rap in different ways. You have the families and the wives and girlfriends of the rappers, they've seen them go through the struggle, that's why Ludacris got prompted to make that song ["Runaway Love" (2006)]. But then you got that "pussy poppin'" where he's trying to get at the whole aspect of the strippers and the groupies and all that. I feel like women are kind of getting portrayed in hip-hop for what they are. (George, b3)

> You had people like 'Pac [Tupac], came out and called all these girls bitches and hos and stuff, but you got to think about the people that were around him, the women that were around him at the time. They were around him because he was famous, because he was making money. (Roy, w2)

There's bitches and hos everywhere. There's a difference between a good woman and a bitch or a ho, and she'll tell you that herself. But rappers, that's what they're around, that's all they get, that's all they want, because they're not trying to be tied down. (Nate, b1)

There's a difference between a bitch, a ho, and a regular lady. I don't think the artists are really talking about girls in general, unless they really say that . . . There's someone that fits in all those categories. I think people just try to take it as something negative and blow it up to something bigger than what it is. Like, there's real hos out there, and that's who they're talking about. (Nolan, b3)

There's a lot of disrespect for little girls who think they're going to sleep with a lot of men and get money. That's who they're disrespecting. That's who they call bitches, basically. (Dwayne, b3)

I don't think it's completely, like, a rapper's fault or anything, because that's sometimes the way that women carry themselves. We all have different perspectives on the way that women should carry themselves. You know, dress nice in the truest sense of being a lady could be. I think most MCs when they degrade women it's because that woman is not being a lady. (Darryl, b1)

According to both black and white respondents from different social classes, degrading representations of women are rooted in the reality that there are certain types of women who act in degrading fashion. This understanding falls in line with interview data from chapter 1 illustrating that part of what enables respondents to relate to hip-hop is that they believe the narratives reflect something true about the real world. More often than not, the defining characteristics of dishonorable women are predatory sexuality and desire and to exploit men they enter into relationships with for financial gain. Commercially successful rappers interact with such women on a regular basis, according to respondents, and it should be no surprise that they voice their resentment for women who attempt to take advantage of them. Respondents' insistence that degrading representations of women are rooted in reality is intertwined with the belief that many women *choose* to play these degrading roles, which absolves hip-hop culture and individual performers of moral blame.

As far as the videos, girls scantily dressed, doing what they're doing, how can you fault the dudes making the songs, like they're forcing the females into these roles? These females are willingly showing up for video shoots, wanting to be in the roles. If they don't want to walk around half naked, they say no, or if they really want her in the video, they going to accommodate her, respect her wishes. For the videos, I don't think there should be so much flack on the artists and on the industry, because females want to do it, and they're doing it. (Nolan, b3)

Everyone knew women are being called bitches and hos and shit like that in the videos, but the girls are going and doing the videos. They know what they're doing. They know what they're talking about. They're getting paid for it. (Russell, w1)

If you look at these videos, the lines are out the door with beautiful women, just to get twenty seconds of camera time. If they're going to do that to themselves, of course men are going to take advantage of that. "Here's fifty dollars, go shake your ass a little bit, get in there, grind up on me." And they'll do it, for the money and the fame. They get to hang around with stars. For them, that's a come up, but really you bring yourself down, and they don't realize that. (Steven, b4)

Some of it is degrading, some of it is put on by guys. It depends on how that female handles the situation. I don't think anybody is forcing anything that they don't want to do. (Ryan, b4)

It's ridiculous, and it gets me pissed, but I would do the same thing if I was them [rappers]. Talk about girls liking their money, wanting to give them head all the time. Or how they just shit on girls and the girls will come right back like nothing happened. How do you justify the girls that are involved? Not the dudes. If you're a dude and this shit keeps happening to you, you're going to turn into a cocky prick, and there's nothing you can do about it. (Brandon, w3)

A lot of these women do these things and don't want to be referred to as "bitch," "ho," stuff like that. But that's what you're inciting by doing these things. I'm not saying that because you want to be in a video, that makes you a bad person. But you already know before you even start that that's how you're going to be looked at. Don't get mad when people call you; we're only calling it like we see it. (Jack, b2)

All the videos you got the females in there dancing and shaking their ass, just not respecting themselves. They feel . . . that it's degrading black women or whatever, but I don't know. They just show more and more skin, but if these women are willing to do it, and being a part of it, they're making money, they're having fun while they're doing it, I don't understand the problem. (Fred, w3)

I think that whole discussion is based on the way certain, can't say all, but the way certain women portray themselves. And if you allow yourself to be portrayed that way, that's why you get spoken about. (Tim, b2)

Bikari Kitwana asserts that men born and raised in the hip-hop generation lack interest in or knowledge of feminism (2002, 102). Respondents' unwillingness to tie representations of women in hip-hop to a larger system of gender oppression certainly speaks to a lack of feminist analysis. In contrast, one might argue that women's sexual agency, a crucial concept in feminist politics, is central to the discussion about women's degradation in hip-hop contexts and that women who allow themselves to be portrayed in a sexual manner are simply comfortable with their sexuality. But T. Denean Sharpley-Whiting strikes down such readings by highlighting the exploitative context in which women's sexual agency is exercised, pointing out that black women's sexuality in the hip-hop marketplace is subjugated to male desires at best and completely discounted at worst (2007, 66). As respondents note, women may choose whether to participate in hip-hop sex marketing, but this choice to perform cannot be read as an accurate representation or performance of women's sexual desires or of their labor preferences within the hip-hop industry.

Too frequently, the objectification and insult of women in rap music is considered the only or primary example of sexism, when in fact hip-hop is defended as male space in other ways as well. The most famous and influential hip-hop music labels, such as Def Jam, Interscope, and Bad Boy, were founded and are run by male executives who sign and develop primarily male talent. Compounding women's exclusion in the industry, Rose (1994) points out that women have been denied access to the technological spaces where music is produced and recorded. Further, the physical spaces where hip-hop is performed are frequently male dominated. Men's preference for a particular genre of music or art is not necessarily evidence of sexism, but Cheryl Keyes notes that when conducting participant interviews at hip-hop concerts and clubs for her study, despite her high personal comfort level she often felt unwelcome by the men in such spaces, who warned her that these gatherings were "no place for a lady" (2002, 10).

In addition to narrative insult and physical exclusion/marginalization from spaces of production, there is strong defense of hip-hop as male space in the realm of aesthetics. Put bluntly, the men in my sample do not hold female artists in high regard. In total, 115 men placed their names and contact information on the original sign-up sheets for the interview project. The sign-up sheet contains a column where respondents are asked to list one or more of their favorite rap artists. Not one respondent in 115 men listed a female rap artist or group among his favorites (see appendix). This disregard is reinforced during the interviews, where the number of unprompted mentions of female artists is staggeringly low.[8] Part of the challenge of making sound qualitative inferences is combing through data to look for patterns, frames, and stories that consistently present themselves during interviews. But it is equally important to apprehend what is *absent* from the data, and the fact that female hip-hop artists are almost entirely ignored by the cohort of men I talked with is a significant finding.

In McLeod's (1999) authenticity rubric discussed in chapter 4, gender presents itself as one of the dimensions of authenticity, as realness in hip-hop connotes a male and "hard" disposition, while being "soft" and feminine is read as fake. My interview data affirm the distinction between commercialism and anticommercialism as the strongest theme in respondents' discussion of hip-hop authenticity, but the emphasis on commercialism does not render gender irrelevant. The excerpts below reveal respondents' collective anticommercial and antimainstream sentiment as a gendered construct and confirm the importance of masculinity to ideas of authenticity.

I think 50 [50 Cent] has done the best, because he'll come with his hard stuff on the mix tapes and make his money there, but when it's album time, he's making hits, joints for the ladies. He'll have a couple songs on there for the hood, or whatever, but he's a business man. (Nate, b1)

Like Sisqo came out with a CD, and all these typical teenage white girls are just into hip-hop, and thinking they're like "down" now. And they're like banking off their fathers' payrolls, they got a Lexus from their daddy, haven't worked for a dime in their life, have no, like, thought of a struggle. And what rap basically is, is a giant struggle to make it out. (Marc, w1)

MICHAEL: So what do the ladies like and what is street credibility?
DAVID (b4): Basically the ladies, the type of beat that they have is on the dancing type. It's played out in the club. They play it, girls love it. "You

can meet me in the *ehhhhh*, it's goin' *downnnnn*" [*disparagingly*]. [This is a reference to Yung Joc's smash hit "It's Goin' Down" (2006).]

KEVIN (w4): Females just want to listen to reggaeton and dance all day [*laughs*]. I don't got none of that, I got the best of the Lox.

MICHAEL: How do you explain that?

KEVIN: They just like to follow everything, and they just listen to have a good time, you know? Like you ever see a white girl listening to Spanish music, driving, singing the words and she don't know what anything means? It's like, come on, she's just doing it to follow, she just likes what's hot . . .

MICHAEL: Is there a type of hip-hop that you think women can relate to like you relate to it, or is the idea of women putting on the Lox just ridiculous?

KEVIN: No. Because when I put on a CD when I'm with my girlfriend, she'll turn it off. So now I bring my iPod with me and say, "You listen to what you want, I'll listen to what I want."

MICHAEL: So you wouldn't expect a girl to relate to it at all?

KEVIN: What?

MICHAEL: The Lox.

KEVIN: No.

The thing is that I hate it, but if you go to a party or something, like fifteen girls will be dancing, getting crazy, and you're like, "I'll go over there." . . . So whatever they're doing, they're doing something right. They're making catchy songs, songs that people want to hear, so it can't be bad, but it goes against what I like in hip-hop. (Brandon, w3)

MICHAEL: Another topic in hip-hop is women in hip-hop. What comes to your head when I mention that topic?

ZACK (w1): They can't rap. I can't rap either, but generally, I think women can't rap. I've heard a couple of chicks that can rap. MC Lyte, talented chick. As far as being in the community, more power to them. If you're talented, speak up. I just can't say that I've heard too many talented chicks from my personal experience.

The quotations above, drawn from respondents of both racial groups and a range of classes, provide additional insight into the workings of gender in hip-hop. As chapters 2 and 3 illustrate, the influence of hegemonic masculinity lays itself bare in the narratives and accompanying imagery of commercially successful rap. But explicit affirmation of domination-driven masculinity in hip-hop performances texts prescribes a limited model for how gender operates within hip-hop. This limited traditional gender discourse says that men have power over women, and their primary means for maintaining power are economic exploitation, control over visual representations of women in hip-hop contexts, and physical and verbal violence. Women within hip-hop culture resist the degrading representations put forth by male acts either by demanding respect as human beings rather than sexual objects or, more recently, by celebrating their sexual power over men and rhetorically switching the gender of pimp and ho. Hip-hop artists, executives, and fans who perpetrate these abuses of power do so publicly and without remorse, and for this reason they must be chastised and held accountable. Willful and unapologetic sexism is the main cause of women's suffering in hip-hop contexts, and those concerned with social justice work to eliminate misogyny, striving toward a politics of decency and respect between the sexes.

Interview data suggest that this understanding of gender dynamics within hip-hop culture should be adjusted. There is no doubt that willful public demonstrations of sexism and violence toward women should be condemned, and men who perpetrate these acts should be held accountable, along with the corporations that fund, package, promote, and sell them. But the *silent* and *implicit* operation of gender in the aesthetic realm of hip-hop is a second front in the battle against hip-hop sexism.[9] Respondents do not simply report that women are only good for sex or that they have no place in hip-hop because they are weak.[10] Instead, their mental maps reveal slick and occasionally subconscious connections between disgraceful, inauthentic commercialism and femininity, connections that are central to masculine identification and engagement with hip-hop. Though absolutely necessary, it is not enough to speak up against the sexism made plain in the raps and images of hip-hop music. We need to speak to the often silent, insidious masculine shame that often accompanies awareness of one's affinity for a catchy "female-friendly" mainstream party jam. The male anxiety and anger that leads to sexism grows from a paranoid need to preserve social position, and this social position is cemented by identity differences and distance between men's and women's enjoyment of hip-hop. It is dangerous and damaging to men's masculine self-concept to affirm that they derive the same sort of pleasure as women do from a wildly popular hip-hop club anthem. The empathetic web between "real" hip-hop artists and men who use their music as social technology can never be extended to include women with similar emotional needs. Hip-hop's gender problem is not only about the degradation and insult that women are subject to; it is also about men's profound inability to recognize the ways gender operates on the male body and psyche, limiting the range of performances and identities that allow for self-recognition, self-affirmation, and connection to other (nonmale) hip-hop listeners.

In my explanation of complex coolness, I emphasize that the complexity inherent in commercially successful hip-hop does not excuse or counterbalance sexism. This bears repeating. Interview data suggest that despite the conflict and discursive multiplicity of commercial hip-hop, many of the most prominent gender discourses are quite troubling. Though a great deal of attention is paid to gender throughout this chapter, this ends discussion of the moral panic specifically surrounding women in hip-hop, as we turn to the debate over the words *nigger* and *nigga*.

The "N-Word"

On November 17, 2006, actor/comedian Michael Richards, of *Seinfeld* fame, infamously responded to a heckler during a performance at a Los Angeles comedy club by yelling:

> Shut up! Fifty years ago we'd have you upside down with a fucking fork up your ass! You can talk, you can talk, you can talk, you're brave now mother-fucker! Throw his ass out, he's a nigger! He's a NIGGER! He's a nigger! A nigger! Look, there's a nigger![11]

The fallout from the Richards fiasco was swift and neat, as the comedian was publicly chastised and shamed by media and political commentators of every ideological ilk. He apologized profusely and claimed something close to temporary insanity, stating that he could not recognize himself on tape, utterly subject to his comedic alter ego, oozing rage and spewing hate.[12] The American public absorbed this moral shock, inflicted by a discourse of racism it assumed had been left behind decades ago. Fortunately, the Richards incident seemed to be an open and shut case: a crazy man who shouted a disgusting word that has no place in civil society was humbled, shamed, and righteously silenced. Moral order was restored.

This tenuous order was disturbed roughly six months later in April of 2007 by the Imus fiasco, which once again brought issues of racism and black English to the forefront of mainstream discussion. There are similarities and differences between the Richards and Imus incidents. Both white men used shocking language in the service of comedy, and both were chastised by a multiracial collection of morally outraged objectors. The obvious difference was that Richards's use of "nigger" was not intended as or derived from mimicry, while Imus's use of "hos" was at least partially intended as a wink to black vernacular. Despite this crucial difference, many public commentators connected the words *ho* and *nigger* to one another in the context of a discussion about hip-hop's role in the proliferation of such hurtful language. In this context, the NAACP took a dramatic stance against the n-word during its July 2007 convention in Detroit by holding a ceremonial public burial. NAACP delegates marched through downtown Detroit with a horse-drawn casket decorated with black roses, in a display designed to symbolize the final resting place of the word *nigger*. Detroit mayor Kwame Kilpatrick proclaimed, "We gather burying all the things that go with the n-word. We have to bury the 'pimps' and the 'hos' that go with it" (Associated Press 2007). NAACP chair Julian Bond added, "While we are happy to have sent a certain radio cowboy [Imus] back to his ranch, we ought to hold ourselves to the same standard. If he can't refer to our women as 'hos,' then we shouldn't either" (Associated Press 2007). CNN's *Anderson Cooper 360* covered the NAACP burial as one of its feature stories later that night, making hip-hop culpability crystal clear for anyone yet to connect the dots for him or herself. The transcript for the opening portion of the *360* segment reads:

NAACP CONVENTION SPEAKER: "Nigger" has terrorized us, but he has not beaten us. We have overcome him, and we celebrate the end of his existence in our community. We officially declare him dead.

JASON CARROLL (CNN REPORTER/NARRATOR): Many still consider the word deeply offensive, but it's been used often, some say far too often, by some of hip-hop's biggest-selling artists. Rappers like 50 Cent make no apologies for using it.

50 CENT (RAPPER): Sure, the music is a mirror, and hip-hop's a reflection of the environment that we grew up in. It's the harsh realities.

T.I. (RAPPER): But there are bitches, niggers, and hos that live in America. And, as long as that fact exists, I think rappers deserve the right to talk about it. (Cooper 2007)

Hip-hop is the eye of the storm, but the complexity of the controversy surrounding the n-word is lost in the summation of the NAACP burial and Anderson Cooper's news segment. There is no definitive etymology of the word *nigger*, but we do know that from its earliest recorded usage it bears a specific reference to labor (Kennedy 2002; Judy 2004). R. A. T. Judy takes care to point out that *nigger* was historically used to refer to property, or an object: "the nigger is that *thing*." He contrasts this use with that of *ne-gro*, a word he argues designated human identity in the antebellum period, rather than objecthood. However, even before the Civil War, black Americans practiced what Judy calls "ironic misnaming," or what we might call signifying, referring to each other as "niggers" in order to claim and use the word for self-affirmation and community building (2004, 111). This humanizing use of the distinctly antihuman word *nigger* continues in the present day and is the source of much confusion and debate about the extent to which black people's reclamation of the word constitutes an act of resistance or internalized self-hatred.

When spoken or written today, however, the n-word is often presented differently, with an *a* rather than *er* at the end. This change in conceptualization of the word and the implicit distinction between *nigger* and *nigga* has momentous implications for our understanding of its meanings, use, and power. It is impossible to account for every single meaning of *nigger*/*nigga*. Any project that strives to do so misses the point—meanings are determined by context and reference.[13] *Nigger*/*nigga* is one of many floating signifiers in the hip-hop universe, but in order to grasp how *nigger*/*nigga* works within other discourses, namely class and gender, it is useful to consider a few of the ways it has been treated in scholarly conversations about hip-hop. To begin, Cheryl Keyes writes, "The meaning of this term is solely determined by the adjective or possessive that precedes it: *my* nigga, *main* nigga, *real* nigga . . . 'house nigga' (an Uncle Tom), 'fake nigga' (phony person), or 'sucka nigga' and 'bitch nigga' (flimsy person)" (2002, 137). Meaning can be drawn not only from the word(s) that precede it but also from those that follow. This is a minor correction, one that Keyes is sure to concede considering her well-established main point, which is that context matters. However, her statement is still useful for cautionary purposes, because it presents an opportunity to infer too much from our commitment to context, thus erasing the significance of the n-word itself. In the phrases Keyes presents, the adjective certainly imparts meaning to the word, but this doesn't mean that *nigger*/*nigga* communicates nothing on its own, or that it simply refers to anybody, like the word *person*. *Nigger*/*nigga* is always an identity claim or assignment, even when such claims are not the intentional focus of the rap or speech act in question. Jabari Asim's criticism of the ascendance of "nigga" identity illuminates the importance of gender to the meaning of the n-word:

Little gangsta rap produced in the years since N.W.A.'s emergence differs much from the guidelines they laid down. In many instances, they use "nigga" to refer to mere ordinary, law-abiding men or to lowlifes unworthy of respect. "Real niggas" is an appellation reserved for those who have earned it. In the N.W.A. cosmos, life is only about "bitches and money." To get plenty of both, real niggas must run the streets, smoke weed, guzzle malt liquor, trust no one except members of their clique, and be prepared to kill without a moment's hesitation. (2007, 220–21)

As one of the first rap groups to use the n-word as a promotional tool, N.W.A. (Niggaz with Attitude) are to *nigger/nigga* in hip-hop as Richard Pryor is to *nigger/nigga* in standup comedy. The readings presented in chapters 2 and 3 challenge Asim's version of the gangster rap ethos, but this excerpt is nonetheless important because it reveals *nigga* as a gendered noun. It reminds us that the public moral battle over the n-word is as much about respectable masculinity as it is about blackness. Asim's explicit effort to tie what many understand to be blacks' subversive appropriation to a larger commitment to criminality and nihilism is as significant as, and strikingly similar to, conservative efforts to reduce the black urban experience to hedonistic, antisocial practice that shreds the moral fiber of American civilization.

Robin Kelley provides a contrasting understanding of the word *nigga*, emphasizing the spatial and class dimensions of its ascendance:

"Nigga" is not merely *another* word for black. Products of the postindustrial ghetto, the characters in gangster rap constantly remind listeners that they are still second-class citizens—"Niggaz"—whose collective lived experiences suggest that nothing has changed *for them* as opposed to the black middle class. In fact, "Nigga" is frequently employed to distinguish urban black working-class males from the black bourgeoisie and African Americans in positions of institutional authority . . . To be a "real Nigga" is to have been a product of the ghetto. (1996, 137)

The class dimension highlighted by Kelley cannot be ignored. In the song "Sucka Nigga" (1993), which deals largely with the use of the n-word within the black community, Q-Tip of A Tribe Called Quest raps, "You know the word, dummy / Upper niggas in the community think it's crummy." More than a decade after Q-Tip's and Kelley's words, comedian Eddie Griffin had his routine cut short during an event hosted by the highly acclaimed *Black Enterprise* magazine because he not only used the n-word too regularly for his bourgeois black audience but crafted a routine that explicitly addressed the trepidation about the word within the black community. The founder and publisher of *Black Enterprise*, Earl Graves, exemplified this trepidation, dismissing the comedian in the middle of his set and announcing to the crowd, "We will not allow our culture to go backwards. *Black Enterprise* stands for decency, black culture and dignity" (quoted in Pilkington 2007).

J. Martin Favor's (1999) elucidation of black authenticity as nonbourgeois folk-ness, discussed in chapter 2, is directly applicable to the *nigger/nigga* debate. The distinction between *nigger* and *nigga* is important to authenticity, not because merely knowing the word *nigga* or knowing that *nigger* is being signified on, validates blackness, but because *pronouncing and using the word properly, demonstrating natural, preconscious command* of *nigga*, signals familiarity with the imagined black folk experience. The more naturally *nigga* rolls off the tongue, the more readily the listener assumes the speaker to have grown up and learned to speak in the company of black people. This imagining of black people en masse, as a large group or community, often implies an image of the folk, and of poor or working-class black folk more specifically, because black people, en masse, are not bourgeois. The symbolic repertoire provided by mainstream American culture makes it difficult to picture a group of well-to-do "articulate" blacks who pronounce each word with "proper" English intonation. By contrast, imagining a large group or community of poor, desolate blacks is not difficult at all thanks to the collection of racist images and narratives that document the stereotypical black American experience (enslaved, destitute, shiftless, criminally inclined).

Outrage over the word *nigger*, pronounced and employed as racial insult, is simple to understand, but indignation over *nigga* is a bit more complex. For example, imagine a group of black and white academics engaged in scholarly conversation about the meaning of the word *nigger/nigga*. Over the course of the conversation, people who don't normally or usually use the word *nigger/nigga* may say it a number of times in the context of the discussion for the purpose of exposition or clarification. In these circumstances, there is no confusion about why the academics use the word because they are using it to pontificate on its meaning. When use of the word occurs in the context of "civilized" conversation, there is far less moral panic about its invocation. Context matters for people who are confused and upset about usage of the n-word. It is fair to assume that the panic-stricken are far less concerned about intellectuals discussing the merits and meaning of the word than they are about casual use in unregulated settings.

This context-specific concern or confusion points to a genuine social distance, perhaps along lines of race, class, or generation, between those who are perplexed and troubled by the word *nigga* and those who are not. Cultural distance is a two-way street. For example, an analog for black folks raised in a "nigga"-literate culture using the word (in a phrase such as "What's up, my nigga?") might be the use of a word like *dude* ("What's up, dude?") among whites. It goes without saying that *nigga* and *dude* do not have the same meanings, etymologies, or range of linguistic functions. The point is that each of us lacks understanding about some of the things that come naturally for those raised in communities and spaces other than our own.

There are many words and slang expressions across cultures and communities that outsiders do not understand, so the question becomes "Why is mainstream American society so interested in this particular word?" Perhaps the most reasonable answer is that *nigger/nigga* is unsettling because it evokes the country's history of racial exploitation, oppression, and violence, and disgust with the word is connected to sincere disgust with the injustices and mistreatment black Americans have endured. A more radical possibility is that it is not simply one's memory of racial oppression that causes panic, but that when black people use *nigga*, black discontent, resistance, and agency become audible and transparent through signifying, and this revelation of black agency is unsettling to observers and listeners. More pointedly and polemically, one might argue that the confusion or discomfort felt by nonblacks is actually the feeling of racial privilege being challenged, and racial identity destabilized, by a reconfiguration of nigger-speak that is distinctly nondegrading. Or less radically, discomfort is not necessarily anxiety regarding, or remorse for, lost and ill-begotten racial privilege but a reflection of the disturbance caused by the reality that race still matters and racial injustice is still with us. *Nigger/nigga* forces discussions of racial identity and privilege into a mainstream public sphere that is ill-equipped and reluctant to accommodate them.

My interview respondents, however, are not at all reluctant to discuss the significance of the n-word, both in hip-hop contexts and in the context of their everyday lives. It comes as no surprise that the most widely shared understanding of the popular emergence of *nigger/nigga* is that black people are signifying on the original racial insult and changing its meaning from a negative slur to a positive term of endearment. Respondents from each racial group and multiple social classes make a case for this meaning. The first four quotations that follow come from black respondents, the second four from white respondents.

They're [rappers] saying it more like "homey." They done switched it around. And that's what hip-hop does too. Well, black people period. Black, Hispanics, minorities, I don't know if that's the right word to say. The culture—we switch things around to make it look good. (Greg, b4)

You could say "my nigga" chilling with your friends, but then there's also negative ways that people use it. Like, you say something outrageous, and I'm like, "Nigga, what the fuck you talkin' 'bout?" Like, if you're mad, you say "nigga," it shows you're pissed. And if you say, "This is my *nigga*," it's like, "This ain't just my friend, this is *really* my nigga." (George, b3)

We just kept that word and use it all the time. That's probably the word that was used most of anything. It got to the point where you say what's up to someone, you say, "What's up, nigga?" (Ryan, b4)

I think what black people did is try to take that word and change it to a positive. Because that word was so painful, I can imagine, and it still is for some people, so painful, so powerful, for us to be able to take that word and change it to a positive . . . We turn it into a positive so we can call each other and not hurt us, so that's taking power away from the oppressor. (Nolan, b3)

I guess what I've heard is it's a way of getting a word that's used to demean you, a word that's supposed to demean a group of people, or a race, or a culture. They adopt that word as their own slang and use it. When rappers use it, it's supposed to mean, like, "brother," or something like that. (Wally, w1)

They [black people] know what the term came from, they know what it really means. If they want to switch the meaning of it and use it as a term of endearment, who am I to tell them not to? (Zack, w1)

White people used to call black people that word back in slavery, and it went from a negative word to being a positive word. People in our generation call each other that word out of spite, because they got called that word so much, they turned it around, and in retrospect it's now being used as a positive word. (Marc, w1)

I guess hip-hop has kind of succeeded because it doesn't really mean a whole lot anymore. No one ever really acts surprised these days when you hear it.

There's the classic argument about taking back a word, and people do that with "dyke," "fag," you know, everything. In some ways, it's almost like drawing a line in the sand, like, "This is us, this is our family." (Isaac, w1)

The final quotation from Isaac points to the capacities of the n-word as a boundary-making tool for blacks who use it. Controversy arises, however, when this rhetorical boundary-making practice occurs publicly, in realms where *nigger/nigga* can be decontextualized and reinterpreted by those who fall outside the lines of the n-word community. Asim writes, "My concern is with the public square, where I believe the N word and other profane expressions have no rightful place . . . Conversely, if you are white, whether you refer to me as a 'nigger' when you're at home is of little consequence to me . . . I'm willing to acknowledge a distinction between private speech and public behavior" (2007, 230). Among black respondents who use the n-word, the public/private distinction emerges as a key consideration with reference to when and where it is used.

Me personally, I'm not against the word. I use it in certain situations. I don't think it should be a word that is free to use. It was something negative coming up, but I feel like black people have flipped it, claimed it as their own. So I feel like it's something that keeps us together. That's something that we can relate to each other on. It's something so small, but that word shouldn't be free to use. That's a saying that we got, it's exclusive to us. (Steven, b4)

I use that term myself, but at the same time, it's not something that's going to go away. If you use that term [*pauses*], among your group of friends. For me, I'll say it, but I'll use that term around my peers, instead of walking down the street like, "Yo, nigga!" If dude is white, I'm not going to say that around them. (Neil, b4)

I try to use it less now. It depends on who I'm around too. It's just me and my boy, I'll say it. But if there's other people in the room, especially white people or other races, I won't use it . . . You could talk about your mother and your brother, that's your family, that's yours. But you can't let me talk about your mother and your brother, because I'm out of that circle. That word, I feel that's how our people think of that word. (Nolan, b3)

I try not to say it around white people too much. It's kind of like smoking weed and then telling your kids, "Don't smoke." It's like, "How you going to tell me? You telling me not do something you do." (George, b3)

I use the word myself and don't take offense to it, but I have a problem with playing it out publicly. What we do amongst ourselves is what we do amongst ourselves. But playing it out in front of three hundred, two hundred people and not all of them are African American, I don't want to give them no reason to think that we foolish. (Andre, b4)

I use that word. I don't say it around certain people out of respect for myself and respect for them, but it's just a word that people get called in their households, like by their mothers. (Nate, b1)

At least one black respondent from each socioeconomic level reported using the n-word in his personal life. This consistency speaks to the unifying potential of black vernacular and the capacity of linguistic performance to solidify racial bonds across class lines (Patillo-McCoy 1999, 10). Data speak to the boundary-making potential of the word *nigger/nigga*, as respondents strongly suggest that the n-word is now the property of blacks, who have the exclusive right to say it.[14] However, even among those comfortable with the n-word, there is concern about African Americans' public image and significant ideological support for a politics of respectability, which suggests that black people's public standing is dependent on their embodiment of a respectful, reserved, and implicitly bourgeois public self-presentation. Closer examination of interview data calls further attention to class dynamics among black hip-hop listeners, as the only three black respondents who issue a firm statement against the word *nigger/nigga* are either middle class without mobility or cultural elites. Their statements are presented below.

I think the word is degrading no matter who uses it. I don't understand a lot of people. They won't get offended if another black person calls them that, but they get offended if someone of another race, like, say a white person, calls them that . . . If you're going to get mad at one person, get mad at everyone. If you're not going to use it, then everyone can't use it. It's degrading no matter who says it, no matter how they say it. (Tim, b2)

I was brought up differently, I wasn't raised to call my women bitches. Another thing is all my friends are like, "What's up, my nigga?" I don't use that word. I remember when I was in college, on campus I had a couple of white roommates, and he's on the phone like, "Yeah, my nigga, yeah!" And I'm in the room, he's looking at me: "Yo, are you okay with that man?" I'm like, "Shit, that's kind of awkward." If a white person says the word *nigger*, he says

it differently, he says "niggerrrrrr." To me it's no different. If that person cannot use it, I can't use it. (Evan, b1)

I don't like saying it. I think it's—they say they're using it in a positive way
when most rappers say it. They say when white people use it, it gets us down
and stuff like that, so like, why would you start using it as a way to pick
yourself up? Why would black people start using it to like, you know, like
I'm saying it in a positive way . . . It's just like when you've got white friends
and they ask you, "Well, what do you think, can I call you that? Could we be
cool, and I can call you my nigga?" I'm like, "No, you can't." I don't even like
my black friends saying it. I'm not going to kill a white person for calling me
a nigger or things like that, because it gets tossed around so much. Honestly
I kind of want to just be like, "Black people, it's your fault. You put it out
there, and people just think it's cool to say now." (Darryl, b1)

In each of these cases, respondents give two reasons for their objection
to the n-word. First, the word is degrading and offensive in and of itself.
Second, each expresses specific concern about white people's use of *nigger*,
implying that white people's use of the n-word is rooted in their desire to
mimic black use or count themselves among those "down" with black folks.
According to these respondents, this affinity for blackness is no excuse for
sustaining the racist history of such a troubling word. A small number of
white respondents admit to using the word among their peers. One might
expect white respondents who use *nigger/nigga* to be solely of working-
class standing, considering the objections lodged by the black bourgeoisie.
However, this is not the case, as two of the five white respondents who feel
comfortable with the n-word (Marc and Eric) are from the cultural elite
category, with middle-class social origins and advanced education.

It's a word that I call my friends. Like one of my friends is black. To other
black people, they take it offensive, but to my friend, he don't take it offensive. (Abe, w4)

You're not going to change your vernacular just because it might not be
acceptable. I think these days, people don't even look at it as being a slur.
I'm not afraid to use the word at all, not that I use the word, but if I did, I
wouldn't have any qualms about it. (Eric, w1)

I got a bunch of African American friends and bunch of Puerto Rican friends,
and they call me that name and I call it back to them. Like I said, there's a

time and a place for that word. If you're in Harlem, and you're walking up to some random dude on the street wearing an Ecko jacket and tilted New York Yankees hat and you say it to them, he's probably not going to find it as appealing as someone who you're friends with, you say it to them on an everyday basis. (Marc, w1)

MICHAEL: Do you use it?

FRED (w3): Sometimes. I got a lot of black friends, grew up with a lot of black people. It's not like I can't say it. If we're hanging out, I'm not going to use it in a derogatory term to degrade anybody by any means.

It doesn't bother me, like, I'll never say it [*pauses*]. Actually, with my real close friends I might. (James, w3)

Again, the public/private distinction looms large as respondents discuss when and why they say "nigger/nigga," and for white respondents, friendship and mutual understanding with nonwhite people who use the term regularly is grounds for one's own use. These respondents notwithstanding, the majority of white men in the sample (all fifteen other white respondents) do not feel comfortable using the n-word in any context, be it their everyday lives or when engaging hip-hop specifically. Black respondents who express disdain for the n-word believe it is degrading and that it mistakenly gives nonblacks the impression that they can use it. White respondents also cite the word's basic negativity as a key reason not to use it, but there are two instances wherein respondents describe blacks' use of the n-word as related to black folks' resentment of white people.

JAMES (w3): I think some rappers are like, racist towards white people. Like Lauryn Hill and stuff like that. I don't know. I'm not racist, but I think that some rappers are racist. Like there's movies and stuff, like they'll make a joke out of somebody that's white.

MICHAEL: What does that have to do with the word itself?

JAMES: Because I was trying to think of what bothered me about it. That would bother me, like in a movie or something, and they're always saying "nigga," and they'll make a joke out of somebody that's white.

When people say it, you feel like they kind of just, I don't want to be rude. I think the blacks feel like still kind of resentment and pissed off towards white people still. If I went to Roxbury and didn't know somebody that I was going to see, I'd be pretty fucked . . . I feel like the reason they say it back and forth with each other is to kind of just associate, like, the brothers between themselves. Discard all whites and everyone else who can't say it. It's kind of like a personal thing, like a nickname between two people that only they would know, and if someone else is saying it, you're not allowed to say it . . . It's kind of like, a sarcastic, like, "Yeah, I'm this, whatever. This is what white people used to do to me, and we're going to call each other that, but you could *never* say it to us." It being wrong to say is kind of like their own little empowerment over it, and I respect that, because I feel like I don't want us saying that word. I think it's wrong for me, myself, and I think what they do is fine. I think they deserve it. Give them reparations, you know? [*Laughs*]. (Russell, w1)

Each of these excerpts speaks to the complexity revolving around ownership, use, and purpose of the n-word. James admits to occasionally using the n-word around his friends but finds its proliferation troubling because it indicates a double standard whereby rappers are not held accountable for racially insensitive language or representations that celebrate blackness at the expense of whiteness. Russell's commentary is even more complicated, as his fear of merely stepping foot in a black neighborhood (Roxbury) hints at racist stereotypes about black criminality. However, he also offers thoughtful analysis of the n-word's development and utility, as he acknowledges racial injustice and identifies the "nigga" phenomenon as a form of boundary-making through signifying among blacks who use the term. Both black and white respondents discuss the unifying and boundary-making potential of *nigga* as a cultural distinction without antipathy for white people. But unlike the majority of his peers, Russell finds the boundary-making problematic because he thinks it speaks to black resentment of white people (thus his fear of being alone in black neighborhoods). James and Russell are only two of the twenty white respondents, but their comments are significant because similar observations are not made by black respondents, who affirm the n-word as a boundary-making tool but do not connect black collective identity to black resentment of white people.

Respondents of both races and all classes argue that the n-word found its way into hip-hop thanks to the speech habits of performers, who are believed to be speaking in a manner that is comfortable and natural to them. *Nigga* operates as a marker of black authenticity because rappers prove their hood origins by naturally including the n-word as part of their vocabulary.

Black culture, a lot of these people are being pulled out of the ghetto, and that's the message they're taught and surrounded with, and that's the terminology they're brought up around. (Paul, w1)

Because that's a part of keeping it real as well, how you would talk normally. Because everybody knows you write best about what you know. So if that's how you talk on a normal basis, incorporate that in your music, but you don't have to use it every other word. (Jack, b2)

It's interesting how that has become a trope, but it also puts up a wall between certain people and certain other people: black artists and white artists. If you're really speaking concretely, there is something that African American artists can do that other artists can't do. It's that authenticity: "I can say this because this is how I identify myself, my friends, who I'm with, and certain people can't." (Richard, w1)

You got to understand, like 90 percent or 85 percent of hip-hop artists come from the hood. That word is used and there's no consequences, it's just used. And if you don't use it, you're considered corny, or whatever. That's pretty much a way to prove your blackness or prove your hood credibility, by dropping n-bombs all over the place. (Steven, b4)

I think they say it because that's, as silly as it sounds—to get in a discussion about the n-word would take forever—it validates their hood credibility, to just throw it in there. Like, "Yeah, he's talking the way we talk." (Andre, b4)

Recall that findings presented in chapter 4 suggest the discourse of race exerts a lower than theorized impact on considerations of hip-hop authenticity, especially relative to commercialism. The four quotations presented above restore the importance of race as a channel through which hip-hop authenticity flows. Not surprisingly, respondents suggest that "natural," "authentic" blackness is dependent on the ghetto as a spatial site, where rappers learn to talk the way black folk do. However, though these excerpts show a different range of meanings for each group of respondents' understanding of hip-hop authenticity, it is crucial to understand how racial authenticity compares with authenticity concerns rooted in commercialism and gender.

In the Case of Commercialism

· In chapter 4, respondents state that authenticity is a positive attribute that connotes a high-quality musical performance.
· Respondents explicitly and implicitly suggest that distancing oneself from mainstream commercialism is authentic and therefore aesthetically desir-

able. The operative authenticity question is "What sort of an artist are you?" And after all data connecting commercialism and authenticity are analyzed, the answer that confirms authenticity in hip-hop performance for respondents is "I am an artist who cares about the quality of my art more than making money." Despite these claims, respondents express affinity for a number of rappers who brag about their wealth and spending habits.

In the Case of Gender

· In chapter 4, respondents cite examples of skilled signifying that are reliant on domination-driven masculinity. Close reading of examples of good raps cited by respondents suggests that the ability to cleverly convey one's manly dominance is one of the elements of quality MC-ing.

· In chapter 5, respondents implicitly link femininity with the inauthentic by describing women's preference for mainstream, commercial, and poor-quality hip-hop.

· Respondents believe that degrading representations of women are based in reality and are therefore authentic. The operative authenticity question is "What sort of gendered person are you?" When all data connecting gender and authenticity are analyzed, the answer that confirms authenticity in hip-hop performance for respondents is "I am a man capable of dominating others in the realm of competitive lyricism. I am markedly different from women, who are less invested in hip-hop and, in many cases reported by rappers, unworthy of my trust and respect."

In the Case of Race

· In chapter 4, respondents state that it is important to be true to oneself, and retaining social-psychological authenticity aids in arriving at a positive evaluation of a given rapper.

· For a commercially successful MC, one means of displaying this type of authenticity is talking the way he naturally talks. In chapter 5, respondents state that hip-hop performers are often socialized in communities where using the word *nigga* is standard practice, so when rappers use it, they are being true to themselves as black people.

· Respondents do not discount the ability of nonblack hip-hop practitioners to "be real," nor do they blame the plague of hip-hop fakeness on white corporate control of the music industry, white consumers, or systemic racism. However, the claim to blackness as an element of hip-hop authenticity is reflected not only in this rhetorical, performative commitment to being oneself but in the definition of hip-hop as something distinguished by black performers (and originators), as stated in chapter 1.

- The operative authenticity question is "What sort of racialized person are you?" When all data connecting race and authenticity are analyzed, the answer that confirms authenticity in hip-hop performance is "I am a black person whose racial identity is bound to my self-identification as a hip-hop head. You can tell I am being myself and laying claim to blackness by the way I rap and the words I use."

These three formulations are imperfect, and perhaps their greatest fault is the unfortunate appearance of these three categories as firmly bounded and separate from each other when in fact the discourses intersect. Undoubtedly racial authenticity is informed by the rules of gender performance and vice versa. In material reality, understanding these dynamics requires attention to their commonalities, but few of my respondents speak about authenticity in a way that explicitly foregrounds intersectionality during interviews.

In this section, I have argued that the moral panic surrounding the n-word has a great deal to do with its power as a performative device that brings racial identity, authenticity, and racial inequality and racism into public focus. The last section of this chapter addresses a third topic in the discussion about hip-hop and moral panic: gangsterism and criminality in hip-hop.

Gangsterism and Criminality

As noted in previous chapters, residential segregation and criminal justice practices combine to produce perhaps the most important mechanism sustaining black American socioeconomic marginalization and social death. As a complement to these structural affronts, the discourses of race and crime are historically linked in America, and disadvantaged black men have become the quintessential symbol of criminality and threat to American moral order. Mainstream hip-hop acts that perform gangster/thug/criminal narratives are well compensated by the record industry for doing so, and it is tempting to read such performances as uncritical tributes to degrading stereotypes of black masculinity. In chapter 3, I argue that close readings of hip-hop gangster/thug/criminal performances within this structural, discursive, and commercial context both reinforce and contest the most troubling notions of essential black masculinity. More specifically, my claim is that complex cool hip-hop performances are reliant on domination-driven hegemonic masculinity while simultaneously concerned with black male vulnerability, existential reckoning, and affirmations of thug collectivity, loyalty, and love. Respondents both affirm and reject my claims about black criminality and thug life in hip-hop.

I asked respondents to talk about what it means when they hear a rapper refer to himself as either "gangster" as an adjective or as a "gangster" or a "thug" as nouns. The term *gangster* has more traction than *thug* during interviews, perhaps because of its implicit importance to rap resulting from the naming of gangster rap as a genre. *Gangster* is identified as an overused, ubiquitous rhetorical phenomenon similar to the phrase "keep it real" and the word *nigger/nigga*. For this reason, discussion of gangster talk is seasoned with skepticism about the validity of such claims or the qualifier that such performances are carried out for the sake of image. However, this status as a hip-hop trope and the resultant skepticism that comes from hearing "gangster" so frequently does not rob the word of its meaning, as men in the sample agree on the importance of tough, violent, nihilistic, masculinity to hip-hop gangsterism.

> I think it's image. If I were a popular rapper and I wanted to project a tougher attitude, I would use certain terminology. (Pete, w1)

> To say you're a gangster means you'll do anything to better yourself. I would say 50 Cent is a gangster. You'll rob, you'll do whatever to get your dividends, to diversify your portfolio and your bonds. If you want to rob, cheat, steal, you're going to do it. (Marc, w1)

> Well, me and you both know, all that tough talk, stuff like that, you can't be a gangster and be a rapper. That just doesn't make sense. If you're still selling drugs or killing people, shooting people left and right, if you really did do these things, if you're doing these things currently, then the authorities are going to come and get you. (Neil, b4)

> They're trying to convey that they're tough. They're the "Billy Badass," they're not scared. They're going out shooting like Tupac [*skeptically*]. (Nolan, b3)

> Keeping it gangster? I don't know, that they're hardcore. Don't fuck with them. Their way of life is, like, selling drugs, and they don't want people to fuck with them. (Damien, w4)

> A lot of times rappers like to boast about whether or not they've been shot, or if they're in a gang, or something like that. I guess "gangster" or "thug"

says that they're not really making this stuff up, also establishing a harder image for themselves. (Eric, w1)

A character he wants to portray, because there's no real thugs out there. You can do this or that, sell a little drugs, get a little tattoo, that's just how he wants to characterize it, to me. (Sean, b2)

They're trying to say that they're hard, that they're tough, that they got street credit. Most of them don't, though. (Roy, w2)

Someone says they're gangster, it means they'll do anything at any given moment. They might have a gun on them, they'll shoot you, they'll do whatever . . . Gangsters have no heart. They don't care. (Steven, b4)

Respondents' statements about gangsterism do not break down neatly along race and class lines, as they believe hip-hop artists' collective obsession with gangsterism reflects the pressure to portray oneself as an imposing figure in a world full of other would-be intimidators. In this sense, it more closely aligns with the notion of coolness as a coping mechanism than the explanation of complex coolness I offer in chapter 3. While hegemonic masculinity is endemic to my explanation of the gangster/thug phenomenon, what is missing from the excerpts above is an emphasis on the real-life structural and discursive contexts within which these narratives are created. I argue that part of the reason thugs employ antisocial discourses is that residents of the hyperghetto find themselves in circumstances where the assumptions and rules of "civilized" society do not apply. Rhetoric about one's capacity to inflict harm is born from circumstances in which the thug narrator himself is subject to harm. Only three respondents, all of whom are black, discuss the social harm inflicted upon gangster/thug narrators as part of their definition of what a gangster/thug is.

> BILL (b4): Keeping it gangster, I would say keeping it gangster is just keeping it real. Even a Harvard kid could keep it gangster. But "I'm a thug?" I think they're just twisting up the definition. Basically people have rough pasts, they been through things in their life, they're sharing life stories and shit.
>
> MICHAEL: So thug has more to do with your [the imagined subject's] personal experiences?
>
> BILL: I would say that. A lot of dudes been wounded in war, they talk about it. And if you've been wounded in war, you're a thug. That's basically

what it is. That's what I think it is. I don't think it's, you know, snatching purses. None of that.

MICHAEL: What does it mean to be a thug? To be gangster, to be a gangster, what does that mean to you?

ALLEN (B1): Surviving by any means necessary in a bad situation. You may not have the opportunities that other people in other places would, not just because of your skin, but just because of where you're at, and an inability to get out of that situation.

Today, a gangster is a gangster. It's a man who holds his own, who takes care of his business. In certain neighborhoods, you got to step up. You're taught being raised in a single-parent home, or without a parent, you had to step up for yourself and hold your own. Instead of being taught to aspire to go to Harvard, you never really thought of it, because that was way out there in another world. (Dwayne, b3)

None of the white respondents discuss gangsterism or thug life in the ways that these three black men do. What makes their collective understanding of the gangster/thug phenomenon unique and important is that they discuss lack of opportunity, marginalization, and personal suffering as part of the *definition* of what it is to be a thug. Further, though the interview question is directed toward gangster/thug representations in hip-hop, these three men give answers that blend hip-hop narratives with a more universal definition of gangsterism drawn from real life. Both Allen and Dwayne speak to gangsters' placement in a social location that bears no relation to civil society and offers no legitimate opportunities for self-improvement. Later in the interview, Dwayne, who is an ex-offender from a high-poverty, high-street-crime neighborhood continues:

There's a lot of barriers. As a young black man, I could still go to Harvard and graduate with honors, and still have a lot of problems at the workplace, like people will never really respect my work. That's talking from a professional sense. To the extent I feel like, "What the fuck am I doing here anyway?" You feel like that shit wasn't built for you. (Dwayne, b3)

Dwayne's admission that he sometimes feels "like 'What the fuck am I doing here anyway?'" and "this shit wasn't built for you," combined with Bill's definition of a thug as someone with a rough past who has been "wounded in war," certainly presents the potential for depression and nihilism born from marginalized social existence. When we consider these connections, drawn exclusively by black respondents, between the definition of a thug/ gangster and the suffering and frustration that breeds and colors thug life, it is slightly surprising that one of the most striking articulations of the thug life concept comes from a white respondent from a privileged background. As Kenny endeavors to explain what makes Notorious B.I.G. a good MC, he foregrounds the existential cost of life as a social outcast.

> The way that he [Notorious B.I.G.] uses those ominous beats, and his own tone and voice, which always seems to at once embody this nostalgia for the way things were and a knowledge of his own impending death makes that record really powerful . . . "Things Done Changed" (1994) where he describes the way that things were and how they've become. You think about it in terms of the ghettos of America becoming more and more overfilled, and less and less light getting in, and more and more depressing, and there are no prospects, and that change, he describes it right at the beginning . . . And then when he starts talking about the present in comparison to that idyllic past, there's this really amazing feeling that he conveys about his reluctance that he feels. You really get this sense that he is incredibly nostalgic for this lost past and hesitant to engage with the present that is all around him, but he has no choice. I think the way that he conveyed that on the song is very powerful. I hate sounding like some clueless kid who grew up in Cambridge, trying to imagine what it's like to grow up where he did, but at the same time after having listened to that song I think that I can say I have some idea what that means. (Kenny, w1)

Again, what distinguishes Kenny's explanation of Notorious B.I.G.'s narrative from black respondents' discussion of thug life is that Kenny does not speak to marginalization and suffering as part of the definition of what a thug is. However, Kenny ties the structural disadvantage of American ghetto experience directly to Notorious B.I.G.'s personal depression and intimacy with death. Further, the notion that Biggie "has no choice" but to engage his dangerous surroundings speaks to the lack of moral culpability for ghetto dwellers born into such conditions. It is also significant that while Kenny values the empathy he feels as a result of engaging hip-hop thug life, he emphasizes his social distance from such circumstances, identifying himself as "clueless" about, but "understanding" of, such experiences.

Despite data points that reinforce textual analysis about the thug phenomenon in hip-hop music, respondents' characterization of thug life bears two crucial dissimilarities to my arguments in chapters 2 and 3. First, my analysis emphasizes the discursive bond between gangster/thug protagonists. Collective "thug love," I argue, is indispensable both to what a thug is and to thugs' rhetorically warding off injury, coping with vulnerability, and escaping structural and godly damnation. Respondents do not discuss thug solidarity and connectedness during interviews either as a major discursive theme or as what it means to be a thug.

Second, even among respondents who describe hip-hop thug subjectivity in ways that reflect the links between disadvantage, depression, and gangsterism, the hyperghetto/prison as residential space does not present itself as a major structural force in the molding of hip-hop thugs. However, when specifically asked about the relationship between the police, the court system, and hip-hop, men of both races and all classes emphasize the unfairness of the criminal justice complex, especially with regard to race.

> They have a different reason for "fuck the police." In ghettos and things of that nature, the police have been more racial. There's a lot of racial profiling. (Pete, w1)

> It's still going to be a racist form, there's still racists today. Basically, where it came from, pigs, back in the day, police were known to be wild and do whatever they want, because they're on the opposite end of the law. (Sean, b2)

> I think it's definitely something hip-hop should be talking about. The prison population quadrupled since 1980, and it's mostly black youths. The rates of imprisonment for young black men are through the roof, and it's usually for a lot of nonviolent drug instances, or the violence that comes from the drug trade. (Isaac, w1)

> Like N.W.A., when they came out with "Fuck tha Police," that was justified. That was madness. A lot of people have problems with the police and they talk about it. I think that's fine, because that's what hip-hop is, expression, like I said. (Chris, w4)

> For the most part, hip-hop artists, that culture, doesn't mesh well with the law, court systems, justice. I think a lot of that has to do with the feeling that they're not getting equal trial. A fair, equal, even plane. They feel like they're being persecuted, pinpointed based on the obvious things: how they look, what kind of car they're driving, those types of things. (Paul, w1)

Because the police, their job is supposed to be to protect and serve us, but if anything, all they do is just try to bring us down more than help us out. They think you can't have anything. Some people, they come from the hood and everything, but they get money and they change they lives. It has nothing to do with you, they just look at you as a regular black person or whoever you are, if you got money they think you're selling drugs, you're doing this, start following you, and that's why they say that ["fuck the police"], because they get harassed all the time. (Ben, b4)

I think about it as part of a long countercultural tradition. It's particularly applicable to hip-hop, because most rappers, MCs, DJs . . . many of these guys have been young black men from inner cities. And I think that they're from a group that it's common knowledge has been systematically discriminated against by the criminal justice system, not only culturally, but systematically discriminated against by police officers and courts. (Kenny, w1)

Through personal experience and what I saw, I think the justice system, it's unfair, there's no justice in it realistically. Hip-hop has made a whole bunch of people from humble beginnings rich, and now they have the spotlight, they just blowing it spending money buying jewelry, buying liquor, advocating other people to do that. I think they target them because they have money, they have power, they have the people's respect. I think it's just a big target for the government. You take all the money away, they still look at us like niggers, whether we're rich, whether we're poor. (Nolan, b3)

There is a lot of racism out there. Even me being a white male, the way I dress, the way I look, I don't know. Police don't seem to like it and it always seems that I'm a target . . . They might be trying to bring down the culture. Something they don't understand. They're probably afraid because of the gangster rap. (Fred, w3)

There's a lot of innocent dudes in jail. Then, there's a lot of dudes in jail that hustle just to get by, like, they needed it. It's something they got to figure out. Got to change the system, because it's fucked up. I could see why they say that, because maybe they been through the system or they seen they peoples go through it. It's just shady. (Greg, b4)

My friend, when a cop pulls him over, he always puts on a rock station. Cops, they hate that lifestyle, they really do. (James, w3)

Both black and white respondents connect the rift between the criminal justice complex and hip-hop to personal experience, with two basic dimensions. In one respect, discussion about hip-hop is a proxy for discussing racial discrimination more generally, as respondents talk about the racial inequity manifest in criminal justice trends and personal experience with stereotyping and discrimination. Second, hip-hop is cast as part of a countercultural tradition that symbolizes a threat to order rooted in the worn tropes of black male danger. Commercial success makes hip-hop and those who represent it targets for persecution, driven by the jealousy of those who identify hip-hop consumption and "bling" culture as indicators of illicit activity. The offense of mistreatment is even more objectionable to respondents who compare hip-hop's criminal justice plight to the ways in which other wealthy high-profile cultures are dealt with, as excerpts from Roy and George illustrate.

> I think that a lot of the stuff people get upset about is Tupac and Biggie. Two of the biggest people in hip-hop, both murdered, and both unsolved. Why? You can solve all these other cases, and you can't solve two murders that happened in two heavily populated areas, one of which happened in Vegas, and you have 5 million security cameras and you can't tell who shot Tupac. The police, they pay a little bit more attention to people in hip-hop nature. You see a lot more hip-hop, slash rap, get arrested, drug charge, gun charge, when you know a lot of their rock and roll counterparts are doing the same thing. (Roy, w2)

> They have a hip-hop book of all the rappers that they feel might be a threat to commit a crime or a threat to themselves or society. All their whereabouts, their addresses, where they live, what types of cars they have, and it's just like they're automatically labeled . . . To have a hip-hop log, they don't have a white-collar businessman log. Like I understand, you know, within the hip-hop genre or the rap industry there is a lot of violence, so because they put that out there we have to keep an eye on these people, but to label them like that? It's almost like walking into a store as a black man, and as soon as you walk into a store you're being followed because you're going to steal something. (George, b3)

The double standard identified by George and Roy suggests serious skepticism of the moral panic surrounding hip-hop. Mainstream celebrity culture and corporate crime could just as easily provide fodder for those up in arms about the socially destructive influence of hip-hop's moral transgressions, but hip-hop is unfairly singled out by authorities for poisoning the hearts and minds of its young consumer base. However, frustration with the moral panic double standard and the criminal justice system's treatment of hip-hop does not result in deep resentment of criminal justice authorities. Further, despite personal experience with racial discrimination and awareness of racial inequity in criminal justice processes and outcomes, black respondents specifically emphasize the importance of personal responsibility in the context of both racial injustice and the antisocial performances of commercially successful hip-hop acts. Both working-class and middle-class black respondents are represented in the excerpts below.

> The majority of America I think does not like hip-hop. I see a lot of people feel it to be offensive and degrading and just all in all a bad vibe. People say that it causes violence, but I don't believe music at all causes violence, violence is caused by the person. Just like you can't say a gun killed somebody, if there's no on behind the trigger of the gun then it's not going to do anything, it's going to sit there. You can't blame the music for the way people act . . . I can listen to anything else, you could say heavy metal causes violence, that's very violent in it's own way, but it's all about how you take it, and how you choose to react based on what you're listening to. (Tim, b2)

> Once you get to a certain level, certain status, I think if they were living that way, they should really give it up. You could hire security if you feel you're not safe, you have the means to keep yourself out those situations . . . I think that's another reason the government targets them, because they're doing stupid stuff. Like nine times out of ten they're going to have mad weed in their car, or going to have a gun on someone in their entourage. At first I think it was probably done unfairly, but now, they're like, giving them reason to. (Nolan, b3)

> Don't get me wrong, there are bad cops out there that pick on certain things. But for the most part, everybody's not going to go against you, and even if they are against you, don't give them something to talk about. It's one thing [if] you're driving fast, it's another if you're driving fast, you got a gun, or you got weed. They don't care who you are, you're getting locked up. (Jack, b2)

> Police brutality is a reoccurring theme in hoods throughout America in general, so that's just natural. But I don't like when they say, "The law is trying to hold me down." You hold yourself down. The policeman did not put a gun in your hand, put you in a store to go rob it, then wait for you to come

out and arrest you. People got to start taking responsibility for their own actions. Yeah, you're being harassed, but don' t give them a reason to arrest you. (Steven, b4)

These statements challenge conventional political ideologies on the "black crime" problem. Conservatives are thought to have a stranglehold on the discourse of personal responsibility, and more often than not, emphasis on personal responsibility trumps any and all concerns about race-based mistreatment and inequality. Left-leaning commentators often point to structural inequality and discrimination as the only issues worth discussing if we wish to understand the discourse of black crime. When discussing the relationship between hip-hop and criminal justice, respondents of all races foreground racial discrimination and inequality and suggest that hip-hop is viewed as a racialized culture by criminal justice authorities and other public policemen of morality. A number of black respondents pair this analysis with an emphasis on personal responsibility, challenging not only the conventional belief that personal responsibility rhetoric is incompatible with an analysis of racism but also the stereotype that blacks cultivate a culture of complicity and comfort with criminal behavior among themselves.

Summary

This chapter addresses three issues that consistently arise during episodes of moral panic prompted by the explicit content in rap music: treatment of women, use of the word *nigger/nigga*, and representations of gangsterism and criminality. No significant differences emerge along lines of race and class with respect to women's degradation in hip-hop. Respondents state that when rappers degrade females in their performances, they are not insulting all women but are talking about a specific type of dishonorable woman who is worthy of disrespect. There is no grand narrative that connects these objectionable representations of women to larger systems of gender oppression or corporate influence, and respondents believe that women who participate in such representations are partially to blame for the abuse they incur, because they choose to participate of their own free will. In addition, interview data reveal a subtle, implicit connection between commercial and inauthentic rap and female experience, such that the rules and results of hip-hop engagement and identification differ substantially along gender lines. Masculine authenticity in hip-hop demands not only that rappers construct a hegemonic masculinity based on domination for the purpose of rhetorical quality and commercial marketability, but that male listeners build a discourse of aesthetics with firmly established lines between male and female hip-hop engagement and appreciation.

Race and class distinctions are far more important to discussions about use of the n-word in hip-hop circles. There is general agreement about the actual meaning of the n-word as a floating signifier that has been reclaimed by black people and is now employed to communicate a variety of ideas dependent on context. As expected, all black respondents from the cultural elite to the working class are uncomfortable with white people using the word *nigger/nigga*, but a number of white respondents of various classes admit to using the word in what they believe to be a nondegrading way. Class distinctions do not determine white respondents' interpretations of the n-word debate, but almost all of the statements that no one, black or white, should use the word *nigger/nigga* come from black respondents of middle-class standing or above, which is consistent with a politics of racial uplift that emphasizes a bourgeois model of respectability as the key to black people's improving their standing.

When discussing the proper context for saying "nigger/nigga," both black and white respondents affirm that private use among one's friends is far more appropriate than indiscriminate public use. This public/private distinction is especially important to black respondents, some of whom suggest that among the most important reasons for only using *nigger/nigga* in the company of blacks is that if the n-word becomes too popular, non-black people will feel as though they are allowed to say it. Based in part on these data, I argue that the great significance of the word *nigger/nigga* as a performative device with respect to moral panic is that it forces racial identity, and by extension, stigma and power, into the public sphere.

Respondents' discussion of the n-word brings racial authenticity to the fore, and their engagement with questions of racial authenticity complements prior conversation about other authenticity spheres. The operative authenticity questions drawn from interview data in chapters 4 and 5 are worth restating:

On commercialism: The operative authenticity question is "What sort of an artist are you?" And the answer that confirms authenticity in hip-hop performance is "I am an artist who cares about the quality of my art more than personal wealth."

On gender: The operative authenticity question is "What sort of gendered person are you?" And the answer that confirms authenticity in hip-hop performance is "I am a man capable of dominating others in the realm of competitive lyricism. I am markedly different from women, who are less invested in hip-hop, and in many cases, unworthy of my trust and respect."

On race: The operative authenticity question is "What sort of racialized person are you?" And the answer that confirms authenticity in hip-hop performance is "I am a black person whose racial identity is bound to my self-identification as a hip-hop head. You can tell I am being myself and laying claim to blackness by the way I rap and the words I use."

Finally, respondents discuss thug life, gangsterism, and criminality in ways that both support and challenge my analysis of complex cool in chapters 2 and 3. According to men in the sample, the prevalence of the gangster persona is an effort on behalf of hip-hop acts to craft themselves as imposing figures, reinforcing the importance of masculinity claims as a coping mechanism that imparts hip-hop legitimacy. In chapter 3, I argue that vulnerability and the admittance of injury or struggle is just as vital to understanding hip-hop coolness as are claims to manly pride. Overall, there is little support for this interpretation of thug life in the interview data, and the only respondents who acknowledge pain and vulnerability as part of the definition of hip-hop thug life are black men. Further, there is no significant support for understanding thug life as a demonstrably collective discourse, and the notion of thug love or solidarity does not present itself in interview data.

Another major difference between respondents' interpretations of thug life and mine is that the structural context of the hyperghetto/prison is not emphasized, even when respondents discuss the unfortunate conditions from which many hip-hop narrators arise. However, data strongly support a shared understanding of racial inequity and mistreatment within the criminal justice complex. Respondents (black men in particular) speak to this mistreatment with reference to both personal experience and the hip-hop industry in general, which is unfairly cast as a threat to public safety. Despite shared understanding of racial inequity and hip-hop's mistreatment by the police, data do not suggest that hip-hop listeners of all racial and class locations condone criminal behavior or harbor antipolice attitudes. In fact, this understanding of criminal justice inequity and mistreatment is paired with commitment to personal responsibility for a number of black men.

The Last Verse

People be asking me all the time,
"Yo, Mos, what's getting ready to happen with hip-hop?" I tell them,
"You know what's going to happen with hip-hop?
Whatever is happening with us."

—Mos Def, "Fear Not of Man" (1999)

Research Summary

As stated in the introduction, the research questions that drive this book are "How should we understand narratives about ghetto life, 'thuggin', courtship, and material excess performed by black men in commercially successful hip-hop?" and "Are there significant differences between the ways black and white men interpret rap music and the meaning of hip-hop?"

Chapters 2 and 3 specifically address concerns about black masculinity as represented in commercially successful hip-hop, using the idea of complex coolness as a frame. A number of critics essentialize hip-hop as cool pose in its purest form: an empty, pseudorevolutionary culture that reveals black male disillusion, neurosis, and self-defeating pathology. My textual analysis of hip-hop representations advances three specific criticisms of hip-hop as cool pose: (1) performances affirm a black male collective built upon connections to others as a source of strength rather than a neurotic projection of the invincible, supercool self; (2) performers advance narratives of black authenticity as a means of establishing the boundaries of their social worlds, but authenticity comprises a wide range of context-dependent messages and is not fundamentally oppositional to mainstream notions of success or status attainment; and (3) hip-hop narratives explicitly communicate vulnerability, existential anxiety, and thug love, which are antithetical to cool pose posturing.

While cool pose is inadequate, it is disingenuous to ignore the ways black masculine coolness is celebrated and prioritized in commercially successful rap music. The character of contemporary black masculine coolness draws on previous theories, including those related to cool pose. In addition to theories of black masculinity that highlight the frequency with which coolness is employed as a coping mechanism, complex cool incorporates elements of Thompson's "aesthetic of the cool," which celebrates an all-encompassing composure, smoothness, luminosity, and stylin'. In the end, complex cool is a combination of these two intellectual traditions of black coolness, complete with the distinction it allows for the transparent portrayal of strife, conflict, complexity, and insecurity by cool performers, whereas previous iterations of black masculine coolness require the exclusion of such expressions from public purview.

In chapters 1, 4, and 5, interviews with everyday hip-hop listeners illustrate differences and diversity in hip-hop meaning and interpretation. Questions of cooptation and mimicry are central to racial politics and hegemony, and documenting interpretive differences between black and nonblack hip-hop respondents serves as an empirical springboard for discussions about hip-hop's cultural significance. The interview-driven chapters document how respondents define, evaluate, and interpret hip-hop. These data are important because the voices of everyday listeners are conspicuously absent from many book-length projects in hip-hop studies. In addition, respondents' voices are useful as a check for my textual analysis and the salience of complex cool. As I document the ways race, class, and gender influence understandings of hip-hop, I highlight instances where respondents' analyses support and challenge my understanding of complex cool.

Chapter 1 argues that the men in my study understand hip-hop primarily as a "culture" and a form of expression or communication and generally agree that hip-hop originated with economically disadvantaged African Americans in urban areas. Both sets of respondents affirm hip-hop as part of their identities and as a culture that they live on a daily basis. But black respondents from each class build a racialized collective hip-hop identity and believe they are connected to other hip-hop enthusiasts because hip-hop is, in part, about black experience. White respondents do not link their appreciation of and experience with hip-hop to collective racial identity, indicating a different correspondence between their personal identities as whites and members of the hip-hop communities they belong to. Black respondents also affirm a collective ownership claim that does not exist within the range of white respondents' description of what hip-hop is.

Black collective identity is a crucial element of the arguments advanced in chapters 2 and 3, as is the black ghetto as a heavily used trope of black experience and signifier of authenticity. Shared "hood" experience is not at the core of collective identity articulated by respondents, but the importance of racial identity to both white and black men's understandings of hip-hop remains a significant finding.

Respondents relate to hip-hop because they believe it reflects real-life truths and because they hear and see representations that echo personal experiences. Given the importance of collective racial identity to their definitions of hip-hop, it is not surprising that black men recount race-related experiences or events among those recast in hip-hop music. While there is no analog to black respondents' race-based experiences for white respondents, both groups describe a variety of reasons for listening to hip-hop music, which may be purposely used to achieve different mental and physical affects and may become constitutive of specific emotional states. Respondents' definitions of, and uses for, hip-hop directly challenge the idea that hip-hop can be understood as shallow oppositional posturing and cool pose. Data suggest it is appropriate to understand hip-hop as a tool for identity building with multiple uses.

Chapter 4 focuses on how respondents evaluate hip-hop music and allows men in my sample to intervene in the debate on hip-hop authenticity. Both privileged and disadvantaged respondents appreciate narrative and technical skill when making aesthetic judgments about rap, which runs counter to the notion that only consumers of high class status are concerned with the technical dimensions of the art they consume. The ability to signify is the technical skill that respondents look for most when evaluating rap music. Despite its rightful placement in the black vernacular tradition, signifying is critical for both black and white respondents, and this finding challenges the notion that white people cannot fully understand hip-hop and that their affinity for hip-hop is purely naïve, voyeuristic fascination with black machismo. Both groups of respondents affirm the importance of the verbal game in play within rap music.

Authenticity is vital to aesthetic judgments, and respondents across race and class groups regularly employ a psychosocial understanding of authenticity and believe that both people in real life and hip-hop performers should be themselves. Men in my sample report that inauthentic and "bad" hip-hop is characterized by commercialism, mainstream appeal, and the pursuit of wealth as a primary goal. When rappers are motivated purely by money, respondents claim the art suffers, though their stated preferences and evaluations of individual artists include statements that celebrate the work and skill of many rappers who have achieved commercial success and celebrate their financial accomplishments in their songs. This contradiction between stated preference for "real" rappers who do not prioritize financial gain and an affinity for rappers such as Jay-Z illustrates that authenticity is enabled by subjective and fluid moments of connection between artist and consumer rather than static, objective qualities such as the lyrical content of texts.

While anticommercial sentiment emerges as a stated aesthetic principle for respondents, antiwhite sentiment does not. Moreover, listeners do not explicitly state that they judge the quality of a hip-hop performance based on its racial (black) authenticity. However, when data from chapter 4 are combined with data from chapter 5 about the use of the n-word, we see that natural, authentic command of black vernacular is one of the standards by which rappers are judged. So although there is no clear affirmation of racial authenticity as one of the dimensions of aesthetic appraisal, a closer look at respondents' mental maps reveals that racial realness is important to rap aesthetics. Narratives about black authenticity and white corruption of hip-hop do not present themselves in direct comments from respondents, but multiple black respondents lament stereotypic black male thug performances that have come to symbolize real blackness in hip-hop. However, these respondents do not tie the proliferation of stereotypic black thuggery to white or corporate control of hip-hop or systemic racism and express more disappointment with the black communities for allowing them to thrive.

Toughness and the ability to rhetorically dominate one's opponent are also important to aesthetics, and respondents' emphasis on domination-driven masculinity complements the textual analysis in chapters 2 and 3 as well as previous research on hip-hop as male space. While gender emerges as a subtle and implicit consideration in discussion with respondents about authenticity in chapter 4, it receives more thorough treatment in chapter 5, where interview data on the position of women in hip-hop are presented as the first of three sections on explicit content and moral panic.

Respondents across lines of race and class state that when rappers degrade women in their performances, they are insulting a specific cohort of women, a cohort that behaves dishonorably and is worthy of disrespect. None of the respondents draw explicit connections between degrading representations of women and greater systems of gender oppression. Further, men in my sample report that women who participate in objectionable representations bear a significant amount of the blame for their debasement, because they freely choose to participate in their humiliation. Data also reveal implicit connections between commercial/inauthentic rap and feminine aesthetics, as they suggest that women enjoy low-quality rap music more than men and have trouble recognizing the value of real hip-hop. Masculine authenticity is manifest both in rappers' construction of imposing and marketable domination-driven masculinity and in respondents' insistence on clear boundaries between male and female hip-hop engagement and appreciation.

The final section of chapter 5 focuses on thug life, gangsterism, and criminality, and respondents both support and challenge my arguments in chapters 2 and 3. Hip-hop performers' desire to project toughness is commonly understood as a major reason for the proliferation of gangster representations in rap music, which affirms the importance of domination-driven masculinity to trends in commercial hip-hop. However, respondents do not highlight collective thug caretaking and personal vulnerability as key elements of thug performance. And though there is general agreement about race-based mistreatment at the hands of the criminal justice system, there is very little emphasis on the structural and discursive context of the hyperghetto/prison as a starting point for defining thug life. Industry pressures to reenact gangster tropes are discussed as part of the reason that so many rappers act hard, and respondents are certainly skeptical about many of the claims that performers make. But on the whole, respondents do not advance the notion that a white patriarchal corporate machine is actively producing these insulting representations of black masculinity in order to reinforce racist ideologies and racial inequality.

This summary of findings should not be read as a denunciation of the many convincing arguments about the ways industry structures and the dynamics of hegemony influence representations of blackness in American popular culture. Rather, this book shows that these arguments have not made an especially deep impression on the everyday listeners I interviewed.

This study is not designed to make sweeping, categorical generalizations about racial differences, but a crude breakdown of the most significant similarities and differences between the mental maps of black and white respondents looks something like the following.

Similarities

· Respondents from both racial groups love and understand hip-hop. They have similar schemas for evaluating rap music and a special appreciation for signifying, wordplay, and layered meaning as an aesthetic principle.

- Respondents from both groups use hip-hop in diverse ways as emotional technology and as a means for understanding themselves and their worlds.
- Neither group of respondents advances a firm understanding of the proliferation of objectionable representations of blackness in commercially successful hip-hop primarily as an outcome of white patriarchal oppression of people of color.
- Neither group of respondents prioritizes the political economy of the music industry as a driving explanation for trends in commercially successful hip-hop.
- Both groups of respondents sorely lack voices that offer a feminist analysis of gendered subjects in commercially successful hip-hop.

Differences

- Black respondents use hip-hop to understand themselves as racialized subjects and to interpret race-related experiences. Whites do not report such uses.
- Black respondents make racially derived collective ownership claims about hip-hop, indicating a correspondence between their collective racial identity and their membership as part of a hip-hop community. White respondents do not make ownership claims, and data do not point to correspondence between their racial identity and hip-hop identity.
- Black respondents are sensitive to, and reflexive about, the ways black people are portrayed in and affected by commercial hip-hop representations. In general, white respondents are hesitant to discuss the racial significance of these representations. Though both groups are skeptical about authenticity claims, black respondents' skepticism leads to a more focused discussion about the stereotypes of black coolness and thug life.

Methodological and Theoretical Contributions

With so many academic studies of hip-hop's history, content, and cultural significance already available, the major contribution of this book is its emphasis on the voices of everyday hip-hop fans. Other researchers have studied the substantive topics I cover, and a number of hip-hop studies rely on ethnography and qualitative data drawn from researchers' interactions with respondents. However, this study is rife with excerpts from my in-depth interviews, and respondents are presented not merely as data sources but as analysts who both undercut and reinforce my own take on the issues at hand.

While this book represents a meaningful contribution, with justification for its interview methodology and a manageable range of topics addressed, its value is significantly diminished if the research model is not improved and expanded to tap other groups of people who engage hip-hop and make it their own. In the interest of comparative feasibility, my respondent sample is restricted by gender, sexuality, age range, race, and region. There is ample reason to conduct similar interview studies by sampling with concentrated attention to at least three other identity markers.

The first of these is gender and sexuality. Part of the reason for exempting women from this study is that studies of and conversations about gender are typically considered feminist territory, and in order to reveal the power and problems of masculinity, it is vital to study men's gendered understandings of themselves and their social worlds. But studying masculinity and sexuality without attention to gay, lesbian, bisexual, and transgendered people constitutes a conspicuous blind spot. Additionally, in privileging men's voices, my study further marginalizes women from discussions of popular hip-hop, a world where they are already considered second-class citizens. A comparative or exploratory study of women's interpretations and understandings is desperately needed, as is a book-length study of nonstraight hip-hop communities.

Second, hip-hop is traditionally treated as a youth movement, thanks to the age of the majority of its consumers and those who founded the culture. However, hip-hop music began in America roughly forty years ago, and we can no longer treat it as exclusively youth culture with so many hip-hop listeners over the age of thirty. It would be useful to focus on older hip-hop loyalists to reveal generational diversity and distinction, but it is perhaps more pressing that we study people under eighteen years of age who engage today's hip-hop in all its commercial and commoditized glory. It could be argued that focusing on young people's interpretations would only validate much of the moral panic surrounding hip-hop, which is most harmful for children who "don't know any better." Despite this danger, there is legitimate reason to investigate young people's interpretations of hip-hop performances, considering the emphasis on authenticity within hip-hop circles. Many of the respondents in this book cannot discuss authenticity without stating their skepticism of "keep it real" claims as a qualifier for their analysis. Men in my study know that the cars and jewelry in music videos are often rented and that the outlandish claims made by rappers are artistic embellishments. It is conceivable that younger people do not make these distinctions, but it is possible to study the same set of questions without stirring up moral panic.

Finally, styles of hip-hop and hip-hop tastes differ by region, as do discourses of race, class, and gender. Studies conducted with more locally specific samples (for example, one specific urban or suburban tract or neighborhood) or in different geographic sectors of comparable size are sure to produce different data sets. More broadly, this book is focused explicitly on the American context, ignoring the international scale and scope of hip-hop as a social and corporate movement. It would be useful to study the American context as a case for comparison, especially when one considers the global influence of American popular culture and the likelihood that hip-hop listeners in other nations make such comparisons for themselves as they reckon with hip-hop's American-ness. Additional intrigue springs from the centrality of language and signifying to hip-hop appreciation and appraisal. Hip-hop studies outside of the United States have much to teach us about the significance of signifying within other linguistic and rhetorical communities and how those unfamiliar with both English and American cultural references derive their appreciation for globally celebrated MCs like 50 Cent and Jay-Z.

I hope that the utility of interview methodology is evident, and I would be doubly pleased if this book might serve as a humble example of the ways textual and qualitative analysis can be usefully paired. As noted in the introduction, I am sensitive to the shortcomings of purely textual analysis, especially where hip-hop is concerned. Treating texts as inanimate objects, unaffected by human performance, reception, and interpretation is dangerous analytic practice. When researchers offer no justification for the texts they select and treat their own readings as the last word on the topic in question, their work is open to even deeper criticism. Textual analysis is utilized here to develop and communicate my understanding of commercial hip-hop in the current structural and discursive context. But my analysis is the beginning rather than the end of the project, as the ideas put forth in chapters 2 and 3 serve as points of comparison for the explanations offered by respondents. Moreover, the textual analysis chapters provide a number of theoretical frames that are used throughout.

Substantive Implications

Hip-hop retains its status as a social movement because it is so vital to both collective and personal identities. The global expansion of hip-hop combined with new communications technologies allows those in the hip-hop world to connect with each other in unprecedented ways. When we examine what brings people to hip-hop and what this imagined community shares, we find that respondents are drawn to hip-hop for many of the same reasons. It is undoubtedly true that the emphasis on domination-driven masculinity, immediate gratification, and consumption plays some role in hip-hop's command of Americans' attention. But affinity for rap music cannot be attributed purely to voyeuristic fascination, and though signifying is rooted in black vernacular tradition, respondents of all race and class categories love the work and play of rap music and relish the affect of a bangin' beat or boast.

While findings point to the things that respondents in different socio-economic and racial groups have in common, results also show that hip-hop does not eradicate inequality; dissolve race, gender, and class boundaries; or lead to liberating knowledge of self for either black or white listeners. The resilience of these boundaries is clear when we examine the ways respondents discuss race and gender. Respondents who interpret their life experiences with attention to race find reinforcement for racial thinking in their engagement with hip-hop, and those for whom race is not a primary lens do not necessarily come to race consciousness or heightened awareness of racism through hip-hop.

Though definitive statements about the effect of hip-hop on respondents' life outcomes are beyond the scope of this book, one of the strongest points we can glean from the data is that degrading and marginalizing women is a clear trend in contemporary mainstream hip-hop. Respondents' comments about the position of women in hip-hop, in combination with more subtle distinctions and connections that make up their mental maps of gender and selfhood, suggest that hip-hop enthusiasts have much to be concerned about with regard to gender relations. Heterosexual male supremacy exerts a powerful force within hip-hop communities, and respondents I spoke with are both effects and producers of this phenomenon.

The encouraging news is that everyday hip-hop listeners are not brainwashed or brain dead. Respondents think critically about the virtues and vices of the culture and reflexively about their position in it. The political significance and potential of hip-hop will always be an open question as researchers, critics, and fans debate hip-hop's influence on power relations. So far, the most convincing argument comes from Rose and others who highlight the impact of bringing hidden and marginalized transcripts into the public sphere, where they challenge and ultimately change dominant discourses of race, space, and justice. But rap music is not just significant because it comprises hidden transcripts with oppositional ideologies. Hip-hop's cultural dominance and the moral panic that surrounds it can push those who engage it toward self-examination and into discussions about race, gender, sexuality, criminal justice, materialism, and consumption. Hip-hop does not wage a cogent and directed battle against the forces of conservatism, capitalism, or racism; it is the political battlefield itself, a field of breaks, raps, sound, and fury, home to armies of all creeds and loyalties.

Obama as Hip-Hop Icon

My President is black, my Lambo is blue
And I'll be God damned if my rims ain't too.

—Young Jeezy, "My President" (2008)

In October 2007, the NAACP and a host of prominent black political figures, including Jesse Jackson, expressed their discontent about the title of rapper Nas's forthcoming album, to be called *Nigger*. Nas responded, "We're taking power away from the word. No disrespect to none of them who were part of the Civil Rights Movement, but some of my niggas in the streets don't know who Medgar Evers was . . . [T]hey know who Nas is" (quoted in Reid 2008). In July 2008, after Jackson's off-air criticism of presidential hopeful Barack Obama was captured and broadcast by Fox News, Nas took the opportunity to revisit the point, asserting, "Jesse Jackson, he's the biggest player hater . . . All you old niggas, time is up. We heard your voice, we saw your marching, we heard your sermons. We don't wanna hear that shit no more . . . We don't need Jesse; I'm here. I got this. We got *Barack*. We got [rapper/producer] David Banners. We got Young Jeezys. We're the voice now" (quoted in Reid 2008; emphasis added).

Nas's comments reveal his generational distance from the political leadership and ideology of the civil rights movement. Americans aged fifty and over, and black Americans in particular, may find this disconnect offensive and argue that it is disrespectful to Jackson and his civil rights movement compatriots. Further, the dismissive tone of Nas's statement is thought to be typical of hip-hop culture by those unfamiliar with it, an example of boisterous oppositional posturing without any discernable political agenda.

Enter Obama. The community-organizer-turned-president who played a Jay-Z song at his Iowa caucus victory party.[1] By virtue of his unique biography and historical moment, Obama bridges the black American civil rights generation and the hip-hop generation. Just as Nas lays claim to Obama by grouping him with fellow rapper Young Jeezy, Jackson's contemporaries might compare him to Martin Luther King Jr. In this and other ways, Obama stands as a symbol of political redemption.

While Obama plays the role of redeemer naturally, his reluctant turn as a hip-hop icon has been touch and go. Despite overt attempts by many rappers to adopt our president into the hip-hop fold both before and after his electoral victory, the marriage between Obama and hip-hop is an uneasy one. On the surface, hip-hop's relationship with Obama is based on the following faulty logic: Obama is a cool black celebrity, hip-hop features plenty of cool black celebrities, and therefore, Obama and hip-hop fit together. The irony here is that though faulty, this line of thought is not completely incorrect when one considers the specific character of "cool" that both Obama and hip-hop embody. Though the bond is tenuous, Obama and hip-hop are linked by the complex cool I describe in the opening chapters of this book. Its trademark is the revelation of vulnerability and complexity as the foundation of stylized luminosity and swagger. In this epilogue, I recap the ways Obama is represented by hip-hop celebrities during and immediately after his campaign, describe how Obama has positioned himself relative to mainstream American hip-hop, and explain how Obama came into his own complex coolness.

During the early stages of Obama's campaign, hip-hop celebrities' support was far from a given. In a *New York Times* interview published on April 29, 2007, founder and CEO of Def Jam Records Russell Simmons had more flattering words for John Edwards and Dennis Kucinich than for Obama. Simmons expressed doubt about the source of Obama's campaign dollars, stating that in the end, Obama was "a mouse too, like everybody else," controlled by corporate interests. Simmons was not alone—the night before Super Tuesday (February 5, 2008), 50 Cent appeared on *The O'Reilly Factor* and threw his support behind Hillary Clinton, expressing enthusiasm about the return of both Clintons to the White House. He added that he did not think the country would embrace a black president and that he feared Obama would be assassinated, though his support for Clinton was primarily based on his belief that she would perform well in the role.

Obama's hip-hop bandwagon grew crowded after the votes from Super Tuesday were tallied, following a larger trend among moderate and left-of-center voters. By the end of March, 50 Cent had switched from the Clinton camp to team Barack, citing Obama's landmark speech on race, "A More Perfect Union," as a turning point. He joined long-standing (read:

since 2007) Obama supporters such as Common and Talib Kweli, as well as those who became more boisterous in 2008 through their music, such as Young Jeezy, Nas, and Ludacris. When asked about the phenomenon of rappers' dropping Obama's name in their songs, Common stated that Obama and hip-hop were natural partners as symbols of struggle and progress, and Kweli cited Obama's youth and multiculturalism as qualities that appealed to the hip-hop generation (Hamby 2007).

Kweli also noted that the name Obama is "a nugget of lyrical gold," meaning that it is convenient and fun to use in rap lyrics (Hamby 2007). No doubt, the sound of Obama makes for convenient signifying material, but many Obama raps pack substance along with rhyme style. The most famous Obama-rap song is "My President," released by Young Jeezy in September 2008 and recorded long before Obama won the presidential election. The song features Young Jeezy and guest star Nas, and much of the content delivered by Jeezy in the first two verses has little to do with Obama himself, save a brief criticism of George W. Bush and celebration of Obama as a hopeful figure. The now famous chorus, which begins, "My president is black," seems similarly distant from the realm of the political, though it constitutes a prescient example of the subtle mechanisms that link Obama with coolness. Jeezy raps:

> My president is black
> My Lambo is blue
> And I'll be God damned if my rims ain't too.

Obama's blackness is thus constructed as trendy and hip, as his racial composition complements Jeezy's blue Lamborghini with blue custom wheels. Further, Jeezy's exhortation that he will be "God damned" if his rims don't match the Lambo (and the president) is meant to communicate the pride he takes in achieving coolness, which is linked to his own blackness, as well as Obama's, through the stylin' and stuntin' hip-hop tradition.

Nas's verse on "My President" is more explicitly attentive to the politics of race, as he raps, "My history, black history / No president ever did shit for me." The verse continues, cautioning Obama not to let his ego get the best of him and imploring the president not to forget where he came from. Nas repeats his call for Obama to remain accountable to African Americans on a solo effort entitled "Black President" (2008), released after Obama was elected. "Black President" contains vocal samples from Obama himself ("They said this day would never come"), and from Tupac Shakur ("Though it seems heaven sent / We ain't ready to have a black president").

The second verse of "Black President" is dedicated entirely to Obama, and in addition to calling for accountability, Nas imagines Obama's fear that the president might become the target of violence and touches on Obama's capacity to spur interracial empathy.

The range of content in Obama-rap songs includes celebrations of Obama as a trendy and politically promising figure as well as calls for presidential accountability and realism about how much change he is capable of bringing. Very few songs served as unofficial campaign advertisements for Obama during his White House run, but one such song by Ludacris, entitled "Politics (Obama Is Here)" (2008), set off a political firestorm the Obama team felt compelled to respond to. The track is just over two minutes long and contains only one verse. Ludacris begins by bragging about Obama's admission that Luda is one of the artists on the president's iPod, and the general theme of the song is that an Obama victory is unavoidable. In the course of this boast-filled prognostication, Ludacris chides Jesse Jackson for his aforementioned appearance on Fox News and takes potshots at Obama's chief adversaries. He dismisses Hillary Clinton ("Hillary hated on you so that bitch is irrelevant") and John McCain ("don't belong in any chair unless he's paralyzed") before referring to George W. Bush as "mentally handicapped."

The Obama team reacted with swiftness and severity to the release of the song, as campaign spokesman Bill Burton issued the following statement on July 30, 2008:

> As Barack Obama has said many, many times in the past, rap lyrics today too often perpetuate misogyny, materialism and degrading images that he doesn't want his daughters or any children exposed to. This song is not only outrageously offensive to Senator Clinton, Senator McCain and President Bush, it is offensive to all of us who are trying to raise our children with the values we hold dear. While Ludacris is a talented individual, he should be ashamed of these lyrics. (quoted in Yao 2008)

This statement is among the most extreme invocations of hip-hop as cause for moral panic by Obama or his representatives during the campaign. The president consistently displayed enough knowledge of hip-hop events and personalities to build connections with young voters, all the while maintaining a politically astute detachment from the hip-hop generation as someone more musically identified with rhythm and blues and soul music. In his interview for the cover story of *Vibe* magazine with hip-hop journalist Jeff Chang, Obama explains, "You know I haven't been buying new music lately. Because I don't have time. Look, I'm impacted by my generation. Most of my iPod probably is either jazz classics—Coltrane, Miles Davis—or it's got the songs of my youth . . . But every once in a while I will find something that's out right now that moves me, and then I'll pull that down" (quoted in Chang 2007).

For someone who merely dabbles in hip-hop, Obama demonstrates admirable command of its current trends, promise, and pitfalls. At a rally in Georgia, he told younger audience members, "Maybe you are the next Lil' Wayne, but probably not, in which case you need to stay in school."[2] Perhaps his most celebrated hip-hop shout out came in April 2008, when he paused to brush his shoulders off in the middle of a speech in order to indicate that he is unfazed by critics, coolly signifying the hip-hop dance move from Jay-Z's "Dirt off Your Shoulder" (2003). Obama has been unafraid to comment on hip-hop controversies, as he acknowledges the argument that moral panic over language in hip-hop serves as a distraction from the social conditions that produce the performers who might use such language. At the same time, he laments the celebration of materialism and casual sex in representations that emphasize immediate gratification rather than values that are helpful in achieving social mobility. Obama states that not only is hip-hop a reflection of reality, in some cases it shapes reality, and for that reason it is something worth paying attention to, even if he has more pressing items on his agenda as a public servant (Chang 2007).

But why should this basic command of hip-hop confirm Obama as a hip-hop icon when he never suggests that he identifies with the hip-hop generation, or with hip-hop itself? In addition to the unlikely possibility that hip-hop community members applaud Obama purely on the basis of his political positions, another explanation is that regardless of whether Obama identifies with the hip-hop generation, hip-hoppers identify with him because of his age. In truth, there are multiple hip-hop generations, but it is fair to assume that the vast majority of people who engage hip-hop on a regular basis are under the age of thirty-five. According to exit polls, Obama won 66 percent of the votes from people aged eighteen to twenty-nine, a landslide margin by historical standards.[3] If hip-hop is largely the domain of people under thirty, hip-hop listeners (including famous rappers) may simply find it easier to see themselves in a forty-seven-year-old candidate than in John McCain, who was seventy-one at the time of the election.

I want to suggest that it is not only Obama's age but also his biography and personal affect that made him an instant hip-hop celebrity. The explanation is not simply that hip-hop is a black art form, Obama is black, and racial loyalty or solidarity catapulted him to the top of the hip-hop world. Nor does a parallel story about shared underdog status fully explain hip-hop's embrace. While age, race, and underdog status are certainly components of his hip-hop appeal, Obama's *coolness* is indispensable to his status as a hip-hop icon.

Obama's narrative fits within the paradigm of complex cool, wherein exposing vulnerability and inner conflict is essential to cool performance. In his two books, *Dreams from My Father* (1995) and *The Audacity of Hope* (2006), Obama is painstakingly candid in discussing his personal struggle to reconcile his relationship with his absent father, arrive at a comfortable racial identity, and accept Christianity as his religion. *Newsweek*'s Richard Wolffe suggests that Obama's emotional detachment from the perils of public life was essential for the campaign's success. Moreover, Obama's ability to achieve and manage this detachment is born first from the distance between himself and his father and later from the distance between Obama and his white mother and grandmother as he struggled with self-doubt and came to grips with his racial identity (Wolffe 2009). As explained in chapters 2 and 3, we hear echoes of each of these struggles in the detachment, racial identity, faith, and family throughout hip-hop during the thug era, and in some cases the narratives are strikingly similar. On "December 4th" (2003), an autobiographical song by Jay-Z, the MC eerily channels Obama's experience:

> Now all the teachers couldn't reach me,
> And my momma couldn't beat me
> Hard enough to match the pain of my pop not seeing me, so
> With that disdain in my membrane
> Got on my pimp game
> Fuck the world, my defense came.

Again, the key to this coolness is not just that Obama and thug narrators showcase their personal unflappability; it is that these figures are forthright about the experiences that produce a cool response, which invalidates understandings of hip-hop coolness as a shallow and self-defeating facade. To the contrary, these performances are self-affirming, as narrators summon the courage to make their private struggles public business. The "cool" element of these performances is not simply the outward projection of detachment; it is the entire *process* that each performer goes through.

In Obama's case, the revelation of his personal flaws, struggles, and reconciliations humanized him as a candidate, an important step that allowed voters to build sincere (rather than authentic) connections between themselves and a candidate with a relatively undistinguished record as a legislator. Though hip-hop communities seem to have adopted Obama as their own, complex cool hip-hop performances are often received with less fanfare, and mainstream society seems less willing to humanize and empathize with commercially successful MCs than they are with Obama and other politicians with indiscretions on their records and skeletons in their closets. This stems in part from the fact that rap superstars strive to be larger than life and, in some ways, more than human, and it is more difficult to drum up empathy for someone bragging about his $100,000 car and endless casual sexual encounters with women. Again, we would be wise not to romanticize contemporary hip-hop's inherent political value and not to excuse objectionable performances that make commercially successful MCs susceptible to criticism. With earnest engagement of hip-hop culture, however, comes recognition of its layers, contradictions, and complexity, and even if people are not moved to empathize with Jay-Z in the same way they are moved by Obama, respect is due.

Qualitative Methodology

No idea is original
There's nothing new under the sun
It's never what you do, but how it's done.

—Nas, "No Idea's Original" (2002)

Cultural Sociology and Hip-Hop Ethnography

Both critical theorists and cultural studies scholars have taken issue with sociology, primarily because of sociology's claim to objectivism or positivism and disregard for the interpretive process. This criticism is unfounded. In qualitative sociological studies, the art of interpretation is at the center of the analytic project. First, the researcher must acknowledge his agency as an interpreter as he places the research in theoretical and historical context and interacts with the sample, and second, the ethnography itself is fundamentally about respondents' or subjects' interpretations—the goal of ethnography is to represent subjects' social worlds as clearly as possible. For political reasons, many of which I am sympathetic to, critical theory and cultural studies have consciously framed themselves as oppositional disciplines, the voices of the unheard shouted up through the ivory tower. But sound qualitative sociology about everyday cultural practices should be viewed as the best cultural studies has to offer rather than an elitist, nonreflexive antagonist.

Jason Kaufman's explication of recent developments in cultural sociology situates this book firmly within the relatively new tradition of "endogenous explanation." He explains:

The sociological approach to culture has of late backed away from a style of reasoning that presumes to explain culture through extra-cultural factors

such as social structure (DiMaggio 1982), the economics of artistic production (Peterson 1976), the institutional makeup of criticism and dissemination of the arts (Griswold 1981), and so forth. Endogenous explanations
focus instead on causal processes that occur *within* the cultural stream:
mechanisms such as iteration, modulation, and differentiation, as well as
processes of meaning making, network building, and semiotic manipula-
tion. (2004, 336)

In the introduction I recount how changes in the music industry have
changed hip-hop and how these changes relate to the types of hip-hop
criticism and concern we see today ("economics of artistic production"
and "dissemination of the arts"). In chapter 3, I describe the hyperghetto/
prison as crucial for contextualizing the content of contemporary rap lyrics ("social structure"). However, these explanations and acknowledgments
are not a comprehensive definition of what hip-hop actually means because it must be endogenously explained by those who engage it and make
it their own.

Kaufman outlines three types of endogenous explanation, two of which,
"semiology" and "post-hermeneutic cultural sociology," are central to my
research.[1] The two chapters dedicated to textual analysis (chapters 2 and 3)
are exercises in semiology. Kaufman describes semiology by discussing
what it is not. He writes, "The goal here appears to be rejection of aesthetic
historicism, or the attempt to explain the origins of various cultural products, in lieu of a self-conscious focus on semiotic patterns embedded in
those products. Sociologists in this tradition ask not *why* a specific genre of
art appears at a particular time and place but *what* the signs and symbols
embedded in that genre say about that time and place" (2004, 337). While
we need to understand and acknowledge the context in which hip-hop performances are crafted, they do not simply reproduce, describe, or symbolize those circumstances. The question is, what does hip-hop say as it speaks
in our contemporary context?

Posthermeneutic sociology "look[s] not at the values implicit in various cultural tropes but at subjects' search for meaning therein. Thus, the
central project here is to explore the psycho-semantics of perception, emotion, and meaning making on the part of socially situated individuals"
(J. Kaufman 2004, 337). The premise of this approach is that "actors do
not simply consume culture in ways that fit their predominant worldview;
they use cultural products to try and find that worldview, to construct it out
of the items in their grasp" (339–40). The in-depth interview sections of
this book grow from this premise and are expressly concerned with depict-

ing respondents' understanding of hip-hop. The research does not aim to answer questions such as "Does hip-hop cause violence?" The goal is to discover what hip-hop means to respondents and how ideas about hip-hop mesh with other ideas about life.

Tia DeNora's *Music in Everyday Life* (2000) is the best model available for such a study. DeNora is leery of semiotic approaches that suggest there is no need for ethnography or that music can be read or decoded to predict how it will influence social life, actions, emotional conditions, or judgments (DeNora 2000, 21).[2] In a book that includes both commentary on cultural sociology and a collection of interviews studying everyday listeners, DeNora builds on the foundation laid by Paul Willis (1978), exploring the ways in which music works for and shapes the identities of respondents. DeNora urges readers to recognize music as "an active ingredient of social formation" and a force capable of moving listeners from one social state—sitting and listening—to another, like dancing, or from a space of unfettered aesthetic enjoyment to a state of mental contemplation or nostalgia (2000, 7). Her study uses in-depth interviews to uncover the meanings that listeners form through music. She asks people when they choose to play music and why and what the music does for them both physically and emotionally when they access it. Data reveal that not only do people use music to change their mood at a given time—getting them in the mood to party or clean or work out—but also that "musical materials provide terms and templates for elaborating self-identity—for identity's identification" (68). For instance, one of DeNora's respondents identifies gangster rap as a type of "boy music" that she despises but is often subjected to because her boyfriend plays it when he is in the company of male friends to affirm his masculinity (116).

There is no ethnomusicological study of hip-hop that follows DeNora's lead in using in-depth interviews to foreground the voices of everyday listeners, and my research aims to fill this gap. However, as noted throughout this book, a number of important hip-hop ethnographies do exist. Cheryl Keyes's *Rap Music and Street Consciousness* (2002), a participant observation study of hip-hop culture, is one of the first book-length hip-hop ethnographies.[3] Keyes makes the distinction between traditional studies of hip-hop and their reliance on textual analysis, and ethnomusicology, which lends itself to anthropological immersion. *Rap Music and Street Consciousness* is primarily based on data collected from time spent at clubs and other concert venues. Keyes's research leads her to a number of informal interviews and conversations with artists, industry insiders, and fans, but it is primarily a participant observation rather than an interview study. As mentioned in the introduction, Joseph Schloss (2004, 2009), Ian Condry (2006), and Marcyliena Morgan (2009) are a few of the hip-hop researchers who follow Keyes's methodological lead.

Participant observation and immersion may be best suited for the goal of Keyes's valuable book, which she describes as an "attempt to capture the essence of rap music tradition by examining its cultural sensibilities within its world of beats, rhymes, and street consciousness" (xv). But participant observation is not the best method for answering my research questions because it does not always provide the sort of methodological consistency needed to draw out boundaries and differences between groups. By sticking to an interview schedule with specific probes, I am more readily able to demonstrate the extent to which patterns repeat or distinguish themselves in data from multiple respondents.

Again, this is not a dismissal of Keyes's work or the work of other ethnographers; the field has progressed by leaps and bounds thanks to the rigor and quality of their qualitative research. *Rap Music and Street Consciousness* is full of useful qualitative data, and its centrality to hip-hop studies is undisputed. I mention Keyes's book in order to distinguish mine; discussions with audience members are cited only once in Keyes's appendix and works cited sections, where she refers to a discussion with two women from one of the many concerts she attended. Keyes engages people in the hip-hop industry including promoters, record executives, DJs, and video directors, while my study focuses on listeners who may be part of one hip-hop scene or another but do not consider hip-hop to be their vocation.

A less thorough but no less important hip-hop ethnography is Greg Dimitriadis's *Performing Identity/Performing Culture* (2001). Dimitriadis situates his study in a community center that provides services for black urban youth, and he engages their hip-hop sensibilities in several ways, from informal conversations to more formal audience response sessions to hip-hop films. This methodology is more useful than Keyes's if the goal of the project is to understand how everyday consumers produce meaning from hip-hop texts. Additionally, by embedding himself in his respondents' space, Dimitriadis is able to observe friendship networks and patterns of social interaction at a collective level, which points to the importance of hip-hop culture as a significant building block of youth identity and network building. Again, I would not mention Dimitriadis's book if it were not so well executed and did not constitute such an important contribution to the field. However, the voices of the children in Dimitriadis's study fail to drive the text, as interview and conversational data are underutilized as evidence for his sound explanations of cultural theory; three of the five chapters are void of substantive ethnographic data. In contrast, the present hip-hop interview project endeavors to highlight the voices of everyday listeners who are not necessarily expert producers of hip-hop but who are equally important.

Stuart Hall's notion of encoding/decoding adds to the theoretical frame for such work. Hall argues that studying media is vital to understanding hegemony and domination because in late capitalist societies attuned to mass media, visual and musical texts are the primary means through which dominant ideologies are reproduced and disseminated and the superstructure (discursive realm of social order) is maintained (1980). Dissemination of ideas from media to the masses entails far more than passive, linear reception of unchanged messages and meanings from media producers to consumers. Meanings and messages are encoded in texts during the production phase and subsequently decoded by the various audiences who receive the texts. During encoding, dominant ideologies, those that comprise the superstructure and maintain social order, are inscribed into media texts for consumption.[4] However, during decoding, audiences receive and interpret these messages and ideologies in different ways, depending on social context. A single text encoded with languages and meaning systems that maintain social dominance may in fact be decoded in such a way that audiences draw meanings and build knowledge systems that challenge social order and social dominance.

Hall developed a typology to describe the range of readings possible for any given text. The preferred reading is the reading encoded during production, which favors the dominant ideologies and the social order. Audience members in favorable social positions who benefit from the preferred reading will produce what Hall refers to as dominant readings, which might be described as inflexible acceptance or affirmation of dominant ideologies. The second type of reading is negotiated reading, in which readers affirm dominant ideologies, or the preferred reading, to some extent but leave room to negotiate or adjust those meanings based on their social contexts. Finally, there are oppositional readings, which challenge the preferred reading not by ignoring the dominant ideologies altogether or pretending they don't exist but by deconstructing the stories or messages transmitted and building meanings that critique the social order. The implication of constructing the typology is that social position influences how one interprets texts and builds meanings. One of the questions this book tries to answer is whether white decoders, who have certain social privileges by virtue of their whiteness, produce a set of readings that is consistently and systemically different from readings produced by black respondents.

However, the question of white readings versus black readings is not the only one at stake in this project, which investigates not only how consumers interpret specific texts but also how respondents define hip-hop music more generally. Additional questions include What is hip-hop's place in consumers' lives? How do listeners evaluate the hip-hop they hear? What do listeners make of the explicit content in rap performances? and What are the categories that respondents use to draw these distinctions?

Answering these questions requires a methodology designed to sketch a wide range of meanings, and in-depth interviewing is the best method for the task. A number of sociologists concerned with qualitative methods have explained the virtues, vices, and processes of this methodology, but Michèle Lamont's discussion of in-depth interviews and boundary making is most instructive. Lamont's work is concerned with "symbolic boundaries—the types of lines that individuals draw when they categorize people—and high status signals—the keys to our evaluative distinctions" (1992, 2). Understanding consumers' hip-hop preferences as symbolic boundaries allows not only for an exploration of the symbolic meaning of hip-hop to different communities of listeners (that is, the role hip-hop plays in social identity and cultural production) but also for an investigation of taste and evaluative mechanisms—what makes good hip-hop music and how listeners arrive at their evaluative decisions.

Lamont's ultimate goal is to connect the boundary-making process to greater patterns of social inequality by looking at the social conditions within which her subjects make their distinctions. She endeavors not only to record the different boundaries that her subjects draw but to evaluate the characteristics of those boundaries in order to gauge their importance as a tool of cultural distinction.[5] This emphasis on evaluating the character of boundaries is crucial for my work as well. For instance, it would be a significant finding if hip-hop consumers consistently identify black identity as grounds for truly understanding hip-hop or being part of the hip-hop community. It is also possible that race is consistently mentioned during interviews without being an especially robust or rigid boundary and without being assigned special status as a requisite for hip-hop knowledge or experience. In both cases, we might say race exists as a boundary, but its importance to respondents' "mental maps" (Lamont 1992, 2000) and notions of self can only be determined by evaluating the context in which race is evoked during interviews. This is the essence of the theoretical frame. Lamont's aim, and mine, is "to describe the *established rules* of upholding claims or the *conventional and widely shared mental maps* that people mobilize to demonstrate an idea" (2000, 271; emphasis in original).

In the study of symbolic boundary making and the investigation of ideologies and tastes, open-ended questions are essential because the researcher can document the choices each respondent makes. An open question like "What does hip-hop mean to you?" gives respondents the opportunity to define hip-hop using any boundaries they wish. If certain boundaries are consistently affirmed and defended across a range of respondents, the researcher can confidently point to them as significant elements of respondents' mental maps and build a robust description of their character. This "small n" study is not aimed at establishing causality, nor does it make definitive statements in the spirit of public opinion surveys (such as "All whites believe x" and "All blacks believe y").

Sampling

It would be more convenient to extol the political importance of fringe, underground, or "indie" rap[6] because of the large number of explicitly political artists who are distributed by independent labels. My textual analysis in chapters 2 and 3 focuses on the most often criticized and readily available hip-hop music. In order to narrow down a collection of artists, songs, and albums to study, I draw from responses of people who listen to popular hip-hop. Data collection began on June 3, 2006, at Summer Jam, a concert sponsored by WJMN 94.5 FM Boston, a hip-hop radio station owned by Clear Channel Communications. Summer Jam is an ideal site for gathering participants because it is a multicity tour organized by Clear Channel Communications, which owns over a thousand radio stations nationwide. Clear Channel and Summer Jam epitomize the corporate takeover of hip-hop and the political stakes of such a takeover, as explained in the introduction. By drawing respondents from the crowd at Summer Jam, I tapped into a collection of consumers who chose to access commercial hip-hop and share a basic knowledge of the commercial hip-hop universe.

At the concert, I approached audience members and asked whether they were interested in participating in the study. I approached men walking alone as well as men walking in groups with either women or men. My initial question was "Do you listen to hip-hop?" If the respondents said yes, my follow up statement was "I'm a student at Harvard University doing an interview project on hip-hop music. It pays twenty dollars per interview, and each interview lasts about one hour. Do you think you might be interested?" I then asked them to write their names and either an e-mail address or phone number where I could reach them on the sign-up sheet. The sign-up sheet contained a column asking participants to jot down their favorite hip-hop act (artist) or album. My initial recruitment failed to yield forty participants, and over the next several months I repeated the recruiting process outside of the following locations:

1   In-store record signing with Method Man at the Underground Hip-Hop Store (which sells all hip-hop, not merely "underground") in Boston on August 15, 2006. Method Man, an original member of the Wu Tang Clan, has reached platinum status numerous times during his fourteen-year career as a hip-hop performer. His commercial success as a rapper has led to roles in sitcoms, feature films, and television drama series.

2   A concert featuring the Clipse in February 2007. The Clipse are under contract with Jive Records, a subsidiary of Sony. Their first album, *Lord Willin'*, was released in 2002 and moved more than 1 million units, earning them platinum selling status. Their second major-label album, *Hell Hath No Fury*, was released in 2006. The Clipse's biggest hit, "Grindin'" (2002), spent over a year on the *Billboard* Hot 100 chart, peaking at number one.

3   Hip-hop nightclubs in Boston. I went on eight recruiting trips to Boston night clubs during the spring of 2007. These clubs shared many of the characteristics of the concert, as they played hip-hop music and attracted a range of hip-hop fans and featured DJs with their own shows on JAM'N (WJMN) 94.5. During recruiting, I did not enter the clubs but waited to recruit visitors as they exited at the end of the night.

4   The Dub Magazine Custom Auto Show and Concert, which took place on July 15, 2007, at the Bayside Expo Center in Boston. *Dub* is an "automotive lifestyles magazine" featuring articles and photographs that highlight the latest trends in custom automotive art and culture. The 2007 concert featured exclusively hip-hop acts, including platinum-selling Bone Thugs-N-Harmony and Rich Boy, both under contract with Universal. Rich Boy's smash hit "Throw Some D's" peaked at number six on the *Billboard* Hot 100 chart in 2006, while Bone Thugs-N-Harmony won an American Music Award in 1999 and produced a string of hits and platinum records in the late 1990s and early 2000s before reappearing on the commercial hip-hop scene in 2006.

5   Finally, I turned to a snowball sampling method, asking those who had been interviewed if they had any friends who might be interested in taking part in the study. Snowball sampling through referral in this case does not pose a methodological problem, as the sample is not designed to be random, and I do not aim to produce a prescriptive and generalizable set of results. Additionally, there are theoretical justifications for snowball sampling, discussed below.

I have explained my decision to focus on the race/gender categories chosen, but age and class also present themselves as key concerns. The interview sample consists of black and white men between the ages of eighteen and twenty-nine. The eighteen-year-old age minimum addresses a practical concern, as it allows for greater ease in obtaining consent from participants. Another reason to focus on this age demographic is hip-hop's history. I am interested in hip-hop music beginning in the mid-1990s, which excludes audience members who came to hip-hop too recently. For instance, a fifteen-year-old consumer born in 1991 might not have come to hip-hop until 2002, which would leave him with a far more limited range of hip-hop knowledge than someone who has followed hip-hop's commercial ascent through gangster rap and into the criminality phase.

This white-versus-black power dynamic also mandates that my sample be theoretically driven. That is, I am investigating the extent to which social boundaries such as spatial location and economic status influence respondents' symbolic boundaries (ideologies, tastes, and evaluative mechanisms). In the process of collecting subjects, I had to ensure that a significant portion of the black men I interviewed had experience as residents of depressed or working-class urban neighborhoods, in which concentrated poverty and an absence of social organization lead to high rates of street crime, police surveillance, and incarceration. Conversely, a significant portion of my white respondents are from communities that do not suffer from the neighborhood conditions that produce social disorganization in ghettos. In order to make sure I collected respondents from each of these groups, I used snowball sampling, asking for referrals from respondents on the initial sign-up lists. Subjects' social networks are most likely to include people in similar socioeconomic and spatial locations, and for this reason snowball sampling proved extremely effective. Because my aim is to sketch the full range of boundaries used when discussing hip-hop music, my sampling net is cast wide enough to include people who reside in a variety of socioeconomic locations, but again, the political underpinnings of the project dictate that I make sure to include the two aforementioned groups, whites of socioeconomic privilege and blacks of socioeconomic disadvantage.

The Universe of Hip-Hop Music

In total, 115 respondents signed up to be participants in the research project, and 74 listed a favorite artist or hip-hop group (some listed more than one). The final list of performers from the sign-up sheet appears below. Artists are listed alphabetically, and if they were mentioned more than once, the number of mentions appears in parentheses. In addition to recording the mentions of individual artists, I tallied the number of times artists from a group, clique, or camp, or the camp itself, was mentioned as a favorite. So if someone mentioned 50 Cent, who is a member of G-Unit, as a favorite, 50 Cent is tallied once and G-Unit is tallied once as well.

Artists Listed on Sign-Up Sheet
Aesop Rock
AZ
Beanie Sigel
Big Tymers
Black Milk
Cam'ron (3)
Cassidy
Chamillionaire
The Clipse
The Coup
The Diplomats (3)
Dougie Fresh, El-P
Fabolous (2)
50 Cent (2)
Gille Da Kid
Immortal Technique
J Dilla (2)
Jadakiss
Jay-Z (11)
Juelz Santana
Kanye West
Lil' Wayne
Little Brother
LL Cool J
Lloyd Banks
Ludacris (3)
Method Man (3)
MF Doom
Mobb Deep (3)
Mos Def
Nas (8)
Notorious B.I.G. (7)

Papoose (3)
Project Pat
Rick Ross
The Roots
Styles P (3)
Talib Kweli (2)
Three 6 Mafia
T.I.
Tupac (2)
Wu Tang Clan

Camps/Cliques/Groups by Number of Mentions
(7 mentions) The Diplomats (Cam'ron, Jim Jones, Juelz Santana, Hell Rell, Freaky Zeaky, JR Writer, Duke Da God)
(6) G-Unit (50 Cent, Lloyd Banks, Young Buck,[7] Tony Yayo, DJ Whoo Kid)
(4) The Lox (Jadakiss, Styles P, Sheek Louch)
(4) Wu Tang Clan (RZA, GZA, Old Dirty Bastard, Inspektah Deck, Raekwon the Chef, U God, Ghostface Killah, Method Man, Cappadonna)
(2) Cash Money (Lil' Wayne, Baby, Birdman, Mannie Fresh, Juvenile, Big Tymers)

In addition to this list, I compiled unprompted mentions of artists during interviews with respondents. In order to be counted on the list below, the artist must be introduced by the respondent during the interview without any prior reference by me, and the artist must be different from the artist listed as a favorite by the respondent on the sign-up sheet. Additionally, the artist must be mentioned in the context of contemporary hip-hop rather than as an example of an artist from previous eras. Where applicable, negative or disparaging comments about the artist are noted.

Artists Mentioned in Interviews
Aesop Rock (1)
Akon (1)
Akrobatic (1)
AZ (2)
Beanie Sigel (1)
Benzino (1)
Bone Thugs-N-Harmony (2)
Cam'ron (4)
Cannibal Ox (1)

Chamillionaire (3 total, 3 negative)

The Clipse (7 total, 1 negative)

Common (3)

D4L (2 total, 2 negative)

De La Soul (1)

Dead Prez (3)

DMX (5)

Dose 1 (1)

Dr. Dre (5)

El-P (1)

Eminem (5)

Fabolous (2)

Fat Joe (3 total, 1 negative)

50 Cent (17 total, 5 negative)

Foxy Brown (2)

Franchise Boys (1 total, 1 negative)

G-Unit (20 total, 6 negative)

The Game (2)

Gang Starr (1)

Ghostface Killah (1)

Hell Rell (1)

Hurricane Chris (1)

Ice T (1)

Ja Rule (3 total, 3 negative)

Jay-Z (18 total, 1 negative)

JR Writer (1)

Juelz Santana (1)

Kanye West (6)

Kool G Rap (1)

KRS-One (4)

Lauryn Hill (2 total, 1 negative)

Lil' John (1)

Lil' Kim (2)

Lil' Wayne (5)

Little Brother (1)

LL Cool J (4)

Lloyd Banks (1 total, 1 negative)

The Lox (4)

Ludacris (4 total, 2 negative)

Master P (1)

MC Lyte (1)
Method Man (3)
MF Doom (1)
Mobb Deep (5)
Mos Def (4)
Mike Jones
Mims (2 total, 1 negative)
Missy Elliot (1)
Mystikal (1 total, 1 negative)
Nas (12)
Nelly (2 total, 2 negative)
The Neptunes (3)
Notorious B.I.G. (10)
N.W.A. (2)
Old Dirty Bastard (2)
P. Diddy (2)
Papoose (2)
Paul Wall (1 total, 1 negative)
Q-Tip (1)
Queen Latifah (2)
Rakim (1)
Redman (2)
Rich Boy (1)
Rick Ross (2)
Scarface (2)
Sean Price (1)
Snoop Doggy Dogg (6)
Styles P (3)
Swizz Beatz (1)
Talib Kweli (5 total, 1 negative)
Tech N9ne (1)
Three 6 Mafia (4)
T.I. (5 total, 1 negative)
Timbaland (3)
T-Pain (3)
Tupac Shakur (9)
Ying Yang Twins (1 negative)
Young Buck (1)
Young Jeezy (3)
Yung Joc (1)

Camps/Cliques/Groups by Number of Mentions in Interviews
(19) G-Unit
(13) The Diplomats
(8) Wu Tang Clan
(6) Cash Money
(1) Hieroglyphics

The analysis presented in chapters 2 and 3 focuses exclusively on texts produced by the artists on these lists with the exception of excerpts from Memphis Bleek and Trick Daddy. Though these two artists were not mentioned by respondents, the song I discuss that features them also features T.I., who was mentioned repeatedly and is a major figure in contemporary hip-hop. Further, both Memphis Bleek and Trick Daddy have enjoyed considerable commercial exposure and success. Trick Daddy boasts two albums with platinum status, and Memphis Bleek has reached number one on the *Billboard* Hip-Hop/R 'n' B charts with multiple albums and appears on a variety of other platinum efforts, most frequently with Jay-Z, who plays a role in the reading I give.

The textual sample is primarily concerned with artists who claim East Coast cities as their home. It is fair to say that there are four basic regions commonly understood to make up the hip-hop landscape: East Coast, which includes northeastern cities such as New York, Philadelphia, and Boston; the South, which extends east from Texas to the East Coast and generally excludes areas north of Virginia; the Midwest, where Saint Louis and Chicago are the most relevant cities; and the West Coast, which includes rappers from California and the Pacific Northwest. Considering that the sample is drawn exclusively from respondents near the Boston metropolitan area, the East Coast bias is not surprising and is consistent with other research about the importance of geography and musical taste.[8] However, one of the reasons I recruited at the sites I chose is that concerts such as Summer Jam and the Dub Magazine Auto Show are multicity, multiregion shows, which strengthens the case that there is a core group of commercially successful hip-hop artists who occupy the center of the national hip-hop universe despite regional differences in taste.

The Interview Schedule

The list of questions used for the forty in-depth interviews appears below. I begin each interview with a consent script. Rather than immediately asking questions that force respondents to think hard about aesthetic criteria or boundaries between artists and genres, I ask them to start by telling me about early musical experiences. Each respondent is considered the undisputed authority on his own life experience. Starting with questions along these lines—questions designed to help the respondent realize that he is, in fact, the expert, despite the interviewer's research credentials—sets a positive tone for the interview, as one of the goals is to allow the respondent to speak freely and authoritatively about hip-hop.

I then move to the hip-hop-specific questions that are most pertinent to this book, before closing with more personal biographical questions, which are easier to discuss having established a comfortable rapport. The best interviews unfold as natural conversations, with probes, follow-up questions, and requests for elaboration that may bleed into other questions and disturb the order listed below. Put differently, the schedule is a rough guide designed to make sure the interviewer does not skip any topics, but other than the beginning and end of the interview, the exact order of the questions is subject to the trajectory of the conversation.

Are you at least eighteen years of age?

Do you consent to having portions of this taped interview included in an ethnographic research project designed to investigate listeners' interpretation of hip-hop performance?

Do you consent to portions of this interview being published as part of my dissertation project, and possibly in the future as part of a book or journal article?

Do you understand that you do not have to answer any questions you don't want to, and if you feel uncomfortable, you are welcome to take a break or suspend the interview?

For your privacy, identifying information will be changed during transcription, and the tapes will be destroyed after transcription is complete. All tapes will be stored in a lock box in my home until they are destroyed. I am the only one who will ever have access to the original materials.

When do you remember first starting to listen to music on your own?

What kind of music was it?

How were you introduced to hip-hop?

Do you remember the first album or song you bought?

The most recent album you bought?

How do you decide which music to buy? Where do you usually buy music?

What is your favorite type of music?

How often do you listen to hip-hop?

How would you define hip-hop?

What does hip-hop mean to you?

Do you think other people share your definition?

If someone describes themselves as hip-hop by saying, "I'm hip-hop, my style is hip-hop style," what does that mean?

What makes hip-hop different from other music?

Are there different types of hip-hop? (Probe each type: what are the things that make X different from Y?)

Do you like one type more than others?

Do you listen to one type more than others?

What makes a hip-hop song or album a good record?

How do you know good music when you hear it?

When and where do you listen to hip-hop (radio, TV, concert, in your home on a CD, etc.)?

What is it like to be at a hip-hop concert or club? How do you feel in these places?

Do you have any favorite hip-hop artists/songs/albums? What makes them your favorite?

Do your favorites make you feel differently than other music?

What are these artists/songs/albums about?

You mentioned (X) as one of your favorite rappers/songs/albums when you originally signed up. What makes this rapper/song/album one of your favorites?

Can you think of a specific song that you really like, either by artist X, or by someone else, and tell me what you like about it? (If he can't come up with a song, suggest a song and provide lyrics.)

Can you think of a song/artist/album that you dislike? What is it that makes you dislike it?

Do you watch music videos? On which channels? Which shows do you prefer?

Do you have a favorite music video? What makes the video good?

Is there such a thing as a hip-hop movie? Can you think of one that you like or dislike? Why?

Describe how you dress. Is it hip-hop?

Do your friends listen to hip-hop?

What do they enjoy about hip-hop?

What does "keep it real" mean when rappers say it? Where did it come from? Can you think of a rapper/group who says it frequently? Do you use this phrase in your daily life?

Are some rappers more "real" than others?

What does "thug" mean when rappers say it? Where . . .? Can you . . .? Do you?

What does "gangster" mean when rappers say it? Where . . .? Can you . . .?
Do you?

What does "bitch" mean when rappers say it? Where . . .? Can you . . .?
Do you?

What does the n-word mean when rappers say it? Where . . .? Can you . . .?
Do you?

What does most of America think about hip-hop? What makes you say that?

What do you think are the common critiques of hip-hop? Are they valid?

Is there anything about hip-hop that bothers you?

Do you want to change the things you don't like? How would you do that?

What is your occupation?

Other than your primary job, do you have any other hobbies or activities that
you do on a regular basis? How did you get involved?

Describe your neighborhood for me. What was it like growing up?

What are your parents' or guardians' occupations?

What was your school like? What schools have you gone to? (Probe for level of
education.)

What race do you consider yourself?

How would you describe yourself politically?

Interview Data Analysis

I analyzed interviews using ATLAS.ti, a computer program that allows users
to store large collections of interview transcripts, systematically code interview data, and identify patterns and networks of data points. I knew that
many of the topics of interest that would ultimately appear in my dissertation (and later in this book) were directly targeted by the questions on my
interview schedule, and this fact, in combination with what is a relatively
small sample size, enabled me to use focused coding at the outset of the
project and work deductively. For example, I could begin with the premise that hip-hop authenticity has something to with black authenticity and
then code all interview data for instances where respondents discussed
race while discussing authenticity. The richness and diversity of responses
within this "race and authenticity" code then forced me to recode using an
inductive approach within this data subset, as specific data points, such as
skepticism about authenticity, forced a reconsideration of the initial deduc-
tive code (hip-hop authenticity = racial authenticity).

Researchers who work with in-depth interviews frequently experience
remorse upon completion of a project because we know that ultimately
we are only able to include a fraction of the touching and poignant con-

tributions offered by our respondents. I collected dozens of pages of data about personal musical history, the notion of genre, hip-hop film, and myriad other topics that, in the end, did not serve the purposes of this book. Though I regret that I was unable to present more of what my respondents had to say, I know that I am richer for their contributions, and I thank them sincerely.

NOTES

INTRODUCTION

1. Quoted in Jeffreys (1995).
2. Hip-hop enthusiasts will note that I do not include graffiti as one of the core elements of hip-hop, though it is often linked to MC-ing, DJ-ing, and b-boying as a cornerstone of hip-hop expression. Gregory Snyder (2009) locates the beginnings of the graffiti subculture well before hip-hop was born and emphasizes the diversity of graffiti writers in both their racial and ethnic demographics and their connections to musical taste communities. Marcyliena Morgan (2009) makes a similar argument about the distinction between hip-hop and graffiti subcultures in Los Angeles.
3. I'm thinking specifically of Henry Chalfant (photographer and codirector of the 1982 graffiti documentary *Style Wars*), Michael Holman (club promoter), and Fab Five Freddy, who each connected graffiti to MC-ing, DJ-ing, and b-boying in at least one instance. Fab Five Freddy does so in the 1982 film *Wild Style*, directed by Charlie Ahearn, the first hip-hop movie that prominently featured all four elements as related practices.
4. Quoted in Chang (2005, 130).
5. Throughout the book, I use the term *hip-hop* both to describe the greater cultural phenomenon and as another term for rap music. During interviews, I ask respondents first to describe and define hip-hop and then to talk about rap music specifically. Commercially successful hip-hop music of the sort discussed both by me and the respondents throughout the book is rap music.
6. This quotation comes from Mark Anthony Neal's 2005 article "Rhythm and Bullshit," published online at PopMatters.com. The majority of the "Culture for Sale" section, about record industry history and the commercialization of hip-hop, is a summary of Neal's piece. For his arguments about the changing nature of rhythm and blues as a genre, the cultural significance of these developments, and further reading on this topic, see the entire essay at http://popmatters.com/music/features/050603-randb.shtml.
7. Neal (2005). I would be remiss if I failed to mention the collection of articles and essays on the relationship between hip-hop and big radio written by longtime DJ and hip-hop journalist extraordinaire Davey D. For a bibliography, see http://www.daveyd.com/hiphopradiodirectory.html.

8. 50 Cent made this statement at a press conference during the BET Awards nominations show on March 16, 2007, http://www.hiphopdx.com/index/news/id.5251/title.50-cent-t-i-respond-to-critics (accessed April 10, 2007).

9. Tricia Rose expresses similar apprehension about resurrecting the black/white dichotomy in her 2008 book, *The Hip-Hop Wars*.

10. Cosby has repeatedly attacked hip-hop for glorifying violence, degrading women, and encouraging a general disregard for self-respect among young black people. See, for example, Cosby and Poussaint (2007).

11. Since the debut of *The O'Reilly Factor* on the Fox News network in 1996, O'Reilly has publicly lambasted a number of rappers, including Cam'ron, Ludacris, Nas, and Snoop Dogg.

12. Joseph Schloss (2009, 6) expertly highlights two ideal cases of this phenomenon, in Whitlock's 2007 article about hip-hop and misbehavior among football players and Douglas's 2008 piece about disgraced Detroit mayor Kwame Kilpatrick.

13. Mitchell cites Peter Jackson (1989) as the primary source of this formulation of cultural politics.

14. Those who have made related arguments or addressed related topics of hip-hop commodification/resistance include Baker (1993), Rose (1994), Potter (1995), Martinez (1997), Neal (1998), Boyd (2002), Forman (2002), Keyes (2002), Kitwana (2002), Queeley (2003), Perry (2004), Quinn (2005), and Watkins (2005) among others.

15. "Textual" refers to the lyrics and rhetorical strategies employed by rappers as well as the musical samples and images that accompany hip-hop performances. Whether it takes the form of a song, music video, or album cover, a text contains signs and symbols that we read and draw meaning from.

16. Stuart Hall (1996) argues that Antonio Gramsci's notion of hegemony cannot be understood in opposition to "counterhegemony" because hegemony refers to the social order as a whole. In other words, hegemony is simply the way things are in a late capitalist society informed by mass media, and to be outside of hegemony, or "counterhegemonic," is to be somehow outside of society, which requires a rather extreme poststructuralist/deconstructionist worldview. My use of "hegemonic and counterhegemonic" follows Rose (1994), who uses these terms to point out the potential of a text to insidiously reproduce and maintain power relations to the detriment of structurally disempowered speakers and performers who understand hip-hop production as an act of resistance.

17. The ideas in this paragraph spring from Henry Louis Gates Jr. (1988) as well as Russell A. Potter (1995) and Imani Perry (2004), who are among those who have most effectively employed Gates's theory in analyses of hip-hop. Gates is careful to point out, however, that the tale of the "Signifying Monkey," from which his Afro-American literary theory is derived, should not be read as "a simple allegory of the black's political oppression" (1988, 55), despite its political implications. The foundation for this work on the importance of signifying to black vernacular is laid mostly by linguists and ethnographers such as Thomas Kochman (1972), William Labov (1972), Claudia Mitchell-Kernan (1972), Geneva Smitherman (1981, 1986), and Marcyliena Morgan (2002), who explore the subject in great depth.

18. Christopher Small (1998) and Antoine Hennion (2001) are two scholars who insist and elaborate on this "performative" understanding of music, and Adam Krims (2000) raises similar concerns specifically with regard to rap music. It is crucial to point out the distinction between "performativity" as it pertains to identity, and

"performativity" as it pertains to the cultural study of music. Performativity as a theoretical concept developed by gender theorist Judith Butler (1990) refers to the phenomenon whereby bodily postures, speech acts, styles, and gestures come to make up one's social identity. Identity and the self are thus continuously and unconsciously performed rather than prescribed by one's social category or a universal law of the autonomous and individualized "self." Performativity in the sense used by the aforementioned music scholars is related to Butler's understanding in that meaning is contingent and process driven and not stabilized by the "truth of the text." But traditionally the emphasis on performance in cultural studies of music is not primarily aimed at redefining the individual or the self but at reconsidering music and our relationship to it.

19. Hip-hop texts are contingent upon the musical score or sounds they mesh with and the instruments or technology available and chosen at the time of song production. But more importantly, hip-hop texts are contingent upon sociohistorical (the rise of the postindustrial city and hypercarceral American state) and discursive (hip-hop history and tropes of hip-hop performance like masculine boasting, signifying, metaphoric violence, etc.) contexts.

20. Again, it is not my intent to buttress the myth that hip-hop is a purely black cultural phenomenon.

CHAPTER ONE

1. Erin Trapp builds on Watkins's work, arguing that hip-hop is a social movement with the ability to both "push" and "pull" marginalized participants into the public sphere. The movement "*push*(es) political systems and mainstream culture in the direction of a subgroup," in this case, African American youth (2005, 1483). On the flip side, hip-hop artists "are leaders of a social movement who *pull* and shape identity in their community and foment action for social change" (1483). That is, the push element changes greater society—the world that lies beyond the collective, which must adjust to hip-hoppers' collective action. Simultaneously, the pull element transforms those in the movement by virtue of their inclusion in the collective.

2. I have taken slight liberty with Craig Calhoun's argument here, as he does not directly refer to racial and ethnic minorities in the section of the text from which this excerpt is drawn. However, he is largely concerned with social movements of marginalized groups and writes that "this tends to deflect attention away from those movements concerned largely with values, norms, language, identities, and collective understandings—including those of movement participants themselves" (1995, 176).

3. The crucial passage reads, "Language, the body, dramatic forms are, in a way, both raw material and tools. Symbolic creativity is more fully the practice, the making—or their essence, what all practices have in common, what drives them. This is the production of *new* (however small the shift) meanings intrinsically attached to feeling, to energy, to excitement and psychic movement . . . Symbolic creativity may be individual and/or collective. It transforms what is provided and helps to produce specific forms of human identity and capacity. Being human—human being-ness—means to be creative in the sense of remaking the world for ourselves as we make and find our own place and identity" (Willis 1990, 11).

4. My argument here is *not* that identity itself springs from within us and outside structures, cultures, and discourses are irrelevant. We draw on, and are affected by,

structures, cultures, and discourses as social forces and stimuli as we construct and perform who we are. This *ability to draw from the outside world, to be bricoleurs and sculptors of the self,* is symbolic creativity.

5. This issue is taken up more fully in chapter 4.

6. For the sake of historical accuracy, it bears repeating that hip-hop has always been a multiracial culture, including during the period of its genesis, when many of the major figures from the 1970s hip-hop scene were Latino.

7. Though he mistakes the name of the track, Sean is referring to Rick Ross's "Hustlin'" (2006).

8. The connection between the idea of "real life" and authenticity in hip-hop is an important one and will be explored more fully in chapter 4.

9. It is equally erroneous to argue that hip-hop is "truly" a social critique for the purpose of resisting oppression.

CHAPTER TWO

1. Quoted in Golden (1994, 19). This quotation from Golden also appears in Mark Anthony Neal's *New Black Man* (2005), and I am indebted to Neal for unearthing it.

2. 50 Cent, "Hate It or Love It" (2005).

3. While "hustling" may refer to any number of labor choices within the illegitimate economy, the importance of the drug economy in particular and notions of social isolation are well established in ethnographic work focused on the postindustrial American ghetto. See, for example, Wilson (1996) and Venkatesh (2000).

4. I do not argue that the examples from this song reconfigure "negative" ghetto signs and symbols into "positive" ones. The point is that the tales of poverty, drug dealing, and violence portrayed in the song and video congeal into something more than a painful lamentation about living in the ghetto.

5. Elijah Anderson describes this territorial practice in *Streetwise* (1990, 85).

6. Nas, "Represent" (1994).

7. In addition to legitimacy, Bleek also strives to create authenticity with the symbols he uses.

8. This is but one of myriad songs with similar titles and themes; others include Jay-Z's "Big Pimpin'" (1999), Foxy Brown's "Stylin'" (2002), and Three 6 Mafia's "Stay Fly" (2006), which is also known as "Stay High." "Still Fly" is chosen as an example because of its self-aware, humorous, and ironic tone; the Big Tymers recognize the absurdity of such a celebration of excess juxtaposed with the lives of everyday black folk, but they show and tell us about stylin' in spite of its apparent contradictions and their misgivings.

9. The exact meaning of *fly* depends on context, but generally speaking, it means beautiful, attractive, or cool.

10. Regina Austin (1996) makes for indispensable reading on this topic. Not only does Austin expertly document the consumption-as-resistance versus consumption-as-alienation debate, she illuminates the extent to which historical constructions of black consumption are contained within a discourse of deviance.

11. Michele Lamont and Virag Molnar (2001) highlight the extent to which marketing strategy across a range of industries is driven by this premise.

12. Nas's album *God's Son* reached platinum status in 2003, and "I Can" peaked at number twelve on the *Billboard* Hot 100 chart.

13. "Impeach the President" contains one of the most recognizable and frequently sam-

pled drum riffs in hip-hop history, and the inclusion of this sample (in concert with Beethoven) reinforces the "classic" affect of the song.

CHAPTER THREE

1. Marc Mauer and Ryan King (2007) also note that Hispanics are currently incarcerated at 1.8 times the rate of whites and point out that the dramatic rise in Hispanic incarcerations is one of the dominant storylines in American imprisonment in the last ten years.

2. For the most comprehensive look at racial inequality, crime control, and trends in American punishment, see Bruce Western's *Punishment and Inequality in America* (2006). Western not only reveals the race-driven elements of American crime discourse but finds that the recent increases in punishment and incarceration do not achieve their stated crime control objectives, which greatly contravenes the conservative discourse of law and order.

3. As Tommie Shelby argues, "Moral criticism can be appropriate even when the targeted behavior and attitudes have been shaped and encouraged by unjust conditions and even when those subjected to criticism are not responsible for the fact that these conditions exist . . . But there are legitimate and constructive forms of moral criticism and illegitimate and self-serving forms" (2007, 160). The criticism offered by Bennett and company is illegitimate because the authors fail to recognize "how lack of justice in a basic structure affects what obligations citizens have," (160) they fail to acknowledge the joint effort (by the empowered and the oppressed) needed to rectify conditions, and they rely heavily on racist myths of black criminality.

4. For further discussion of the importance of the black rapist as a complementary image to that of the Uncle Tom and a myth that has shaped American notions of black masculinity for centuries, see Riché Richardson's *Black Masculinity and the U.S. South* (2007).

5. Patricia Hill Collins traces this rhetorical connection between blackness and crime, connecting the discourse on American crime to that of South Africa:

> Black-on-black violence is the site at which the U.S. news media reconstruct Black Africa as "tribal," threatening, savage, and incapable of self-government and democracy, and also Black urban neighborhoods as sites equally incapable of controlling their children and being self-governing . . . In both the South African and U.S. media, news of "black-on-black" violence centers on one type of perpetrator, typically a young, Black male. The struggle against apartheid or against a punitive urban police force, then, is reduced to a "self-perpetuating" rebellion of youth against a bona fide authority. (2004, 165)

6. Additionally, Russell highlights the phenomenon of the criminal hoax, when perpetrators blame their crime on an imaginary criminal. In the widely publicized cases of Susan Smith, Jesse Anderson, and Charles Stuart, the criminal hoax became a racial hoax as black men were blamed for heinous criminal acts. Based on a sample of the most publicized hoaxes since 1989, Russell concludes that black men are overwhelmingly victimized as the supposed culprit, as the perpetrators play on commonly held public fears and collective recognition of the proverbial black male criminal (1998, 75).

7. Portions of this section ("Tupac: Original Thug"), "Bonnie and Clyde Romance," and "Shorty Wanna Thug (No Homo)," appear in an earlier article by the author on representations of love in thug performances published in a 2010 edition of *Women and Language.*

8. Thug Life consisted of Shakur, Big Syke, Macadoshis, Mopreme, and the Rated R. It released its only studio album, *Thug Life: Volume 1*, in 1994. Shakur's use of the word *thug* on record coincides almost perfectly with some of its earliest invocations by popular East Coast acts, as Nas uses the word *thug* on two tracks from *Illmatic* (1994): "One Love" and "Represent."

9. This sort of lyrical content is objectionable, and its malignant potential should not be ignored. It is true that commercial hip-hop is widely controlled by the white men who own record labels and radio stations and that hip-hop's corporate ascension has coincided with a deluge of representations of objectionable and stereotyped black masculinity. But even if white male racism is responsible for rewarding and distributing such representations, it does not render the moral and political implications of this text irrelevant or unobjectionable, nor does it change the fact that a black man is willing and perhaps eager to present himself in this way.

   A more thoughtful and less apologist line of defense might suggest that Harris is merely portraying a character in his raps, and though this particular character happens to be violent and sexist, T.I.'s artistic license allows him to say whatever he wants, and an artist cannot be reduced to one of his many artistic representations. Harris's 2007 album, *T.I. vs. T.I.P.*, is engineered with this sentiment in mind and depicts a battle between the rapper's two personalities—T.I., the shrewd and civilized businessman, and T.I.P., the ruthless, gun-toting thug. But Harris's character is not at issue. The question is, how should we understand such performances, and which social forces and discourses enable us to make sense of the texts that hip-hop thug narrators produce? Among the forces and meanings that render such raps intelligible and, for some, enjoyable are racist and sexist gender scripts that assign a brutish, hypersexual identity to black men and declare the capacity to dominate others the lynchpin of masculine identity. This excerpt from "Undertaker" bolsters these scripts, and we can and should condemn the discourse without crucifying the speaker or hip-hop culture as a whole.

10. Tupac, "Live Freestyle" (1999). This song appears on *The Tunnel*, an album featuring various MCs, produced and released by DJ Funkmaster Flex.

11. Tupac, "My Block" (1995). This song appears on the soundtrack for the movie *The Show* (1995).

12. Elijah Anderson (1990) argues that this shift to drug dealers and petty criminals as primary agents of socialization in poor black communities represents a major difference from prior eras of black communal life, where "old heads" and "neighborhood mothers" maintained social organization in black communities rich and poor.

13. Platinum certification as documented by RIAA at the searchable database at http://www.riaa.com/goldandplatinumdata.php?table=SEARCH (accessed January 5, 2010).

14. Footage of this episode can be found in the documentary *Hip-Hop: Beyond Beats and Rhymes* (2006), produced and directed by Byron Hurt.

15. One might argue that the controversy surrounding Chris Brown's verbal and physical abuse of Rihanna serves as a recent example of this phenomenon.

16. For a brief and humorous history of the phenomenon, see "An Old Person's Guide to No Homo" at http://nahright.com/news/2008/08/16/video-an-old-persons-guide-to-no-homo/ (accessed March 28, 2009).

17. Those who follow hip-hop gossip closely will recall that in 2006, a photograph of Lil' Wayne kissing his mentor, Cash Money Records founder Brian "Baby" Williams,

surfaced on the Internet. The photograph depicts Wayne and Baby leaning forward to kiss each other on the lips, which led to widespread speculation that the men were gay. On October 26, 2006, Baby addressed the photo on a radio interview with Uptown Angela on Q93 New Orleans, explaining that his demonstration of affection for Wayne falls within the bounds of their father-and-son relationship, as Baby considers Wayne one of his children (Wayne has likewise said that he considers Baby his father). Wayne's recent predilection for the phrase *no homo* developed largely in the aftermath of this controversy.

18. "Every Girl" (2009) is performed by Young Money Entertainment, a group that includes Lil' Wayne and other artists signed to his record label, Young Money.

19. Hood-driven paranoia is a robust theme in hip-hop narratives, and perhaps the most influential song on the topic is the Geto Boys' "Mind Is Playing Tricks on Me" (1991).

20. Notorious B.I.G. refers to this movie frequently on his records, adopting Frank White as an alternative name for himself in some cases. Numerous rappers draw on mafia/gangster movies for inspiration and self-styling, with *Scarface* (1983) being perhaps the most heavily sampled and celebrated movie in the genre.

21. Dyson (1996) and Perry (2004, 96) are two among many hip-hop scholars who discuss moral reckoning as a component of the gangsta tradition in hip-hop.

22. From "Everything I Love (Remix)" (2006), featured on P. Diddy's *Press Play*.

23. Though Young Buck was not present at the incident, this line refers 50 Cent's shooting and hospitalization prior to his emergence on the national rap scene.

24. Young Buck is no longer a member of G-Unit, and after a falling out with 50 Cent, he moved to a new record label.

THE BRIDGE

1. Again, I do not mean to imply that these distortions of black manhood carry equal ideological or moral weight. The racist stereotype of brutish black masculinity is far more objectionable and, sadly, more influential than the other notions of true black manhood.

CHAPTER FOUR

1. Becker writes, "Art worlds consist of all the people whose activities are necessary to the production of the characteristic works which that world, and perhaps others as well, define as art" (1982, 34). Further, "works of art, from this point of view, are not the products of individual makers, 'artists' who possess a rare and special gift. They are, rather, joint products of all the people who cooperate via an art world's characteristic conventions to bring works like that into existence" (35). Becker also notes that he has no interest in defining the boundaries of art worlds, and thus it seems perfectly reasonable, in fact necessary, to include everyday listeners and consumers as vital parts of the hip-hop art world.

2. Tricia Rose (1994) and Adam Krims (2000) are two of the most oft-cited resources on this concept.

3. Kenny explains this point even further, as he describes Talib Kweli as an example of an artist he does not like because he fails to exercise the necessary restraint. The excerpt from the interview reads:

> When I think of somebody who's also clearly a smart well-spoken guy but who kind of drowns himself in it, I think of Talib Kweli, who a lot of people like, but I don't really like him that much. And I think that one of the reasons

why I don't like him is he really wears his erudition on his sleeve, and his music becomes sort of about himself, and his range of reference, and what he can say, and what kind of complex rhyme schemes he can develop, hundred-dollar words off of other hundred-dollar words. And a lot of the time it just seems like he's not saying anything. I think that's a problem that's common to all kinds of people, not just in hip-hop, even to literature, I think you have that problem a lot with smart writers, who don't talk about what they're writing about, they just talk about their own vocabulary, basically. So I think that's the other end of that spectrum, not having an understanding of how the music works as a whole package, and not being able to occasionally hold yourself back to create a whole product that makes more sense than if you had just indulged your own desire to use your great vocabulary.

4. Later during his interview, Bill identifies "urban" people as blacks and Hispanics.

5. The notion of managing stigmatized identity, so crucial to oppositional culture and cool pose theory, is largely derived from the work of Erving Goffman (1963).

6. The absence of role models, or middle-class blacks to whom young ghetto residents can look as examples of people connected to legitimate institutions and patterns of social life, is firmly established in the literature on ghetto ecology. William Wilson (1987) and Elijah Anderson (1990) are among those often cited for this work.

CHAPTER FIVE

1. Quoted in Lewis (2007).

2. Sister Souljah's comments, not surprisingly, were taken out of context by Clinton and others.

3. For further explanation of these events, see Chang (2005, 392–99).

4. In addition to the pornographic videos he produced in cooperation with Hustler, Inc., Snoop has also appeared as a host on the *Girls Gone Wild* video series.

5. For more information, see http://www.essence.com/essence/takebackthemusic/index.html.

6. The obscenity label was subsequently overruled by a federal judge on the grounds of free speech, and 2 Live Crew's right to perform their music was upheld by the United States Supreme Court. The list of hip-hop scholars who have written on this topic is quite lengthy, and the exchange between Gates and Crenshaw is considered the formative give and take on the politics of this moment.

7. Ludacris's "Runaway Love" (2006) is frequently cited by respondents as an example of an uplifting song, or one that speaks to women's struggle, in the context of discussions about substantive variety in hip-hop narratives and women in hip-hop culture.

8. The Fugees, and Lauryn Hill specifically, were exceptions to this rule, as one of the few female-inclusive acts heralded by respondents.

9. I do not mean to imply that aesthetics is entirely separate from considerations of social position. As my previous discussions of aesthetics makes quite clear, these concepts are intimately linked by much of the sociological literature. My point is that when gender dynamics in hip-hop are discussed, the subtle, subterranean workings of gender are routinely ignored, though they are clearly complementary to explicit exploitation and violence.

10. Many men, both black and white, from all class locations, express regret about the position of women in hip-hop and objections to misogyny and sexism. In fact, some of these objections take the familiar form of moral panic discourse, as re-

spondents express concern about the effect of such representations on children who cannot fully understand what they are witnessing and are likely to interpret such performances as realistic depictions of male/female interaction.

11. Video of Richards's racist tirade is available at http://www.tmz.com/2006/11/20/kramers-racist-tirade-caught-on-tape/ (accessed September 21, 2009).

12. Richards offered this public apology on *The Late Show with Dave Letterman* on November 20, 2006.

13. Richard Pryor is frequently cited, including by Kennedy (2002, 39), as proof positive of this point on the multiplicity of *nigga*. Pryor's brand of groundbreaking humor was uniquely driven by his linguistic mastery of *nigga*, which he wielded as all-purpose comedic weaponry and currency.

14. This sentiment is robust in the interview data, with many more supporting quotations than those included in this section.

EPILOGUE

1. "Hillary, Barack Rap, and Rock," *New York Post*, posted January 14, 2008, http://www.nypost.com/p/pagesix/hillary_barack_rap_rock_Yj3GsDqpHDEZo54FZp61EP (accessed December 30, 2009).

2. Quoted in "Feist, Smashing Pumpkins, Ludacris, and More," MTV Newsroom, posted July 9, 2008, http://newsroom.mtv.com/2008/07/09/for-the-record-feist-smashing-pumpkins-ludacris-more/ (accessed September 21, 2009).

3. These statistics are documented by the Center for Information and Research on Civic Learning and Engagement at Tufts University, http://www.civicyouth.org/?p=321 (accessed September 21, 2009).

APPENDIX

1. The third type of endogenous explanation, cultural ecology, "supports a general theory of cultural change through the analysis of naturally evolving subdivisions in cultural fields . . . [T]he basic theme is a search for endogenous properties of cultural fields that naturally, if not inevitably, lead to cultural differentiation and innovation over time" (Kaufman 2004, 337). While this frame is not foundational to my research design, related issues of differentiation and innovation present themselves in interview data.

2. As my project employs both semiotics and ethnography, I both agree and disagree with DeNora on this point. I agree that semiotics cannot be used to predict the social actions or judgments of listeners and that because it ignores the meanings that listeners give to music, it lends itself to a biased reading and decoding of musical products, rife with the potential for elitism and moralism to creep into analysis of musical meaning; DeNora rebukes Theodor Adorno for precisely this reason (DeNora 2000, 22). However, my analysis does not aim to predict how hip-hop music influences listeners in the real world but offers suggestions about how we might make sense of what we hear in rap narratives and what are the discursive and structural forces that influence the production of these artistic products.

3. Joseph Schloss's *Foundation* (2009), one of the strongest and most recent contributions to this collection, uses participant observation and interviews to compile data about b-boy and b-girl culture in New York. For excellent examples of committed participant observation and immersion hip-hop studies outside the United States, see Ian Condry's (2006) work on Japan and Derek Pardue's (2008) work on Brazil.

4. Dominant ideologies are not the only ideologies present at every moment of encod-

ing. But media are mass-produced by institutions with a clear stake in the social order, such as large media conglomerates, and these institutions exert their influence during encoding to reproduce the meanings that serve their interests. One might argue that audiences are institutionally constrained during decoding as well, but the direct influence of dominant institutions on personal interpretations of texts is certainly mediated by the variety of social contexts that influence each individual decoder.

5. Lamont notes that "this inductive approach to symbolic boundaries contrasts with that of Bourdieu (1984), who predefines categories of evaluation/identification" (2000, 271).

6. "Indie," short for independent, refers to music acts that are under contract with independent record companies that do not fall under the umbrella of the four major companies discussed in the introduction.

7. Young Buck was a member of G-Unit at the time data were collected but is no longer part of the clique.

8. Given this bias, it is also not surprising that Trick Daddy's name does not appear, as he originates from Miami and is generally considered a southern rapper.

REFERENCES

Adorno, Theodor W. 1938. *The Culture Industry: Selected Essays on Mass Culture*. London: Routledge, 1991.

Adorno, Theodor W., and Max Horkheimer. 1947. *Dialectic of Enlightenment: Philosophical Fragments*. Palo Alto, CA: Stanford University Press, 2002.

Ahearn, Charlie, and Fab Five Freddie. 1982. *Wild Style*. Film. Rhino Entertainment.

Allen, Virginia M. 1983. *The Femme Fatale: Erotic Icon*. Troy, NY: Whitston.

Alexander, Bryant Keith. 2006. *Performing Black Masculinity: Race, Culture, and Queer Identity*. New York: Altamira.

Anderson, Elijah. 1978. *A Place on the Corner*. Chicago: University of Chicago Press.

———. 1990. *Streetwise: Race, Class, and Change in an Urban Community*. Chicago: University of Chicago Press.

———. 1999. *Code of the Street: Decency, Violence, and the Moral Life of the Inner City*. New York: Norton.

Anderson, Eric. 2005. "Orthodox and Inclusive Masculinity: Competing Masculinities among Heterosexual Men in a Feminized Terrain." *Sociological Perspectives* 48, no. 3 (Autumn 2005): 337–55.

Anderson, M. T. 2006. *The Astonishing Life of Octavian Nothing, Traitor to the Nation*. Vol. 1, *The Pox Party*. Cambridge, MA: Candlewick.

Ang, Ien. 2001. "On the Politics of Empirical Audience Research." In *Media and Cultural Studies: Keyworks*, ed. Meenakshi Gigi Durham and Douglas Kellner, 177–97. Malden, MA: Blackwell.

Appiah, Kwame Anthony. 1996. "Race, Culture, Identity: Misunderstood Connections." *The Tanner Lectures on Human Values* 17: 51–136. Salt Lake City: University of Utah Press.

Asim, Jabari. 2007. *The N Word: Who Can Say It, Who Shouldn't, and Why*. Boston: Houghton Mifflin.

Associated Press. 2007. "NAACP Delegates 'Bury' N-Word in Ceremony." July 9. http://www.msnbc.msn.com/id/19680493 (accessed August 20, 2007).

Austin, Regina. 1996. "'A Nation of Thieves': Consumption, Commerce, and the Black Public Sphere." In *The Black Public Sphere: A Public Culture Book*, ed. Black Public Sphere Collective, 229–52. Chicago: University of Chicago Press.

Baraka, Amiri. 1963. *Blues People: Negro Music in White America*. New York: Morrow.

Baker, Houston A., Jr. 1993. *Black Studies, Rap, and the Academy*. Chicago: University of Chicago Press.

Barker, Hugh, and Yuval Taylor. 2007. *Faking It: The Quest for Authenticity in Popular Music*. New York: Norton.

Bauman, Zygmunt. 1989. *Freedom*. Minneapolis: University of Minnesota Press.

Beavers, Herman. 1997. "'The Cool Pose': Intersectionality, Masculinity, and Quiescence in the Comedy and Films of Richard Pryor and Eddie Murphy." In *Race and the Subject of Masculinities*, ed. Harry Stecopoulos and Michael Uebel, 253–85. Durham, NC: Duke University Press.

Beck, Ulrich. 1992. *Risk Society: Towards a New Modernity*. London: Sage.

Becker, Howard S. 1982. *Art Worlds*. Berkeley: University of California Press.

Beckett, Katherine. 1997. *Making Crime Pay: Law and Order in Contemporary American Politics*. Oxford: Oxford University Press.

Bennett, William J., with John J. Dilulio Jr. and John P. Walters. 1996. *Body Count: Moral Poverty and How to Win America's War on Crime and Drugs*. New York: Simon and Schuster.

Bernstein, Leonard. 1976. *The Unanswered Questions: Six Talks at Harvard*. Cambridge, MA: Harvard University Press.

Bhabha, Homi K. 1994. *Location of Culture*. New York: Routledge.

Bleiker, Roland. 2003. "Discourse and Human Agency." *Contemporary Political Theory* 2: 25–47.

Bobo, Lawrence. 1997. "The Color Line, the Dilemma, and the Dream: Race Relations in America at the Close of the Twentieth Century." In *Civil Rights and Social Wrongs: Black-White Relations since World War II*, ed. John Higham, 31–55. University Park: Pennsylvania State University Press.

Bourassa, Alan. 2002. "Literature, Language, and the Non-Human." In *A Shock to Thought: Expression after Deleuze and Guattari*, ed. Brian Massumi, 60–76. London: Routledge.

Bourdieu, Pierre. 1984. *Distinction: A Social Critique of the Judgment of Taste*. Cambridge, MA: Harvard University Press.

Boyd, Todd. 2002. *The New H.N.I.C. (Head Niggas in Charge): The Death of Civil Rights and the Reign of Hip-Hop*. New York: New York University Press.

———. 2007. "Thug Life and the Effect of Hip-Hop on Language." National Public Radio, February 5. http://www.npr.org/templates/story/story.php?storyId=7179289 (accessed September 21, 2009).

Brown, Timothy J. 2006. "Welcome to the Terrordome: Exploring the Contradictions of a Hip-Hop Black Masculinity." In *Progressive Black Masculinities*, ed. Athena D. Mutua, 191–214. New York: Routledge.

Butler, Judith. 1990. *Gender Trouble: Feminism and the Subversion of Identity*. New York: Routledge.

Calhoun, Craig. 1995. "New Social Movements of the Early Nineteenth Century." In *Repertoires and Cycles of Collective Action*, ed. Mark Traugott, 173–215. Durham, NC: Duke University Press.

Carter, Prudence. 2005. *Keepin' It Real: School Success beyond Black and White*. Oxford: Oxford University Press.

Cashmere, Paul. 2008. "Universal Maintains Lead as Biggest Music Company of 2007." *Undercover*, January 4. http://www.undercover.com.au/News-Story.aspx?id=3766 (accessed March 2, 2008).

Caulfield, Keith. 2008. "Ask Billboard: Kanye West, 50 Cent and Kenny Chesney, UK Artists, Rock Charts." Billboard.com. http://www.billboard.com/search/?Nty=1&Ntx=

mode%2Bmatchallpartial&Ntk=Keyword&Ns=FULL_DATE|1&Ne=125&N=12
6&Ntt=50+Cent&page=3#/news/ask-billboard-kanye-west-50-cent-and-kenny-
1003849640.story (accessed January 5, 2010).

Chalfant, Henry, and Tony Silver. 1983. *Style Wars*. Film. Public Broadcasting Service.

Chang, Jeff. 2005. *Can't Stop, Won't Stop: A History of the Hip-Hop Generation*. New York: St. Martin's.

———. 2007. "Barack Obama Q & A." *Vibe*, August 2. http://www.vibe.com/obama/2007/08/obama_transcript/ (accessed September 21, 2009).

Checkoway, Laura. 2007. "Weezy F. Baby: Uncut." *Vibe*, October 2. http://www.vibe.com/news/news_headlines/2007/10/lil_wayne_excerpts/ (accessed September 21, 2009).

Clarke, John, et al. 1989. "Subcultures, Cultures and Class: A Theoretical Overview." In *Resistance through Rituals: Youth Subcultures in Post-War Britain*, ed. John Clarke et al., 9–74. London: Unwin Hyman.

Clay, Andreana. 2003. "Keepin' It Real: Black Youth, Hip-Hop Culture, and Black Identity." *American Behavioral Scientist* 46, no. 10: 1346–58.

Collins, Patricia Hill. 2004. *Black Sexual Politics: African-Americans, Gender, and the New Racism*. New York: Routledge.

———. 2006. "A Telling Difference: Dominance, Strength, and Black Masculinities." In *Progressive Black Masculinities*, ed. Athena D. Mutua, 73–97. New York: Routledge.

Condry, Ian. 2006. *Hip-Hop Japan: Rap and the Paths of Cultural Globalization*. Durham, NC: Duke University Press.

Connell, Raewyn. 1987. *Gender and Power*. Stanford, CA: Stanford University Press.

———. 1995. *Masculinities*. Berkeley: University of California Press.

Connell, Raewyn, and James Messerschmidt. 2005. "Hegemonic Masculinity: Rethinking the Concept." *Gender & Society* 19: 829–59.

Cooper, Anderson. 2007. "Iraq: Reality Check; War over Iraq; Burying the 'N' Word; U.K. Terror Plot; Cameras Watching You." *Anderson Cooper 360*, July 9. http://transcripts.cnn.com/TRANSCRIPTS/0707/09/acd.02.html (accessed January 3, 2008).

Cornyetz, Nina. 1994. "Fetishized Blackness: Hip Hop and Racial Desire in Contemporary Japan." *Social Text* 41: 113–39.

Cosby, Bill, and Alvin F. Poussaint. 2007. *Come On, People: On the Path from Victims to Victors*. Nashville: Thomas Nelson.

Crane, Diana. 1992. "High Culture versus Popular Culture Revisited: A Reconceptualization of Recorded Cultures." In *Cultivating Differences: Symbolic Boundaries and the Making of Inequality*, ed. Michèle Lamont, 58–72. Chicago: University of Chicago Press.

Crenshaw, Kimberle. 1991. "Beyond Racism and Misogyny: Black Feminism and 2 Live Crew." *Boston Review*. http://www.bostonreview.net/BR16.6/crenshaw.html (accessed November 3, 2007).

Dawson, Michael. 2001. *Black Visions: The Roots of Contemporary African-American Political Ideologies*. Chicago: University of Chicago Press.

De Genova, Nick. 1995. "Gangster Rap and Nihilism in Black America: Some Questions of Life and Death." *Social Text* 43: 89–132.

Del Barco, Mandalit. 1996. "Rap's Latino Sabor." In *Droppin' Science: Critical Essays on Rap Music and Hip Hop Culture*, ed. William Eric Perkins, 63–84. Philadelphia: Temple University Press.

Deleuze, Gilles, and Félix Guattari. 1987. *A Thousand Plateaus: Capitalism and Schizophrenia*. Trans. Brian Massumi. Minneapolis: University of Minnesota Press.

DeNora, Tia. 2000. *Music in Everyday Life*. Cambridge: Cambridge University Press.

———. 2003. *After Adorno: Rethinking Music Sociology*. Cambridge: Cambridge University Press.

Dibben, Nicola. 1999. "Representations of Femininity in Popular Music." *Popular Music* 18, no. 3: 331–35.

DiMaggio, Paul. 1982. "Cultural Entrepreneurship in Nineteenth Century Boston: The Creation of an Organizational Base for High Culture in America." *Media, Culture, and Society* 4: 33–50, 303–22.

Dimitriadis, Greg. 2001. *Performing Identity/Performing Culture: Hip Hop as Text, Pedagogy, and Lived Practice*. New York: Lang.

Douglas, Deborah. 2008. "Hip-Hop Attitude Leads to Mayor's Downfall." *Chicago Sun-Times*, March 28. http://www.sun-times.com/news/douglas/865969,CST-EDT-douglas 28.article (accessed March 29, 2008).

Du Bois, W. E. B. 1903. *The Souls of Black Folk*. New York: Norton, 1999.

Dunbar, Paul Laurence. 1896. "We Wear the Mask." In *The Collected Poetry of Paul Laurence Dunbar*, ed. Joanne M. Braxton, 71. Charlottesville: University Press of Virginia, 1993.

Durand, Alain-Philippe, ed. 2002. *Black, Blanc, Beur: Rap Music and Hip-Hop Culture in the Francophone World*. Lanham, MD: Scarecrow.

Dyson, Michael Eric. 1996. *Between God and Gangster Rap: Bearing Witness to Black Culture*. Oxford: Oxford University Press.

———. 2001. *Holler If You Hear Me: Searching for Tupac Shakur*. New York: Basic Books.

Ellison, Ralph. 1952. *Invisible Man*. New York: Vintage Books, 1995.

Emerson, Rena. 2002. "'Where My Girls At?' Negotiating Black Womanhood in Music Videos." *Gender & Society* 16: 115–35.

Entman, Robert, and Andrew Rojecki. 2000. *The Black Image in the White Mind: Media and Race in America*. Chicago: University of Chicago Press.

Eyerman, Ron, and Andrew Jamison. 1991. *Social Movements: A Cognitive Approach*. University Park: Pennsylvania State University Press.

———. 1998. *Music and Social Movements: Mobilizing Traditions in the Twentieth Century*. Cambridge: Cambridge University Press.

Favor, J. Martin. 1999. *Authentic Blackness: The Folk in the New Negro Renaissance*. Durham, NC: Duke University Press.

Fernandes, Sujatha. 2006. *Cuba Represent! Cuban Arts, State Power, and the Making of New Revolutionary Cultures*. Durham, NC: Duke University Press.

Fiske, John. 1987. *Television Culture: Popular Pleasures and Politics*. London: Methuen.

———. 1994. *Media Matters: Everyday Culture and Political Change*. Minneapolis: University of Minnesota Press.

———. 2000. "Shopping for Pleasure: Malls, Power, and Resistance." In *The Consumer Society Reader*, ed. Thomas Schor and Douglas Holt, 306–28. New York: Free Press.

Forman, Murray. 2002. *The 'Hood Comes First: Race, Space, and Place in Rap and Hip-Hop*. Middletown, CT: Wesleyan University Press.

Fordham, Signithia, and John Ogbu. 1986. "Black Students' School Success: Coping with the Burden of Acting White." *Urban Review* 18, no. 3: 176–206.

Frankenberg, Ruth. 1993. *White Women, Race Matters: The Social Construction of Whiteness*. Minneapolis: University of Minnesota Press.

Frith, Simon. 1987. "The Industrialization of Popular Music." In *Taking Popular Music Seriously*, ed. Simon Frith, 93–118. Hampshire, UK: Ashgate, 2007.

———. 1996. *Performing Rites: On the Value of Popular Music*. Cambridge, MA: Harvard University Press.

Fryer, Roland G., and Steven D. Levitt. 2004. "Understanding the Black-White Test Score Gap in the First Two Years of School." *Review of Economics and Statistics* 2: 447–64.

Gans, Herbert J. 1991. *People, Plans, and Poverty: Essays on Poverty, Racism, and Other National Urban Problems*. New York: Columbia University Press.

Gates, Henry Louis, Jr. 1988. *The Signifying Monkey: A Theory of Afro-American Literary Criticism*. Oxford: Oxford University Press.

———. 1989. "Canon Formation, Literary History, and the Afro-American Tradition: From the Seen to the Told." In *Afro-American Literary Study in the 1990s*, ed. Houston A. Baker and Patricia Redmond, 14–38. Chicago: University of Chicago Press.

Geertz, Clifford. 1973. *The Interpretation of Cultures*. New York: Basic Books.

Gilroy, Paul. 1993. *The Black Atlantic: Modernity and Double Consciousness*. Cambridge, MA: Harvard University Press.

———. 2000. *Against Race: Imagining Political Culture beyond the Color Line*. Cambridge, MA: Harvard University Press.

Gines, Kathryn. 2005. "Queen Bees and Big Pimps: Sex and Sexuality in Hip-Hop." In *Hip-Hop and Philosophy: Rhyme 2 Reason*, ed. Derrick Darby and Tommie Shelby, 92–104. Chicago: Open Court.

Goffman, Erving. 1963. *Stigma: Notes on the Management of Spoiled Identity*. Englewood Cliffs, NJ: Prentice-Hall.

Goldberg, David Theo. 2000. "Surplus Value: The Political Economy of Race and Prisons." In *States of Confinement: Policing, Detention and Prisons*, ed. Joy James, 205–21. New York: St. Martin's.

Golden, Thelma. "My Brother." In *Black Male: Representations of Masculinity in Contemporary American Art*. New York: Whitney Museum of American Art, 1994.

Griswold, Wendy. 1981. "American Character and the American Novel: An Explanation of Reflection Theory in the Sociology of Culture." *American Journal of Sociology* 86, no. 4: 741–65.

Grossberg, Lawrence. 1991. "Rock and Roll in Search of an Audience." In *Popular Music and Communication*, ed. James Lull, 152–75. Newbury Park, CA: Sage Publications.

———. 1992a. "Is There a Fan in the House? The Affective Sensibility of Fandom." In *The Adoring Audience*, ed. Lisa A. Lewis, 50–68. New York: HarperCollins.

———. 1992b. *We Gotta Get Out of This Place: Popular Conservatism and Postmodern Culture*. New York: Routledge.

Hall, Stuart. 1980. "Encoding and Decoding in the TV Discourse." In *Culture, Media, Language*, ed. Stuart Hall, 128–38. London: Hutchinson.

———. 1996. "What Is This 'Black' in Black Popular Culture?" In *Stuart Hall: Critical Dialogues in Cultural Studies*, ed. David Morely and Kuan-Hsing Chen, 465–75. London: Routledge.

Hamby, Peter. 2007. "Barack Obama Gets Name-Dropped in Hip-Hop." CNN, August 17. http://www.cnn.com/2007/POLITICS/08/17/obama.hip.hop/index.html (accessed December 30, 3009).

Harcourt, Bernard. 2001. *Illusion of Order: The False Promise of Broken Windows Policing*. Cambridge, MA: Harvard University Press.

Harper, Phillip Brian. 1996. *Are We Not Men? Masculine Anxiety and the Problem of African-American Identity*. Oxford: Oxford University Press.

Harris-Lacewell, Melissa V. 2004. *Barbershops, Bibles, and BET: Everyday Talk and Black Political Thought*. Princeton, NJ: Princeton University Press.

Hartigan, John. 1999. *Racial Situations: Class Predicaments of Whiteness in Detroit*. Princeton, NJ: Princeton University Press.

Hebige, Dick. 1991. "Subculture: The Meaning of Style." In *Media and Cultural Studies: Keyworks*, eds. Meenakshi Gigi Durham and Douglass Kellner, 198–216. Oxford: Blackwell.

Hennion, Antoine. 1997. "Baroque and Rock: Music, Mediators, and Musical Taste." *Poetics* 24, no. 6: 415–35.

———. 2001. "Music Lovers: Taste as Performance." *Theory, Culture, and Society* 18, no. 5: 1–22.

Hochschild, Jennifer L. 1996. *Facing Up to the American Dream: Race, Class, and the Soul of the Nation*. Princeton, N.J.: Princeton University Press.

hooks, bell. 1994. *Outlaw Culture: Resisting Representations*. New York: Routledge.

———. 2004. *We Real Cool: Black Men and Masculinity*. New York: Routledge.

Horvat, Erin N., and Kristine S. Lewis. 2003. "Reassessing the 'Burden of Acting White': The Importance of Peer Groups in Managing Academic Success." *Sociology of Education* 76, no. 4: 265–80.

Hunt, Scott A., and Robert D. Benford. 2004. "Collective Identity, Solidarity, and Commitment." In *The Blackwell Companion to Social Movements*, ed. David A. Snow, Sarah A. Soule, and Hanspeter Kriesi, 433–57. Oxford: Blackwell.

Hunt, Scott A., with Robert D. Benford and David A. Snow. 1994. "Identity Fields: Framing Processes and the Social Construction of Movement Identities." In *New Social Movements: From Ideology to Identity*, ed. Enrique Larana, Hank Johnston, and Joseph R. Gusfield, 185–208. Philadelphia: Temple University Press.

Hurt, Byron, prod. and dir. 2006. *Hip-Hop: Beyond Beats and Rhymes*. Film. God Bless the Child Productions.

Jackson, John L. 2005. *Real Black: Adventures in Racial Sincerity*. Chicago: University of Chicago Press.

Jackson, Peter. 1989. *Maps of Meaning: An Introduction to Cultural Geography*. New York: Routledge.

Jackson, Ronald L. 2006. *Scripting the Black Masculine Body: Identity, Discourse, and Popular Media*. Albany: State University of New York Press.

Jeffreys, Daniel. 1995. "'They're Poisoning Our Kids': Is Gangsta Rap All a White Conspiracy?" *Independent*, July 31, 1995, 2.

Johnson, Devon. 2001. "Punitive Attitudes on Crime: Economic Insecurity, Racial Prejudice, or Both?" *Sociological Focus* 34, no. 1: 33–51.

Jones, Simon. 1990. "Music and Symbolic Creativity." In *Common Culture: Symbolic Work at Play in the Everyday Culture of the Young*, by Paul Willis, 49–83. Buckingham: Open University Press.

Judy, R. A. T. 2004. "On the Question of Nigga Authenticity." In *That's the Joint! The Hip-Hop Studies Reader*, ed. Murray Forman and Mark Anthony Neal, 105–19. New York: Routledge.

Kaufman, Gil. 2009. "50 Cent Brushes Off Soft Sales for *Before I Self Destruct*." MTV News. http://www.mtv.com/news/articles/1627108/20091125/50_cent.jhtml (accessed January 5, 2010).

Kaufman, Jason. 2004. "Endogenous Explanation in the Sociology of Culture." *American Sociological Review* 2, no. 18: 335–57.

Kelley, Robin D. G. 1996. "Kickin' Reality, Kickin' Ballistics: Gangsta Rap in Postindustrial Los Angeles." In *Droppin' Science: Critical Essays on Rap Music and Hip Hop Culture*, ed. William Eric Perkins, 117–58. Philadelphia: Temple University Press.

———. 1998. *Yo Mama's Disfunktional! Fighting the Culture Wars in Urban America*. Boston: Beacon.

———. 2004. "Looking for the Real Nigga." In *That's the Joint! The Hip-Hop Studies Reader*, ed. Murray Forman and Mark Anthony Neal, 119–36. New York: Routledge.

Kennedy, Randall. 1997. *Race, Crime, and the Law*. New York: Pantheon Books.

———. 2002. *Nigger: The Strange Career of a Troublesome Word*. New York: Pantheon Books.

Keyes, Cheryl L. 2002. *Rap Music and Street Consciousness*. Urbana: University of Illinois Press.

King, Ryan D., and Darren Wheelock. 2007. "Group Threat and Social Control: Race, Perceptions of Minorities and the Desire to Punish." *Social Forces* 85, no. 3: 1255–80.

Kilson, Martin. 2003. "The Pretense of Hip Hop Black Leadership." *Black Commentator* 50. http://www.blackcommentator.com/50/50_kilson.html (accessed September 2, 2006).

Kitwana, Bakari. 2002. *The Hip Hop Generation: Young Blacks and the Crisis in African American Culture*. New York: Basic Civitas Books.

———. 2005. *Why White Kids Love Hip-Hop: Wankstas, Wiggas, Wannabes, and the New Reality of Race in America*. New York: Basic Civitas Books.

Kochman, Thomas, ed. 1972. *Rappin' and Stylin' Out: Communication in Urban Black America*. Urbana: University of Illinois Press.

Krims, Adam. 2000. *Rap Music and the Poetics of Identity*. Cambridge: Cambridge University Press.

Kubrin, Charis E., 2005. "Gangstas, Thugs, and Hustlas: Identity and the Code of the Street in Rap Music." *Social Problems* 52, no. 3: 360–78.

Kubrin, Charis E., and Ronald Weitzer. 2003. "Retaliatory Homicide: Concentrated Disadvantage and Neighborhood Culture." *Social Problems* 50, no. 2: 157–80.

Labov, William. 1972. *Language in the Inner City: Studies in English Black Vernacular*. Philadelphia: University of Pennsylvania Press.

Lamont, Michèle. 1992. *Money, Morals, and Manners: The Culture of the French and American Upper-Middle Class*. Chicago: University of Chicago Press.

———. 2000. *The Dignity of Working Men: Morality and the Boundaries of Race, Class, and Immigration*. Cambridge, MA: Harvard University Press.

Lamont, Michèle, and Virag Molnar. 2001. "How Blacks Use Consumption to Shape Their Collective Identity: Evidence from Marketing Specialists." *Journal of Consumer Culture* 1, no. 1: 31–45.

Lareau, Annette. 2003. *Unequal Childhoods: Race, Class, and Family Life*. Berkeley: University of California Press.

Lena, Jennifer C. 2006. "Social Context and Musical Content of Rap Music, 1979–1995." *Social Forces* 85, no. 1: 479–95.

Levine, Lawrence W. 1977. *Black Culture and Black Consciousness: Afro-American Folk Thought from Slavery to Freedom*. Oxford: Oxford University Press.

Lewis, John, with Wynton Marsalis. 2007. "Shock of the New." *Guardian*, March 2. http://arts.guardian.co.uk/filmandmusic/story/0,,2024037,00.html (accessed April 10, 2007).

Long, Phalary. 2009. "KRS-One: Obama, Execution, and the Sneak Attack." *Allhiphop*, July 16. http://allhiphop.com/stories/features/archive/2009/07/16/21806442.aspx (accessed September 21, 2009).

Majors, Richard, and Janet Mancini Bilson. 1992. *Cool Pose: The Dilemmas of Black Manhood in America*. New York: Touchstone.

Martinez, Theresa. 1997. "Popular Culture as Oppositional Culture: Rap as Resistance." *Sociological Perspectives* 40, no. 2: 265–86.

Martinson, Robert. 1974. "What Works: Questions and Answers about Prison Reform." *Public Interest* 35: 22–54.

Massey, Douglas, and Nancy Denton. 1993. *American Apartheid: Segregation and the Making of the Underclass*. Cambridge, MA: Harvard University Press.

Massumi, Brian. 2002. *Parables for the Virtual: Movement, Affect, Sensation*. Durham, NC: Duke University Press.

Mauer, Marc. 1999. *Race to Incarcerate*. New York: Norton.

———. 2003. "The Crisis of the Young African American Male and the Criminal Justice System." In *Impacts of Incarceration on the African American Family*, ed. Othello Harris and R. Robin Miller, 199–218. New Brunswick, NJ: Transaction.

Mauer, Marc, and Ryan S. King. 2007. "Uneven Justice: State Rates of Incarceration by Race and Ethnicity." The Sentencing Project. http://www.sentencingproject.org/template/page.cfm?id=107 (accessed September 21, 2009).

McDermott, Monica. 2006. *Working-Class White: The Making and Unmaking of Race Relations*. Berkeley: University of California Press.

McLeod, Kembrew. 1999. "Authenticity within Hip Hop and Other Cultures Threatened with Assimilation." *Journal of Communication* 49: 134–50.

McWhorter, John H. 2003. "How Hip-Hop Holds Blacks Back." *City Journal*, Summer. http://www.city-journal.org/html/13_3_how_hip_hop.html (accessed December 6, 2006).

———. 2008. *All about the Beat: Why Hip-Hop Can't Save Black America*. New York: Gotham Books.

Mendelberg, Tali. 2001. *The Race Card: Campaign Strategy, Implicit Messages, and the Norm of Equality*. Princeton, NJ: Princeton University Press.

Mitchell, Don. 2000. *Cultural Geography: A Critical Introduction*. Oxford: Blackwell.

Mitchell-Kernan, Claudia. 1972. "Signifying, Loud-Talking, and Marking." In *Rappin' and Stylin' Out: Communication in Black America*, ed. Thomas Kochman, 315–35. Urbana: University of Illinois Press.

Morenoff, Jeffrey, Robert J. Sampson, and Stephen Raudenbush. 2001. "Neighborhood Inequality, Collective Efficacy, and the Spatial Dynamics of Urban Violence." *Criminology* 39: 517–60.

Morgan, Joan. 1999. *When Chickenheads Come Home to Roost: My Life as a Hip-Hop Feminist*. New York: Simon and Schuster.

Morgan, Marcyliena. 2002. *Language, Discourse, and Power in African American Culture*. Cambridge: Cambridge University Press.

———. 2009. *The Real Hip-Hop: Battling for Knowledge, Power, and Respect in the L.A. Underground*. Durham, NC: Duke University Press.

Murphie, Andrew. 2002. "Putting the Virtual Back into VR." In *A Shock to Thought: Expression after Deleuze and Guattari*, ed. Brian Massumi, 188–214. London: Routledge.

Mutua, Athena D. 2006. "Theorizing Progressive Masculinities." In *Progressive Black Masculinities*, ed. Athena D. Mutua, 3–42. New York: Routledge.

Neal, Mark Anthony. 1999. *What the Music Said: Black Popular Music and Black Public Culture*. New York: Routledge.

———. 2002. *Soul Babies: Black Popular Culture and the Post-Soul Aesthetic*. New York: Routledge.

———. 2005. "Rhythm and Bullshit." *Pop Matters*, June 3. http://popmatters.com/music/features/050603-randb.shtml (accessed October 10, 2006).

Obama, Barack. 1995. *Dreams from My Father: A Story of Race and Inheritance*. New York: Three Rivers.

———. 2004. *The Audacity of Hope: Thoughts on Reclaiming the American Dream*. New York: Vintage.

Pardue, Derek. 2008. *Ideologies of Marginality in Brazilian Hip Hop*. New York: Palgrave-MacMillan.

Patillo-McCoy, Mary. 1999. *Black Pickett Fences: Privilege and Peril among the Black Middle Class*. Chicago: University of Chicago Press.

Patterson, Orlando. 1982. *Slavery and Social Death: A Comparative Study*. Cambridge, MA: Harvard University Press.

———. 1999. *Rituals of Blood: Consequences of Slavery in Two American Centuries*. New York: Basic Civitas Books.

———. 2006. "A Poverty of the Mind." *New York Times*, March 26. http://www.nytimes.com/2006/03/26/opinion/26patterson.html (accessed October 10, 2006).

Peffley, Mark, and Jon Hurwitz. 2002. "The Racial Components of 'Race-Neutral' Crime Policy Attitudes." *Political Psychology* 23, no. 1: 59–75.

Perkins, William E. 1996. "The Rap Attack: An Introduction." In *Droppin' Science: Critical Essays in Rap Music and Hip Hop Culture*, ed. William E. Perkins, 1–45. Philadelphia: Temple University Press.

Perry, Imani. 2004. *Prophets of the Hood: Politics and Poetics in Hip-Hop*. Durham, NC: Duke University Press.

Peterson, Richard A., ed. 1976. *The Production of Culture*. Beverly Hills, CA: Sage.

———. 1979. "Revitalizing the Culture Concept." *Annual Review of Sociology* 5: 137–66.

———. 1997. *Creating Country Music: Fabricating Authenticity*. Chicago: University of Chicago Press.

———. 2005. "In Search of Authenticity." *Journal of Management Studies* 42, no. 5: 1083–98.

Peterson, Richard A., and Paul DiMaggio. 1975. "From Region to Class, the Changing Locus of Country Music." *Social Forces* 53: 497–506.

Peterson, Richard A., and Roger M. Kern. 1996. "Changing Highbrow Taste: From Snob to Omnivore." *American Sociological Review* 61: 900–907.

Peterson, Richard. A., and Albert Simkus. 1992. "How Musical Tastes Mark Occupational Status Groups." In *Cultivating Differences: Symbolic Boundaries and the Making of Inequality*, ed. Michèle Lamont and Marcel Fournier, 152–86. Chicago: University of Chicago Press.

Pietroluengo, Silvie. 2008. "How We Chart the Year: Annual Recaps Take the Spotlight as *Billboard* Tracks the Top Artists and Titles of 2008." *Billboard*, December 20, 82.

Pilkington, Ed. 2007. "Black Comedian Cut Short during N-Word Routine." *Guardian*, September 7. http://www.guardian.co.uk/world/2007/sep/07/usa.theatrenews.html (accessed December 3, 2007).

Polletta, Francesca, and James M. Jasper. 2001. "Collective Identity and Social Movements." *Annual Review of Sociology* 27: 283–305.

Potter, Russell A. 1995. *Spectacular Vernaculars: Hip-Hop and the Politics of Postmodernism*. Albany: State University of New York Press.

Pough, Gwendolyn. 2002. "Love Feminism, but Where's My Hip-Hop? Shaping a Black Feminist Identity." In *Colonize This! Young Women of Color on Today's Feminism*, ed. Daisy Hernandez and Bushra Rehman, 85–95. Seattle: Seal.

———. 2003. "Confronting and Changing Images and Representations of Black Womanhood in Rap Music." In *Get It Together: Readings about African American Life*, ed. Akua Duku Anokye and Jacqueline Brice-Finch, 81–84. New York: Longman.

———. 2004. *Check It While I Wreck It: Black Womanhood, Hip-Hop Culture, and the Public Sphere*. Boston: Northeastern University Press.

Pratt, Ray. 1990. *Rhythm and Resistance: Explorations in the Political Uses of Popular Music.* New York: Praeger.

Queeley, Andrea. 2003. "Hip Hop and the Aesthetics of Criminalization." *Souls* 5: 1–15.

Quinn, Eithne. 2005. *Nuthin' but a "G" Thang: The Culture and Commerce of Gangster Rap.* New York: Columbia University Press.

Reed, Adolph. 1999. *Stirrings in the Jug: Black Politics in the Post-Segregation Era.* Minneapolis: University of Minnesota Press.

Reese, Renford. 2004. *American Paradox: Young Black Men.* Durham, NC: Carolina Academic.

Reid, Shaheem. 2007. "Nas Explains Controversial Album Title, Denies Reports of Label Opposition." MTV News, October 18. http://www.mtv.com/news/articles/1572287/20071018/nas.jhtml (accessed September 11, 2008).

———. 2008. "Nas Takes Jesse Jackson to Task for Barack Obama Comments." MTV News, July 10. http://www.mtv.com/news/articles/1590708/20080710/nas.jhtml (accessed September 11, 2008).

Richardson, Riché. 2007. *Black Masculinity and the U.S. South: From Uncle Tom to Gangsta.* Athens: University of Georgia Press.

Rose, Tricia. 1994. *Black Noise: Rap Music and Black Culture in Contemporary America.* Hanover, NH: University Press of New England.

———. 2008. *The Hip-Hop Wars: What We Talk about When We Talk about Hip-Hop.* New York: Basic Civitas Books.

Russell, Katherine K. 1998. *The Color of Crime: Racial Hoaxes, White Fear, Black Protectionism, Police Harassment, and Other Macroaggressions.* New York: New York University Press.

Sampson, Robert J., and Dawn Jeglum Bartusch. 1998. "Legal Cynicism and (Subcultural?) Tolerance of Deviance: The Neighborhood Context of Racial Differences." *Law and Society Review* 32: 777–804.

Sampson, Robert J., and W. Byron Groves. 1989. "Community Structure and Crime: Testing Social Disorganization Theory." *American Journal of Sociology* 94: 774–802.

Sampson, Robert J., and Steve Raudenbush. 1999. "Systemic Social Observation of Public Spaces: A New Look at Disorder in Urban Neighborhoods." *American Journal of Sociology* 105: 603–51.

Sampson, Robert. J., and William J. Wilson. 1998. "Toward a Theory of Race, Crime and Urban Inequality." In *Community Justice: An Emerging Field*, ed. David R. Karp, 97–118. Latham, MD: Rowman and Littlefield.

Sanneh, Kelefa. 2007a. "Don't Blame Hip-Hop." *New York Times*, April 25. http://www.nytimes.com/2007/04/25/arts/music/25hiph.html (accessed September 20, 2007).

———. 2007b. "The Shrinking Market Is Changing the Face of Hip-Hop." *New York Times*, December 30. http://www.nytimes.com/2007/12/30/arts/music/30sann.html?pagewanted=1&_r=1 (accessed September 21, 2009).

Schloss, Joseph. 2004. *Making Beats: The Art of Sample-Based Hip-Hop.* Middletown, CT: Wesleyan University Press.

———. 2009. *Foundation: B-Boys, B-Girls, and Hip-Hop Culture in New York.* Oxford: Oxford University Press.

Schor, Juliet B., and Douglas B. Holt, eds. 2000. *The Consumer Society Reader.* New York: New Press.

Scott, James C. 1992. *Domination and the Arts of Resistance: Hidden Transcripts.* New Haven, CT: Yale University Press.

Shakur, Tupac A. 1999. *The Rose That Grew from Concrete.* New York: Pocket Books.

Sharpley-Whiting, T. Denean. 2007. *Pimps Up, Ho's Down: Hip Hop's Hold on Young Black Women*. New York: New York University Press.

Shelby, Tommie. 2007. "Justice, Deviance, and the Dark Ghetto." *Philosophy and Public Affairs* 35, no. 2: 126–60.

Shouse, Eric. 2005. "Feeling, Emotion, Affect." *M/C Journal* 8, no. 6 (December). http://journal.media-culture.org.au/0512/03-shouse.php (accessed April 11, 2006).

Sidanius, James, and Felicia Pratto. 2001. *Social Dominance: An Intergroup Theory of Social Hierarchy and Oppression*. Cambridge: Cambridge University Press.

Small, Christopher. 1998. *Musicking: The Meanings of Performing and Listening*. Hanover, NH: University Press of New England.

Smith, Christopher Holmes. 1997. "Method in the Madness: Exploring the Boundaries of Identity in Hip-Hop Performativity." *Social Identities* 3, no. 3: 345–74.

Smitherman, Geneva. 1981. "What Go Round Come Round: King in Perspective." *Harvard Educational Review* 11: 40–56.

———. 1986. *Talkin' and Testifyin': The Language of Black America*. Detroit: Wayne State University Press.

Snow, David A., and Doug McAdam. 2000. "Identity Work Processes in the Context of Social Movements: Clarifying the Identity/Movement Nexus." In *Self, Identity, and Social Movements*, ed. Sheldon Stryker, Timothy J. Owens, and Robert White, 41–67. Minneapolis: University of Minnesota Press.

Snyder, Gregory. 2009. *Graffiti Lives: Beyond the Town in New York's Urban Underground*. New York: New York University Press.

Stokes, Martin. 1997. *Ethnicity, Identity, and Music: The Musical Construction of Place*. Oxford: Berg.

Thernstrom, Stephen, and Abigail Thernstrom. 1999. *America in Black and White: One Nation, Indivisible*. New York: Simon and Schuster.

Thompson, Robert Farris. 1966. "An Aesthetic of the Cool." In *Signifyin(g), Sanctifying, and Slam Dunking: A Reader in African-American Expressive Culture*, ed. Gena D. Caponi, 72–86. Amherst: University of Massachusetts Press, 1999.

———. 1974a. "An Aesthetic of the Cool." *African Arts* 7, no. 1: 40–43, 64–67, 89–91.

———. 1974b. *African Art in Motion*. Berkeley: University of California Press.

Tilly, Charles. 2004. *Social Movements, 1768–2004*. Boulder, CO: Paradigm.

Toop, David. 1984. *The Rap Attack: African Jive to New York Hip Hop*. London: Pluto.

Trapp, Erin. 2005. "The Push and Pull of Hip-Hop: A Social Movement Analysis." *American Behavioral Scientist* 48, no. 11: 1482–95.

Twitchell, James. 1999. *Lead Us into Temptation: The Triumph of American Materialism*. New York: Columbia University Press.

Venkatesh, Sudhir. 2000. *American Project: The Rise and Fall of a Modern Ghetto*. Cambridge, MA: Harvard University Press.

Wacquant, Loic. 2001. "Deadly Symbiosis: When Ghetto and Prison Meet and Mesh." In *Mass Imprisonment: Social Causes and Consequences*, ed. David Garland, 82–120. Thousand Oaks, CA: Sage.

Waters, Mary. 1999. *Black Identities: West Indian Immigrant Dreams and American Realities*. Cambridge, MA: Harvard University Press.

Watkins, S. Craig. 1998. *Representing: Hip Hop Culture and the Production of Black Cinema*. Chicago: University of Chicago Press.

———. 2005. *Hip Hop Matters: Politics, Pop Culture, and the Struggle for the Soul of a Movement*. Boston: Beacon.

West, Cornel. 1993. *Race Matters*. Boston: Beacon.

Western, Bruce. 2006. *Punishment and Inequality in America*. New York: Russell Sage Foundation.

White, Shane, and Graham White. 1998. *Stylin': African American Expressive Culture from Its Beginnings to the Zoot Suit*. Ithaca, NY: Cornell University Press.

Whitlock, Jason. 2007. "NFL Buffoons Leaving Terrible Legacy." *Scout*, October 19. http://profootball.scout.com/2/692467.html (accessed August 1, 2009).

Williams, Rhys H. 2004. "The Cultural Contexts of Collective Action." In *The Blackwell Companion to Social Movements*, ed. David A. Snow, Sarah A. Soule, and Hanspeter Kriesi, 91–115. Oxford: Blackwell.

Williams, Saul. 2007. "Open Letter to Oprah Winfrey." *Baller Status*. http://www.ballerstatus.com/article/editorialscolumns/2007/04/2480/ (accessed April 30, 2007).

Willis, Paul. 1978. *Profane Culture*. London: Routledge and Kegan Paul.

———. 1990. *Common Culture: Symbolic Work at Play in the Everyday Culture of the Young*. Buckingham: Open University Press.

Wilson, William Julius. 1987. *The Truly Disadvantaged: The Inner City, the Underclass, and Public Policy*. Chicago: University of Chicago Press.

———. 1996. *When Work Disappears: The World of the New Urban Poor*. New York: Random.

Wolffe, Richard. 2009. *Renegade: The Making of a President*. New York: Crown.

Wyman, Leah, and George Dionisopoulos. 2000. "Transcending the Virgin/Whore Dichotomy: Telling Mina's Story in Bram Stoker's *Dracula*." *Women's Studies in Communication* 23, no. 2: 209–37.

Yao, Laura. 2008. "Ludacris Provides Obama with More Unwanted Help." *Washington Post*, July 31. http://www.washingtonpost.com/wp-dyn/content/article/2008/07/30/AR2008073002960.html (accessed September 21, 2009).

Yousman, Bill. 2003. "Blackophilia and Blackophobia: White Youth, the Consumption of Rap Music, and White Supremacy." *Communication Theory* 13, no. 4: 366–91.

DISCOGRAPHY

Big Tymers. 2003. *Hood Rich*. Cash Money Records (Universal).
Biz Markie. 1989. *The Biz Never Sleeps*. Cold Chillin' (Warner).
Clipse. 2002. *Lord Willin'*. Star Trak Entertainment/Arista Records (Sony).
———. 2006. *Hell Hath No Fury*. Star Trak Entertainment/Jive Records (Universal).
Dr. Dre. 2002. *The Chronic*. Death Row Records/Interscope (Universal).
Eminem. 2000. *The Marshall Mathers LP*. Aftermath Records (Universal).
Fabolous. 2003. *More Street Dreams 2*. Elektra Records (Warner).
50 Cent. 2003. *Get Rich or Die Tryin'*. Aftermath/Interscope Records (Universal).
———. 2005. *The Massacre*. Interscope Records (Universal).
———. 2007. *Curtis*. Interscope Records (Universal).
Foxy Brown. 2002. *Ill Na Na 2* (unreleased). Bad Boy Records (Warner).
Funkmaster Flex. 1999. *The Tunnel*. Def Jam (Universal).
Geto Boys. 1991. *We Can't Be Stopped*. Asylum Records (Warner).
Grand Master Flash and the Furious Five. 1982. *The Message*. Sugar Hill Records (Warner).
Ja Rule. 2000. *Rule 3:36*. Murder Inc./Def Jam (Universal).
Jay-Z. 1998. *Vol. 2 . . . Hard Knock Life*. Roc-A-Fella Records (Universal).
———. 1999. *Vol. 3 . . . The Life and Times of S. Carter*. Roc-A-Fella Records (Universal).
———. 2001. *The Blueprint*. Roc-A-Fella Records (Universal).
———. 2002. *The Blueprint 2*. Roc-A-Fella Records (Universal).
———. 2003. *The Black Album*. Roc-A-Fella Records (Universal).
———. 2006. *Kingdom Come*. Roc-A-Fella Records (Universal).
Lil' Wayne. 2008. *Tha Carter III*. Cash Money Records (Universal).
Ludacris. 2006. *Release Therapy*. Def Jam South (Universal).
Memphis Bleek. 2003. *M.A.D.E.* Roc-A-Fella Records (Universal).
Mobb Deep. 2006. *Blood Money*. Interscope Records (Universal).
Mos Def. 1999. *Black on Both Sides*. Rawkus/Priority Records (EMI).
N.W.A. 1988. *Straight outta Compton*. Priority Records (EMI).
Nas. 1994. *Illmatic*. Columbia Records (Sony).
———. 2002a. *God's Son*. Ill Will Records (Sony).
———. 2002b. *The Lost Tapes*. Ill Will Records (Sony).
———. 2006. *Hip Hop Is Dead*. Def Jam (Universal).
Notorious B.I.G. 1994. *Ready to Die*. Bad Boy (Warner).

———. 1997. *Life after Death*. Bad Boy (Warner).

P. Diddy. 2006. *Press Play*. Bad Boy (Warner).

Ruff Ryders. 2000. *Ryde or Die: Volume 2*. Interscope (Universal).

Run DMC. 1986. *Raising Hell*. Profile/Arista (Sony).

Rick Ross. 2006. *Port of Miami*. Def Jam (Universal).

Styles P. 2006. *Time Is Money*. Ruff Ryder Records (Universal).

Scarface. 2004. *The Fix*. Def Jam (Universal).

Shakur, Tupac. 1995. *Me against the World*. Interscope Records (Universal).

———. 1996a. *All Eyez on Me*. Death Row Records (Sony).

———. 1996b. *The Don Killuminati: The 7 Day Theory*. Death Row Records (Sony).

———. 1997. *R U Still Down? (Remember Me)*. Jive Records (Sony).

———. 2001. *Until the End of Time*. Amaru/Interscope Records (Universal).

———. 2002. *Better Dayz*. Interscope Records (Universal).

Three 6 Mafia. 2005. *The Most Known Unknown*. Sony Records.

Thug Life. 1994. *Thug Life: Volume 1*. Interscope/Atlantic Records.

T.I. 2006. *King*. Grand Hustle Records (Warner).

———. 2007. *T.I. vs. T.I.P.* Grand Hustle Records (Warner).

A Tribe Called Quest. 1993. *Midnight Marauders*. Jive (Sony).

Various Artists. 1995. *The Show: The Soundtrack*. Def Jam Records (Universal).

West, Kanye. 2004. *The College Dropout*. Roc-A-Fella Records (Universal).

Young Jeezy. 2008. *The Recession*. Def Jam, Corporate Thugz Entertainment (Universal).

Young Money. 2009. "Every Girl." Cash Money Records (Universal).

INDEX

Abe (w4), 28; on relating to hip-hop, 48, 49; use of "nigga" viewed by, 172

Above the Rim (film), 90

Adam (w4), 28; on relating to hip-hop, 49

Adorno, Theodor W., 4–5, 233n2

Aerosmith, 2

affect, idea of, 43–44, 49, 50–51, 100, 120, 122, 129, 229n13

African Americans: in American prison population, 80–81; culpability for racist views, 152–53, 164–65, 184–86; cultural commoditization and, 84, 89; cultural dominance of hip-hop, 5–6, 51–52; family instability and, 82–83; hip-hop identity and, 41–43, 55–58, 72–74, 93–95, 133, 151–53, 190–91; hip-hop origins and, 1, 37–39, 42–43, 51, 190; ironic misnaming practice of, 165; middle-class migration to suburbs, 78–79; racial authenticity concept and, 74–76; racist views of, 82–84, 87–88, 152–53, 229n4; reasons for rap appreciation, 8–9, 45, 46–51, 197; semantic reclamation and transformation, 86–87; storytelling tradition, 13, 68–69, 90–91; stylin' as identity marker, 69–70

African roots of cool pose, 59, 60, 115

afterlife and religion in hip-hop narratives, 105–11

Ahearn, Charlie, 225n3

"All about U" (Shakur), 77, 108

Allen (b1), 31, 33–34; hip-hop as defined by, 38, 42; hip-hop gangster image viewed by, 180; hip-hop preferences and appreciation, 135; on relating to hip-hop, 46–47

Allen, Virginia M., 101

Anderson, Elijah, 10, 56, 79–80, 230n12, 232n6(1); *Code of the Street*, 83; *Streetwise*, 228n5

Anderson, Eric, 58, 102

Anderson, Jesse, 229n6

Anderson, M. T., 23

Andre (b4), 30; hip-hop as defined by, 38, 41; hip-hop preferences and appreciation, 124; thug narratives viewed by, 142–43, 144; use of "nigga" viewed by, 171, 175

Anthony (w3), 28; hip-hop as defined by, 37; hip-hop preferences and appreciation, 139, 140, 141

Appiah, Kwame Anthony, 68

Asians, hip-hop and, 6

Asim, Jabari, 165–66

Atlanta, Georgia, 65

Atlantic Records, 153

ATLAS.ti, 223

Audacity of Hope, The (Obama), 204

Austin, Regina, 228n10

authenticity, concept of, 117–49; African Americans and, 84; American Dream and, 71–74; applied to performers, 119–20, 134–41, 145–46, 178–79, 181, 192; commercialism and, 123, 134–36, 145–46, 147, 187; complex cool and, 74–76, 111, 114–15; in

authenticity (*continued*)
    gangsta rap, 86, 92–93, 98, 113; gender
        and, 160–61, 162–63, 176, 186–88;
        heteronormativity and, 101; 'hood and,
        68–71, 73–74, 132, 174–75; mapping
        hip-hop, 132–36; meanings of "real"
        and, 133–34, 145–46; narrative, 119,
        122–23, 146–47, 157–59; "nigga" or
        "nigger" word usage, 166, 167, 168–70,
        187–88; Obama and, 204–5; racial
        identity and, 138–41, 147–48, 175,
        176–77, 188, 191; semantic dimen-
        sions, 134; sincerity and, 117, 132, 137;
        as social construct, 75, 117–18, 146;
        taste and, 118–20, 191–92, 193, 196.
        See also "keeping it real"
Auto-Tune, 102

Baby, "Still Fly," 70
Bad Boy Records, 159
Baker, Houston, 68; *Black Studies, Rap, and
    the Academy*, 13
Banners, David, 199
Baraka, Amiri, 58
Barker, Hugh, 69
Bartusch, Dawn Jeglum, 85
Bauman, Zygmunt, 118
b-boying (break dancing), 1, 6, 8, 34,
    225nn2–3, 233n3
Beavers, Herman, 57
Becker, Howard S., 119, 121, 231n1
Beckett, Katherine, 81
Beethoven, Ludwig van, 72, 229n13
Before I Self Destruct (50 Cent album), 98
Ben (b4), 30; criminal justice system
    viewed by, 183; hip-hop preferences
    and appreciation, 128; on relating to
    hip-hop, 49; on women as portrayed in
    hip-hop, 156
Benford, Robert, 26
Bennett, William, 82–83, 229n3
Bhabha, Homi, 114
Biggie. *See* Notorious B.I.G.
Big L, 128–29
"Big Pimpin'" (Jay-Z), 228n8(2)
Big Syke, 230n8
Big Tymers, the, "Still Fly," 70
Bill (b4), 30; on feelings in hip-hop, 44;

hip-hop as defined by, 34; hip-hop
    gangster image viewed by, 179–80;
    hip-hop preferences and appreciation,
    138, 232n4
Bilson, Janet Mancini, 10, 56, 57, 58–59,
    115, 144
Birth of a Nation (film), 83
"Bitches *vs.* Sisters" (Jay-Z), 156
Biz Markie, 2
Black August Hip-Hop Project, 12
Black Enterprise magazine, 166–67
Black Noise (Rose), 13–14, 15
"Black President" (Nas), 201–2
black studies, 13
Black Studies, Rap, and the Academy (Baker),
    13
Bleek, Memphis: "'Round Here," 64–67,
    108, 132, 220; symbolism used by,
    228n7(2)
"bling." *See* consumption, conspicuous
boasting in hip-hop, 20, 125, 127–28, 130,
    149, 154, 178, 197, 202
Bobo, Lawrence, 87
Body Count (Bennett et al.), 82–83
Body Count, "Cop Killer," 151–52
Bond, Julian, 164
Bone Thugs-N-Harmony, 214
Bourdieu, Pierre, 118–19, 124, 130, 234n5
Boyd, Todd, 86; *The New H.N.I.C. (Head
    Niggas in Charge)*, 11
Brandon (w3), 29; hip-hop as defined by,
    35; hip-hop preferences and apprecia-
    tion, 126, 161; on women as portrayed
    in hip-hop, 158
bravado, masculine, 58
Brazil, hip-hop in, 6, 12, 233n3
break dancing. *See* b-boying (break
    dancing)
Brian (b3), 30; thug narratives viewed by,
    142
Brooklyn, New York, 64–67
Brown, Chris, 230n15
Brown, Foxy, 155; "Stylin'," 228n8(2)
Brown, Timothy, 60
Burton, Bill, 202
Bush, George H. W., 80, 81, 84
Bush, George W., 7, 152, 201, 202
Butler, Judith, 227n18

Calhoun, Craig, 26, 227n2
call-and-response chant, 108
Cam'ron, 226n11
Carter, Prudence, 42, 56, 74, 145
Cashmere, Paul, 3
Cash Money Records, 70, 230–31n17
Caulfield, Keith, 98
Chalfant, Henry, 225n3
Chamillionaire, 137
Chang, Jeff, 12, 202–3
Checkoway, Laura, 103
Chris (w4), 28; criminal justice system
   viewed by, 182; hip-hop as defined by,
   40; hip-hop preferences and apprecia-
   tion, 122, 125–26
Chronic, The (Dr. Dre), 2
Chuck D, 1
civil rights movement: black crime debate
   and, 81, 90; hip-hop and, 11, 199; racist
   views of, 88
Clarke, John, 115
Clay, Andreana, 42
Clear Channel Communications, 213
Clinton, Bill, 81; hip-hop criticized by, 151,
   232n2
Clinton, Hillary Rodham, 200, 202
Clipse, the, 97, 130, 131, 214
Code of the Street (Anderson), 83
Collins, Patricia Hill, 84, 229n5
Color of Crime, The (Russell), 81–82, 84
Columbia Records Groups, 2–3, 97
Common, 201
communicative process, performance as,
   36, 50–51, 61, 119
complex coolness: authenticity and,
   74–76, 98, 163; dissonance of, 60–61;
   explanation of, 60–61, 189–90; in
   hip-hop narratives, 177–78, 'hood in,
   62–64; inequality and, 115–16; Obama
   and, 200, 204–5; social capital in, 67;
   thug love and, 110, 182; transparency
   in, 115–16
Condry, Ian, 6, 210, 233n3
Connell, Raewyn, 57–58
consumption, conspicuous: black identity
   and, 75; complex coolness and, 60–61;
   115; hip-hop listeners' distaste for, 123,
   134–36, 145–46, 147, 175–76, 191–92;

in hip-hop narratives, 9, 48, 62, 69,
   71–74, 98–99, 123, 184, 197, 203, 205;
   thug persona and, 77; women as predators for, 157
cool pose: black identity and, 9, 10; criticism of theory, 61–62, 114, 189–90;
   hegemonic masculinity and, 48, 58,
   66–67, 69, 71–74, 144, 188; hip-hop
   and, 59–62, 114–15, 145–46, 149; as
   mask, 7, 58–59, 105, 114; Obama and,
   200, 203, 204–5; roots of, 58–59, 60;
   stylin' and, 69–71, 115; understanding,
   55–58
"Cop Killer" (Body Count), 151–52
Cornyetz, Nina, 6
Cosby, Bill, 10, 226n10
Crane, Diana, 118
Crenshaw, Kimberle, 154, 155, 232n6(2)
criminality, black, 177–86; black-on-black
   crime, 95; civil rights violations and,
   88, 179, 229n6; culpability for, 185–86;
   drug dealing, 64, 66–67, 79, 96–97,
   145–46, 228n3; in hip-hop narratives,
   62, 64, 78, 86, 88, 94–95, 109–10, 113,
   145–46, 177–86, 188, 193; racist stereotypes of, 174, 177; social isolation and,
   82–83, 141–46; structure and culture of,
   78–80, 182–83; wealth and, 96–99
crossover, 2–5
Cuba, hip-hop in, 6, 12
cultural appropriation, 5–9
cultural ecology, 62, 67, 85, 232n6, 233n1
culture classes, concept of, 118–19, 123,
   130–31, 146
Curtis (50 Cent album), 98

Damien (w4), 29; hip-hop as defined by,
   35; hip-hop gangster image viewed by,
   178; hip-hop preferences and appreciation, 120, 121, 122
Darryl (b1), 31; hip-hop preferences and
   appreciation, 130, 131, 139, 140, 141;
   use of "nigga" viewed by, 172; on
   women as portrayed in hip-hop, 157
Davey D., 225n7
David (b4), 30–31; hip-hop preferences
   and appreciation, 136, 160–61
Death Row Records, 89, 153

"December 4th" (Jay-Z), 204
Def Jam Records, 152, 159, 200
De Genova, Nick, 93–94
"deindustrialization, hip-hop and, 1, 78–79
Deleuze, Gilles, 43
Dem Franchise Boys, 123
DeNora, Tia, 43, 45, 233n2; *Music in Everyday Life*, 209
Denton, Nancy, 56
dialectics: complex cool and, 60–61; cool pose and, 57
Dilulio, John, Jr., 82–83
DiMaggio, Paul, 118, 123
Dimitriadis, Greg, 19–20; *Performing Identity/Performing Culture*, 210–11
Dionisopoulos, George, 101
DJ-ing, 1, 6, 8, 34, 225nn2–3
DMX, 107–8
Domination and the Art of Resistance (Scott), 12
double consciousness, 58, 59–60
Douglas, Deborah, 226n12
Dr. Dre, 2, 86, 97, 120, 121
Dreams from My Father (Obama), 204
dress. *See* stylin'
"Drop It Like It's Hot" (Lil' Wayne), 102
drug dealing. *See* criminality, black
Dub magazine, 214
Dub Magazine Custom Auto Show and Concert, 214, 220
Du Bois, W. E. B., 58, 115
Dunbar, Paul Laurence, "We Wear the Mask," 58, 115
Durand, Alain-Philippe, 6
Dwayne (b3), 31; hip-hop as defined by, 38, 42; hip-hop gangster image viewed by, 180; hip-hop preferences and appreciation, 139–40; on relating to hip-hop, 46, 47–48; understandings of "thug life" and "nigga," 151; on women as portrayed in hip-hop, 157
Dyson, Michael Eric, 11, 89–90, 99, 108–9, 231n21

East Side Boyz, 101
eclecticism, 118–19
educational status, hip-hop understanding and, 32–33

Electric & Musical Industries Limited (EMI), 3–4
Ellison, Ralph, 58
Emerson, Rena, 155
Eminem: Abe's views on, 48; as producer, 3, 97; "Renegade," 90–91
encoding/decoding process, 211–12, 233–34n4
endogenous explanation, concept of, 207–8, 233n1
Entman, Robert, 84
Eric (w1), 29; hip-hop as defined by, 37; hip-hop gangster image viewed by, 178–79; hip-hop preferences and appreciation, 125; on relating to hip-hop, 49–50; use of "nigga" viewed by, 172
Essence magazine, 153
ethnography, 233n2
ethnomusicology, 209–10
Evan (b1), 32; use of "nigga" viewed by, 171–72
Evers, Medgar, 199
"Every Girl" (Lil' Wayne), 104, 231n18
"Everything I Love (Remix)" (Jadakiss), 1, 231n22
Eyerman, Ron, 26–27, 45

Fab Five Freddy, 225n3
fandom, concept of, 24, 104
Favor, J. Martin, 68–69, 167
"Fear Not of Man" (Mos Def), 189
female degradation, 154–63; black culpability argument, 152–53, 164–65; Bonnie and Clyde raps, 99–102; hegemonic masculinity and, 58, 60–61, 92, 98–99, 129–30; in hip-hop narratives, 9, 14, 45–46, 99–102, 149, 157–59, 203, 205; as marketing tool, 153; respondents' views of, 155–56, 186–87, 192, 197, 232–33n10; virgin/whore paradigm, 101–2
Fernandes, Sujatha, 6, 12
50 Cent: career and influence of, 97–99, 104, 108, 111, 152; on demonization of rappers rather than corporations, 4, 226n8; *Get Rich or Die Tryin'* album, 91, 143, 148; "Hate It or Love It," 109–10, 228n2; hip-hop fans' contradictory views of, 143, 146, 148, 160, 178, 196;

'hood viewed by, 62; "I Get Money," 98–99; "In My Hood," 105; Ja Rule and, 98; label of, 3; Lil' Wayne and, 102–3; narrative authenticity of, 122; Obama and, 200–201; "Pearly Gates," 110–11; shooting of, 231n23; "U Not Like Me," 105–6; use of n-word, 164

Filipinos, hip-hop and, 6

"Fireman" (Lil' Wayne), 102

Fiske, John, 118

Flo-Rida, 5

flowing, concept of, 123–25, 146

fly image, 70, 228n9(2)

Fordham, Signithia, 56, 145

Forman, Murray, 63–64

Foundation (Schloss), 233n3

Frankenberg, Ruth, 7

Fred (w3), 28–29; criminal justice system viewed by, 183; hip-hop as defined by, 34; hip-hop preferences and appreciation, 120, 135; use of "nigga" viewed by, 173; on women as portrayed in hip-hop, 158–59

freestyling, 124

Frith, Simon, 36, 132–33

Fryer, Roland G., 56

"Fuck tha Police" (N.W.A.), 182

Fugees, the, 232n8

"Für Elise" (Beethoven), 72

gangsta rap, 6–7; audience for, 51, 209; black culpability argument, 152–53, 164–65, 184–86; changes in, 165–66; genesis of, 85–86; as marketing pose, 86; simultaneous performances in, 20; understandings of, 86–87. *See also* hip-hop; rap

gangster image, 177–86; hegemonic masculinity and, 62, 71–74, 96–97, 193; listeners' skepticism of, 178–79, 184–86; media amplification of, 2, 177–78; success and, 5, 71–74, 184; in white imaginary, 5. *See also* thug image

Gans, Herbert, 35

Gates, Henry Louis, Jr., 68–69, 127–28, 154, 155, 226n17, 232n6(2)

Geertz, Clifford, 35

George (b3), 31, 33; criminal justice system viewed by, 184; on diversity of hip-hop, 50, 51; hip-hop as defined by, 38, 42; hip-hop preferences and appreciation, 120–21; use of "nigga" viewed by, 169, 170; on women as portrayed in hip-hop, 156

Geto Boys, the, "Mind Is Playing Tricks on Me," 231n19

Get Rich or Die Tryin' (50 Cent album), 97, 143, 148

Get Rich or Die Tryin' (film), 98

G-Funk, 86

ghetto: family instability in, 82–83; media representations of, 84; middle-class migration to suburbs, 78–79; as necessary identity element in hip-hop, 62–63, 132; nihilism of, 82, 92–96, 107, 109–10, 180–81. *See also* 'hood; hyperghetto/prison

ghetto hustler image: cool pose and, 56–57; culture of, 78–80; success and, 5, 184

Gilroy, Paul, 11, 19–20

Gines, Kathryn, 101

God's Son (Nas album), 228n11

Goffman, Erving, 232n5(1)

"Go Head" (Ruff Riders), 96–97

Goldberg, David Theo, 80

Golden, Thelma, 228n1

Goldwater, Barry, 81

GOOD Music, 3

Gordon, Thelma, 55

Gore, Tipper, 151

graffiti art, 1, 225nn2–3

Gramsci, Antonio, 226n16

Grandmaster Flash and the Furious Five, "The Message," 62

Graves, Earl, 167

Greg (b4), 31; criminal justice system viewed by, 183; on diversity of hip-hop, 50–51; hip-hop preferences and appreciation, 127–28; use of "nigga" viewed by, 169; on women as portrayed in hip-hop, 156

Griffin, Eddie, 166–67

Griffith, D. W., 83

Grossberg, Lawrence, 24

Groves, W. Byron, 85

Guattari, Félix, 43

guilt and regret in hip-hop narratives, 62, 105. *See also* vulnerability, feelings of
G-Unit, 109–10, 231n24, 234n7

"Half on a Sack" (Three 6 Mafia), 50
Hall, Stuart, 115–16, 211, 226n16
Hamby, Peter, 201
Harcourt, Bernard, 90
Harper, Phillip, 93
Harris, Clifford, Jr. *See* T.I.
Hartigan, John, 7
Harvard Report, 2–3
"Hate It or Love It" (50 Cent), 109–10, 228n2
heavy metal, 151
hedonism, hip-hop, 11–12, 114, 166. *See also* consumption, conspicuous
hegemony, theory of, 57–58, 226n16. *See also* masculinity
Hennion, Antoine, 119, 122, 226n18
heteronormativity, 101
hidden transcripts, concept of, 13
Hill, Lauryn, 173, 232n8
hip-hop: authenticity's importance in, 117–18, 132–36, 191–92; beat in, 120–22; beginnings of, 1–2, 51, 228n6(1); as black vernacular culture, 69, 144, 146–47, 155, 167–68, 192; civil rights movement and, 11, 199; class structure and, 32–33; commoditization of, 2, 37, 71–74, 77, 89, 132–33; content changes in, 2, 6–7, 89, 123; cool pose and, 59–62, 114–15; counterculture and, 183; critical appreciation of, 197–98; critics of, 10–12, 185; cultural appropriation of, 5–6; as culture or lifestyle, 34–35, 40, 51, 144–45, 190; decline in record sales, 5; defenses of, 12–15; defining, 34–43, 225n5; diversity of, 13, 50–51; effect on class-disadvantaged, 11; effect on power relations, 15, 75–76; elements of, 1, 225nn2–3; emotional vulnerability and, 48–49, 61; as escapism, 71; ethnography of, 207–13; evaluating, 120–23, 146–47; feelings and, 43–51; flow in, 123–25, 146; as hidden transcript, 12; identity issues, 23–24, 25, 36–43, 52, 196–97; live performance, 1; as means

of communication and expression, 35–37, 51, 184; methodology and theory of study, 194–96, 207–24; moral panic and, 151–53, 155, 177, 184–85, 187, 195, 197–98, 202–3, 229n3, 232–33n10; multifaceted discourse and meaning in, 61; as music, 37; narrative in, 122–23; neighborhood dynamics and, 32; non-English speakers, 196; Obama and, 199–205; performers favored by respondents, 215–20; politics and, 4, 9, 12, 13–14, 15, 132, 145–46, 171, 199–205; polytextuality of, 14–15; racial identity of performers, 36–43, 51–52; racial interpretations of narratives, 5, 61–62, 113; recording industry and, 1–2; relatability of, 45–48, 52; sex and gender dynamics in, 14, 129–30, 149, 154–63, 176, 187–88, 192; signifying in, 18–19, 123–32, 146–47, 226n17; simultaneous performances in, 20; as social movement, 25–27, 227n1; substantive implications of study, 196–98; suppression of nonblack contributions, 6; texts' contingency, 227n19; textuality problem in, 19–20; thug persona in, 77–78, 141–46, 188; top artists, 2008, 5; "video hos" in music videos, 155, 157–59, 192; in white imaginary, 4, 9; worldview, 11–12. *See also* gangsta rap; rap
Hip-Hop: Beyond Beats and Rhymes (film), 230n14
hip-hop feminists, 14–15, 155, 159
Hip-Hop Summit Action Network, 12
Hip-Hop Wars, The (Rose), 226n9
Hochschild, Jennifer, 71
Holman, Michael, 225n3
homophobia: hegemonic masculinity and, 9, 58, 102, 116; listeners' acceptance of, 14; "no homo" phrase, 102–5
Honeydrippers, the, "Impeach the President," 72, 228–29n13
'hood: authenticity and, 68–71, 73–74, 107, 174–75; concept of, 63–64; hip-hop understanding and, 32; importance of, 62, 110–11, 191; narratives about, 61, 62–68, 94–95, 141–46, 177–78; paranoia in, 105, 231n19; respect in, 67,

79–80, 142–43; stylin' in, 70–71. *See also* ghetto; hyperghetto/prison

hood-making, 67–68

Hood Rich (The Big Tymers), 70

hooks, bell, 12

Horkheimer, Max, 4–5

Horton, Willie, 84

Horvat, Erin N., 145

"How Hip-Hop Holds Blacks Back" (McWorter), 10–11, 12

Hunt, Scott, 26

Hurt, Byron, 230n14

Hurwitz, Jon, 84

"Hustlin'" (Ross), 45, 46, 228n7(1)

hustling: drug dealing and, 228n3; failure of equal opportunity and, 96; in hip-hop narratives, 45, 69, 88, 148; specialness concept and, 111

hyperghetto/prison: characteristics of, 79–80, 188; code in, 140–41, 149, 182–83; rise of, 62; as social death, 88, 94–96, 107, 109, 177, 179–81, 208; survivor image in, 110–11, 193; violence and threat of death in, 109–11; white views of, 82–84

"I Ain't Goin' Back to Jail" (Project Pat), 50

"I Ain't Mad at Cha" (Shakur), 101

"I Can" (Nas), 72–74, 132, 228n11

"I Cry" (Ja Rule), 98

Ice T, 151, 152

identity: collective, 26, 27, 40, 61, 113, 190–91, 196–97; construction of, 39–43, 68, 74–76, 227n18, 227–28n4; hegemonic masculinity, 57–58, 69, 71–74, 75; of hip-hop performer, 86, 119–20; male vs. female preferences and, 162–63, 193; music's role in, 209; "nigga" and, 165–66; social movements and, 25–27, 45, 203, 227n1. *See also* racial identity

"I Get Money" (50 Cent), 98–99

Illmatic (Nas album), 47

"I'm Not You" (Styles P and Pusha T), 97

"Impeach the President" (the Honeydrippers), 72, 228–29n13

improvisation, 133

Imus, Don, 152, 163–64

"In My Hood" (50 Cent), 105

insider/outsider methodology, 148

Internet: discussion on, 103, 134, 231n17; promotion and distribution, 5, 98

Interscope Records, 3, 97, 153, 159

Isaac (w1), 29; criminal justice system viewed by, 182; use of "nigga" viewed by, 169–70

Island Def Jam Music Group, 3

"I Wonder If Heaven Got a Ghetto" (Shakur), 106

Jack (b2), 32; criminal justice system viewed by, 185; on relating to hip-hop, 45–46; use of "nigga" viewed by, 175; on women as portrayed in hip-hop, 158

Jackson, Curtis. *See* 50 Cent

Jackson, Jesse, 199, 202

Jackson, John L., 74, 117, 119, 121, 132, 136, 147

Jackson, Peter, 226n13

Jackson, Ronald, 77

Jadakiss, 1, 108

James (w3), 29; criminal justice system viewed by, 183; hip-hop as defined by, 40; on relating to hip-hop, 45; use of "nigga" viewed by, 173, 174

James, LeBron, 57

Jamison, Andrew, 26–27, 45

Jam Master Jay, 109

Japan, hip-hop in, 6, 233n3

Ja Rule, 50 Cent and, 98

Jason (b1), 32; hip-hop as defined by, 38; hip-hop preferences and appreciation, 122, 123, 134–35; on relating to hip-hop, 46, 47–48

Jasper, James M., 26

Jay-Z: "Big Pimpin'," 228n8(2); "Bitches vs. Sisters," 156; "December 4th," 204; early home of, 64; Knowles and, 99–100; "Money, Cash, Hoes," 107–8; Nas and, 128; "99 Problems," 45, 46; Obama and, 199; "'03 Bonnie and Clyde," 99–100; popularity of, 23, 136, 192, 196; "Public Service Announcement," 55, 92; "Renegade," 90–91; Roc-A-Fella Records, 3; "30 Something," 50, 51

Jeru the Damaja, 156

Jive Records, 214

Johnson, Devon, 81, 84
Judy, R. A. T., 164–65
Juice (film), 90
"Just a Friend" (Biz Markie), 2

Kaufman, Gil, 98
Kaufman, Jason, 207–8
keeping it real: as catch phrase, 137; 'hood
    and, 73–74, 107, 174–75; importance
    in hip-hop, 117–18, 134–41, 147, 157,
    195; thug life and, 75, 89–90, 141–46,
    151, 178–79. *See also* authenticity,
    concept of
"Keep Ya Head Up" (Shakur), 50
Kelley, Robin D. G., 86, 117, 127–28, 166
Kennedy, Randall, 85, 233n13
Kenny (w1), 29; criminal justice system
    viewed by, 183; hip-hop gangster image
    viewed by, 181; hip-hop preferences
    and appreciation, 120, 121, 130–32,
    231–32n3
Kern, Roger M., 118–19
Kevin (w4), 29; on feelings in hip-hop, 44;
    hip-hop preferences and appreciation,
    122, 123, 136–37, 161; on relating to
    hip-hop, 48, 49
Keyes, Cheryl L., 8, 152, 159, 165; *Rap Mu-
    sic and Street Consciousness*, 209–10
Kilpatrick, Kwame, 164, 226n12
Kilson, Martin, "The Politics of Hip-Hop
    and Black Leadership," 11
King (T.I. album), 91–92
King, Martin Luther, Jr., 200
King, Ryan D., 80, 83–84
King of New York (film), 105, 231n20
Kitwana, Bakari, 8, 159
Knowles, Beyonce, 99–100
Kochman, Thomas, 226n17
Kool Herc, 37
Krims, Adam, 226n18, 231n2
KRS-One, 23–24, 34, 42, 86
Kubrin, Charis E., 80
Kweli, Talib, 201, 231–32n3; "Niggas Lie a
    Lot," 126

Labov, William, 226n17
Lamont, Michèle, 212, 228n11, 234n5
Lareau, Annette, 32
Latinos, hip-hop and, 1, 6, 228n6(1)

Lena, Jennifer, 4, 148
Levitt, Steven D., 56
Lewis, Kristine S., 145, 232n1
"Life's a Bitch" (Nas), 47
Lil' Jon, 101
Lil' Kim, 155
Lil' Wayne, 5, 57, 126–27, 203; "Drop It
    Like It's Hot," 102; "Every Girl," 104,
    231n18; "Fireman," 102; "Lollipop,"
    102–4; Williams and, 230–31n17
"Live Freestyle" (Shakur), 230n10
"Lollipop" (Lil' Wayne), 102–4
Long, Phalary, 23–24
love, feelings of: Bonnie and Clyde rep-
    resentations, 99–102; fans and, 104;
    female degradation as flip side of, 154,
    156; homophobia and, 102–5; platonic,
    104–11; in thug narratives, 16–17, 62,
    63, 67, 78, 88, 93–95, 113, 114, 115,
    178, 182, 188, 189
Lox, the, 96–97, 108, 161
Ludacris: O'Reilly's criticism of, 226n11;
    "Politics (Obama Is Here)," 201, 202–3;
    "Runaway Love," 50, 156, 232n7
Lupe Fiasco, 5

Macadoshis, 230n8
Majors, Richard, 10, 56, 57, 58–59, 115,
    144
Mannie Fresh, "Still Fly," 70
Marc (w1), 29; hip-hop as defined by, 34,
    39–40; hip-hop gangster image viewed
    by, 178; hip-hop preferences and ap-
    preciation, 122, 138, 160; hip-hop's im-
    portance to, 23; use of "nigga" viewed
    by, 169, 172–73
Marcy Projects, Brooklyn, 64–67
Marsalis, Wynton, 151
masculinity: cool pose and, 55–58, 66–67,
    189–90; hegemonic, 57–58, 62, 66, 69,
    71–74, 75, 96–97, 98, 115, 128, 129,
    161–62, 177–78, 179, 186–87, 192–93,
    197; hip-hop and, 6–7, 9, 48, 160–61;
    homophobia and, 9, 14, 58, 102–5;
    "nigga" and, 166; thug persona and, 77,
    79–80, 92, 93, 140–46, 148–49, 154,
    188; trope of black man as predator,
    82–84, 229n4
Massacre, The (50 Cent album), 97–98

Massey, Douglas, 56

Massumi, Brian, 43

Mauer, Marc, 80, 81, 229n1

McCain, John, 202, 203

McDermott, Monica, 7

MC-ing, 1, 7, 8, 34, 176, 225nn2–3

McLeod, Kembrew, 134, 137, 147, 160

MC Lyte, 155, 161

McWorter, John, "How Hip-Hop Holds Blacks Back," 10–11, 12

"Me and My Girlfriend" (Shakur), 99–100

Mendelberg, Tali, 84, 86

"Message, The" (Grandmaster Flash and the Furious Five), 62

Messerschmidt, James, 57

Method Man, 50, 120, 214

Miami, Florida, 65

Midnight Marauders (A Tribe Called Quest album), 2

MIMS, 126

"Mind Is Playing Tricks on Me" (the Geto Boys), 231n19

"Miss You" (Notorious B.I.G.), 113

Mitchell, Don, 12, 226n13

Mitchell-Kernan, Claudia, 226n17

Mobb Deep, "Pearly Gates," 110–11

Molnar, Virag, 228n11

"Money, Cash, Hoes" (Jay-Z), 107–8

Mopreme, 230n8

morality, hip-hop and, 82, 88, 90, 105–11, 186

moral panic, hip-hop and, 151–53, 155, 177, 184–85, 187, 195, 197–98, 202–3, 229n3, 232–33n10

Morenoff, Jeffrey, 85

Morgan, Joan, 14, 15

Morgan, Marcyliena, 8, 210, 225n2, 226n17

Mos Def: "Fear Not of Man," 189; "Mr. Nigga," 46–47

Motown label, 2–3

"Mr. Nigga" (Mos Def), 46–47

Music in Everyday Life (DeNora), 209

Mutua, Athena D., 62

"My Block" (Shakur), 94–95, 106, 230n11

"My Brother" (Gordon), 55

"My Brother" (Styles P), 48

"My President" (Young Jeezy), 199, 201

"My Way" (West), 63

NAACP, 164, 199

Nas: "Black President," 200, 201–2; on crack dealing, 64; *God's Son* album, 228n11; "I Can," 72–74, 132, 228n11; Jay-Z and, 128; "Life's a Bitch," 47; *Nigger* album, 199; "No Idea's Original," 207; O'Reilly's criticism of, 226n11; "Represent," 228n6(2)

Nasty as I Wanna Be (2 Live Crew album), 154

Nate (b1), 32; hip-hop as defined by, 38, 42; hip-hop preferences and appreciation, 124, 160; thug narratives viewed by, 142; use of "nigga" viewed by, 171; on women as portrayed in hip-hop, 157

Native Tongues, 6

Neal, Mark Anthony: *New Black Man*, 228n1; "Rhythm and Bullshit," 2–3, 4, 225nn6–7

neighborhoods. *See* 'hood

Neil (b4), 31; hip-hop gangster image viewed by, 178; hip-hop preferences and appreciation, 129, 136; use of "nigga" viewed by, 170

Nelly, 153

New Black Man (Neal), 228n1

New H.N.I.C. (Head Niggas in Charge), The (Boyd), 11

"nigga" (word), 163–77; adjectives or possessives preceding, 165; authenticity and, 167–68, 192; gender and, 165–66; social class and, 166–67; transformation from "nigger," 86, 165; understandings of, 151, 168–70, 187, 233n13; white avoidance of, 170–71, 172–73

"Niggas Lie a Lot" (Kweli), 126

"nigger" (word), 163–77; authenticity and, 167–68; contrasted with "negro," 165; NAACP's stand against, 164; Richards's use of, 163–64; "thug" as stand-in for, 86; transformation to "nigga," 86, 165; usage of, 164–65, 187

Nigger (Nas album), 199

nihilism, 82, 92–96, 107, 109–10, 180–81

"99 Problems" (Jay-Z), 45, 46

Nixon, Richard M., 81

"no homo" phrase, 102–5

"No Idea's Original" (Nas), 207

Nolan (b3), 31, 33; criminal justice system viewed by, 183, 185; hip-hop as defined by, 34, 38–39; hip-hop gangster image viewed by, 178; hip-hop preferences and appreciation, 121, 122; on relating to hip-hop, 47–48, 49; thug narratives viewed by, 143, 144, 145–46; use of "nigga" viewed by, 169, 170; on women as portrayed in hip-hop, 157–58
Notorious B.I.G.: death of, 109, 184; influence of, 39–40; "Miss You," 113; *Scarface*'s influence on, 231n20; Shakur and, 92; "Things Done Changed," 181
N.W.A. (Niggaz with Attitude), 85, 165–66; "Fuck tha Police," 182

Obama, Barack, 7, 199–205
Ogbu, John, 56, 145
"'03 Bonnie and Clyde" (Jay-Z), 99–100
"On My Block" (Scarface), 63
O'Reilly, Bill, 10, 226n11
O'Reilly Factor, The (TV show), 200, 226n11

Pardue, Derek, 6, 12, 233n3
Parents Music Resource Center (PMRC), 151
Parliament-Funkadelic, 86
participant observation, 210
party songs, 2, 45, 50–51, 161, 162
Patillo-McCoy, Mary, 171
Patterson, Orlando, 56, 87–88, 109; "A Poverty of the Mind," 144–45
Paul (w1), 29; criminal justice system viewed by, 182; hip-hop as defined by, 35, 40; hip-hop preferences and appreciation, 121; use of "nigga" viewed by, 174
P. Diddy: *Press Play*, 231n22; "Vote or Die" campaign, 12
"Pearly Gates" (50 Cent and Mobb Deep), 110–11
Peffley, Mark, 84
perception, psycho-semantics of, 208
performative understanding of music, 20, 36, 57, 74–76, 78, 119, 176–77, 226–27n18
Performing Identity/Performing Culture (Dimitriadis), 210–11
Perkins, William E., 117

Perry, Imani, 56, 133–34, 226n17, 231n21
Pete (w1), 29; criminal justice system viewed by, 182; hip-hop as defined by, 37; hip-hop gangster image viewed by, 178; hip-hop preferences and appreciation, 137
Peterson, Richard A., 75, 118–19, 121, 123, 132, 136, 147
Pharrell, 120
Phat Farm, 40
Plies, 5
Poetic Justice (film), 90
"Politics (Obama Is Here)" (Ludacris), 202–3
politics, hip-hop and, 4, 9, 12, 13–14, 15, 132, 145–46, 171, 199–205
"Politics of Hip-Hop and Black Leadership, The" (Kilson), 11
Polletta, Francesca, 26
posthermeneutic sociology, 208–9
Potter, Russell A., 226n17
Pough, Gwendolyn, 14, 15, 101, 155
"Poverty of the Mind, A" (Patterson), 144–45
Power of the Dollar (50 Cent album), 97
Pratto, Felicia, 71–72
Press Play (P. Diddy album), 231n22
prisons: criminal justice policy and outcomes, 80–85, 90, 177; ghetto seen as, 62; Hispanics in, 229n1; hyperghettos seen as, 79–80
Project Pat, "I Ain't Goin' Back to Jail," 50
Pryor, Richard, 166, 233n13
Public Enemy, 1, 6
"public good" (defined), 3
"Public Service Announcement" (Jay-Z), 55, 92
"puerile rap," 4
Puff Daddy, 121
Punishment and Inequality in America (Western), 229n2
Pusha T, 97

Q-Tip, 166
Quayle, Dan, 151–52
Queeley, Andrea, 4, 5, 9
Queen Latifah, 155
Quinn, Eithne, 20, 85–86

racial identity: authenticity concept in, 68–71, 73–76, 101, 138–39, 172–73, 175, 176–77, 188; black cool pose and, 55–58, 61–62, 115–16; black male oppositional, 10–12, 19, 46–47, 56–57, 73, 74, 104, 107, 141–46, 154; boundary-making, 52, 147, 149, 170–71, 174–75, 197, 212–13; embracing of, 139–41; hip-hop definitions and, 36–43, 51, 52, 147–48, 190; 'hood and, 62–64, 174–75; legitimizing myths of, 71–72; as marker, 7; Obama and, 204; race-making, 67–68; use of word "nigga" and, 168–70; white invisibility, 7–8, 55–56, 140, 148

racism: African American views of, 46–47, 72, 96, 192; biological difference argument, 87–88; black cool pose and, 58, 59–60; black criminality and, 174; criminal justice system and, 80–85, 90, 93, 94–95, 177, 182–84; "nigga" usage and, 172–73; "thug" as racially neutral word, 86–87; white distributors and black performers in music industry, 9, 149, 230n8; white uses in comedy, 152, 163–64; white views of black man as predator, 5, 82–84, 90, 229n4

radio: consolidation of, 3–4, 213, 230n9; programming, 4, 51, 135, 152

Raising Hell (Run DMC), 6

rap: commercially recorded, 1–2, 132–33; as element of hip-hop, 1; explicit lyrics in, 151–53, 232n6(2); female performers, 9, 14, 155, 159; live performance, 1; nihilism in, 92–96, 107; puerile, 4; skills in, 111, 123–32, 146–47, 191. *See also* gangsta rap; hip-hop

Rap Music and Street Consciousness (Keyes), 209–10

"Rapper's Delight" (Sugar Hill Gang), 1

Rated R, the, 230n8

Raudenbush, Steve, 85

Reagan, Ronald, 78, 80, 81

real, keeping it. *See* authenticity, concept of; keeping it real

recording industry: boutique labels, 2–3; changes to hip-hop by, 1, 2, 6–7, 132–33, 208, 213; consolidation of, 3–4, 153; crossover and, 2–5; culpabil-

ity of, 153, 177–78; distribution by, 5; hip-hop sales decline, 5; independent labels, 5, 234n6; political economy of, 75; white ownership of, 9, 149, 230n8

Reed, Adolph, 11, 12

Reese, Renford, 145

Reid, Shaheem, 199

Release Yo Delf (Method Man album), 50

Remi, Saleem, 72–74

"Renegade" (Jay-Z and Eminem), 90–91

"Represent" (Nas), 228n6(2)

resistance paradox, 12

respect, concept of, 67, 79–80, 142–43

respondents to study, 27–34; age of, 195, 214; anticommercial sentiment of, 134–36, 138–39, 147, 160–61, 187; black, 30–32, 36, 41–43, 45–47, 51–52, 124–25, 141–46, 170–72, 178–80, 193–94, 214; characterization of thug life, 178–82; class categories for, 33, 171–72, 214; educational status and, 32–33; favorite performers of, 215–20; gangsterism in hip-hop viewed by, 178–86, 188; gender and sexuality of, 195; geographical area, 27–28; hip-hop defined by, 34–43, 52–53, 212; hip-hop evaluated by, 120–46, 147, 190, 191–92; interview data analysis, 223–24; interview schedule, 220–23; location of, 196, 214, 220; neighborhood dynamics and, 32; performer preferences, 120, 160–62; reactions by race, 39–43, 193–94, 197, 214; reaction to interviewer, 148; selection process, 213–15; sexism in hip-hop viewed by, 155–56, 192, 197; social status, 32–33, 51; white, 28–30, 36–38, 39–41, 47–48, 125, 172–73, 178–79, 180, 193–94, 214; women artists and listeners viewed by, 160–62

"Rhythm and Bullshit" (Neal), 2–3, 4, 225nn6–7

Richard (w1), 30; hip-hop as defined by, 37; hip-hop preferences and appreciation, 126–27, 130; on relating to hip-hop, 49; use of "nigga" viewed by, 175

Richards, Michael, 163–64, 233nn11–12

Rich Boy, 214

Rihanna, 230n15

Roc-A-Fella Records, 3

Rojecki, Andrew, 84

Rose, Tricia, 9, 56, 123–24, 159, 197, 226n16, 231n2; *Black Noise*, 13–14, 15; *The Hip-Hop Wars*, 226n9

Ross, Rick, "Hustlin'," 45, 46, 228n7(1)

"'Round Here" (Memphis Bleek, T.I., and Trick Daddy), 64–67, 73, 108, 132

Roy (w2), 30; criminal justice system viewed by, 184; as culture or lifestyle, 40–41, 144–45; on feelings in hip-hop, 44; hip-hop gangster image viewed by, 179; thug narratives viewed by, 142; on women as portrayed in hip-hop, 156

Ruff Ryders, "Go Head," 96–97

"Runaway Love" (Ludacris), 50, 156, 232n7

Run DMC, 2, 6

Russell (w1), 30; on feelings in hip-hop, 44; hip-hop preferences and appreciation, 137; use of "nigga" viewed by, 173–74; on women as portrayed in hip-hop, 158

Russell, Katherine, *The Color of Crime*, 81–82, 84, 229n6

Ryan (b4), 31; hip-hop as defined by, 39, 42; hip-hop preferences and appreciation, 124, 128–29, 135, 137; use of "nigga" viewed by, 169; on women as portrayed in hip-hop, 158

Sampson, Robert J., 85

Sanneh, Kelefa, 153

Scarface (film), 231n20

Scarface, "On My Block," 63

Schloss, Joseph, 8, 210, 226n12; *Foundation*, 233n3

Schoolly D, 86

Scott, James, *Domination and the Art of Resistance*, 12

Sean (b2), 32; on authenticity, 117; criminal justice system viewed by, 182; hip-hop as defined by, 35; hip-hop gangster image viewed by, 179; hip-hop preferences and appreciation, 121, 122, 137; on relating to hip-hop, 45, 46

semiotics, 208, 233n2

sexism: as hip-hop hedonist value, 12, 78, 98, 113, 116, 153, 162–63, 230n9; of record executives, 159; respondents'

views of, 155–56, 192, 197, 232–33n10; signifying and, 154–55; stances against, 62

Shakur, Tupac: "All about U," 77, 108; career and influence of, 88–90, 95–96, 151; death of, 109, 184; gangster image of, 178; "I Ain't Mad at Cha," 101; "I Wonder If Heaven Got a Ghetto," 106; "Keep Ya Head Up," 50; "Live Free-style," 230n10; "Me and My Girlfriend," 99–100; MTV interview, 89; "My Block," 94–95, 106, 230n11; Nas's signifying of, 201; nihilism and, 92–93; "So Many Tears," 89; "Thugz Mansion," 106–7; "When Thugz Cry," 89; women viewed by, 156; word "thug" used by, 230n8

Sharpley-Whiting, T. Denean, 155, 159

Shelby, Tommie, 96, 229n3

Shouse, Eric, 43

Show, The (film), 230n11

Sidanius, James, 71–72

signifying, 18–19; black vernacular narration, 68–69, 127–28, 146–47, 155, 167–68, 192, 226n17; black vs. white listeners' appreciation, 18–19, 124–32; classical music, 72; complexity of, 61; definition, 18, 124–25; encoding/decoding and, 211–12, 233–34n4; ironic misnaming practice, 165, 168–70, 174; "no homo" phrase, 102; non-English speakers and, 196; Obama and, 201, 203; performance skills, 111, 123–32, 146–47, 191; in "'Round Here," 64–67; semantic reclamation and transformation, 86–87, 211–12; sexism and, 154–55

Simkus, Albert, 118–19

Simmons, Russell: culpability of African Americans viewed by, 152; Hip-Hop Summit Action Network, 12; late support of Obama for president, 200

Simpson, O. J., 83

Sisqo, 160

Sister Souljah, 151, 232n2

slavery, as social death, 87, 88

Small, Christopher, 226n18

Smith, Christopher Holmes, 62, 104

Smith, Susan, 229n6

Smitherman, Geneva, 226n17
Snoop Dogg, 153, 226n11, 232n4(2)
snowball sampling method, 214, 215
Snyder, Gregory, 225n2
social capital, 'hood and, 32, 67, 118
social class: "niggas" and, 166–67, 170–72, 187; taste and, 118–20, 124, 130–31, 146, 196
social death, thug life and, 87–88, 94–96, 107, 109, 177, 179–81
social isolation, criminality and, 82–83, 94–95, 182–83, 188
social movements: hip-hop as, 25–27, 52, 196–97, 203, 227n1; as knowledge-building collective praxis, 26–27, 45; types of, 25–26
social pathology, 60
"So Many Tears" (Shakur), 89
Sony Music Entertainment, 3–4
soul music, 10
South Africa, 229n5
spectacularity of hip-hop, 69, 71
Static Major, 104
Stax label, 2–3
"Stay Fly" (Three 6 Mafia), 228n8(2)
Steven (b4), 31; criminal justice system viewed by, 185–86; hip-hop as defined by, 34; hip-hop gangster image viewed by, 179; thug narratives viewed by, 143, 144, 146; use of "nigga" viewed by, 170, 175; on women as portrayed in hip-hop, 158
"Still Fly" (The Big Tymers), 70
street culture, black oppositional identity and, 10–11, 56–58, 73, 141–46, 148, 154. See also 'hood
Streetwise (Anderson), 228n5
Strictly 4 My N.I.G.G.A.Z. (Shakur album), 88–89
Stuart, Charles, 229n6
Styles P, 96–97
stylin': African American tradition of, 69–71, 190; cool pose and, 59, 201; as part of hip-hop, 35, 40–41, 48, 115, 144–45, 183; self-, 90, 115, 231n20
"Stylin'" (Foxy Brown), 228n8(2)
"Sucka Nigga" (A Tribe Called Quest), 166
Sugar Hill Gang, 1

Summer Jam concerts, 98, 135–36, 213, 220
symbolic creativity, 27, 227–28nn3–4

"Take Back the Music" campaign, 153
taste, theories of, 118–20, 124
Taylor, Yuval, 69
Telecommunications Reform Act of 1996, 3
textual analysis, 208, 209; components of, 20; problem of, 19–20; uses of, 15–16, 181–82
Thernstrom, Abigail, 85
Thernstrom, Steven, 85
"Things Done Changed" (Notorious B.I.G.), 181
"30 Something" (Jay-Z), 50, 51
"This Is Why I'm Hot" (MIMS), 126
Thompson, Robert Farris, 59, 60, 69, 115, 190
Three 6 Mafia, 49; "Half on a Sack," 50; "Stay Fly," 228n8(2)
thug image, 77–111; afterlife, morality and, 105–11; authenticity and, 92, 181, 192, 193; black identity and, 75, 76, 140–46, 148–49; changes to, 89; cool pose and, 60; definition of, 180; 50 Cent as embodiment of, 91–92; in gangsta rap, 86–87; as hip-hop persona, 77–78, 188; homophobia and, 102–5; independent agency of, 88; media amplification of, 2; "niggas" and, 165–66; nihilism and, 92–96, 180–81; offensiveness of, 90–92; as outsider/rebel, 89–90, 91, 92–93; recording industry's encouragement of, 177–78; Shakur as embodiment of, 88–90, 151; success and, 113–14, 184; success of, 5; as survivor, 110–11; T.I. as embodiment of, 91–92; violence and, 4, 12, 66–67, 80, 92, 96–97, 100–101, 108, 109–11, 115; in white imaginary, 10–11; word as stand-in for "nigger," 86; word reclaimed by rappers, 87. See also gangster image
Thug Life, 89, 230n8
Thug Life: Volume I (album), 230n8
"Thugz Mansion" (Shakur), 106–7
T.I.: popularity of, 5; "'Round Here," 64–67, 108, 220; "Undertaker," 91–92, 230n9; use of n-word, 164

Tilly, Charles, 25
Tim (b2), 32; hip-hop as defined by, 39; hip-hop culpability viewed by, 185; hip-hop preferences and appreciation, 122–23; thug narratives viewed by, 141; use of "nigga" viewed by, 171; on women as portrayed in hip-hop, 159
TimeWarner, 153
Toop, David, 12–13
"tough on crime" discourse, 81–85, 90
Trapp, Erin, 227n1
Trey Songz, 103–4
Tribe Called Quest, A: *Midnight Marauders*, 2; "Sucka Nigga," 166
Trick Daddy: Miami residency of, 234n8; "'Round Here," 64–67, 108, 220
Tucker, C. Delores, 1
Tunnel, The (album), 230n10
Twitchell, James, 118
2 Live Crew, 154, 232n6(2)
2Pacalypse Now (Shakur album), 88

"Undertaker" (T.I.), 91–92, 230n9
Universal Music Group, 3–4, 214
"U Not Like Me" (50 Cent), 105–6
Uptown Angela, 231n17
urban planning, hip-hop and, 1

vernacular in black narration, 68–69, 127–28, 146–47, 155, 167, 192, 226n17
Vibe magazine, 102, 202–3
"video hos," 155, 157–59, 192
virgin/whore paradigm, 101–2
"Vote or Die" campaign, 12
vulnerability, feelings of: complex cool and, 200, 204; drug dealing and, 131; in hip-hop narratives, 16, 60, 61, 62, 96, 98, 105, 113, 115, 178, 182, 188, 189; love and, 78; nihilism and, 93; respondents', 48–49, 193; in Shakur's raps, 89–90

Wacquant, Loic, 79–80, 85
Walken, Christopher, 105
"Walk This Way" (Run DMC and Aerosmith), 2
Wall, Paul, 135
Wally (w1), 30; hip-hop as defined by, 37; use of "nigga" viewed by, 169; on women as portrayed in hip-hop, 156
Walters, John, 82–83
Warner Music Group, 3–4, 153
Waters, Mary, 56
Watkins, S. Craig, 25, 86, 227n1
"We Don't Care" (West), 96
Weitzer, Ronald, 80
West, Cornel, 93, 94, 95, 101
West, Kanye: GOOD Music label, 3; "My Way," 63; popularity of, 5; "We Don't Care," 96; women in videos of, 101
Western, Bruce, 81; *Punishment and Inequality in America*, 229n2
"We Wear the Mask" (Dunbar), 58, 115
Wheelock, Darren, 83–84
"When Thugz Cry" (Shakur), 89
White, Graham, 69–70
White, Shane, 69–70
white listeners: hip-hop in imaginations of, 4, 5, 9, 10–11; identity construction and, 39–43, 52, 55, 144–45, 183; reasons for rap appreciation, 8–9, 44–45, 47–51; regarded as posers, 8; signifying and, 124–26; thug narratives viewed by, 143–44
white racial identity: hip-hop authenticity and, 138–39, 190; invisibility and, 7–8, 55–56, 140, 148; use of word "nigga" and, 170–71, 172–73, 187
Whitlock, Jason, 226n12
Why White Kids Love Hip-Hop (Kitwana), 8
Wild Style (film), 225n3
Williams, Brian "Baby," 230–31n17
Williams, R., 25
Williams, Saul, 152–53
Willis, Paul, 27, 209, 227n3
Wilson, William Julius, 78–79, 82, 85, 232n6(1)
Winfrey, Oprah, 152
Wolffe, Richard, 204
women, hip-hop and, 154–63; Bonnie and Clyde raps, 99–102; categorization of hip-hop representations, 156–57; "down ass chicks" representations, 100–102, 104; exclusion from music industry, 159, 192; female degradation,

9, 14, 45–46, 58, 60–61, 92, 98–99, 152–63, 186–87, 192, 197, 203, 205, 232–33n10; hip-hop aesthetic preferences, 160, 162; mandated sacrifices, 101–2; marginalization of performers, 9, 14, 129–30, 149, 155, 160–62, 232n8; misogyny as marketing tool, 153; roles in hip-hop videos, 155, 157–59, 186; sexual agency, 159, 162, 232n7; "tricks," "hos," and "bitches" representations, 100–102, 155, 156–57, 163, 164, 186–87, 192; virgin/whore paradigm, 101–2. *See also* hip-hop feminists; sexism

Wyman, Leah, 101

Young Buck, 109–10, 231nn23–24, 234n7
Young Jeezy: "My President," 199, 201; Obama and, 199–201; popularity of, 5
Young Money Entertainment, 231n18

Zack (w1), 30; hip-hop preferences and appreciation, 135, 161; use of "nigga" viewed by, 169